Northwestern University

STUDIES IN *Phenomenology &*

Existential Philosophy

Heidegger and
the Tradition

Werner Marx

Translated by

With an Introduction by

Heidegger and the Tradition

THEODORE KISIEL
and MURRAY GREENE

THEODORE KISIEL

NORTHWESTERN UNIVERSITY PRESS

EVANSTON   1 9 7 1

Originally published in German under the title
*Heidegger und die Tradition: Eine problem-
geschichtliche Einführung in die Grundbestim-
mungen des Seins,* copyright © 1961 by
W. Kohlhammer of Stuttgart, Germany.

First paperback printing, 1982
Second paperback printing, 1989

To the Memory
of My Friend
RUDOLF STRAUSS

Contents

List of Abbreviations

WORKS BY HEIDEGGER

EM	*Einführung in die Metaphysik*
HB	*Brief über den "Humanismus"*
HD	*Erläuterungen zu Hölderlins Dichtung*
HW	*Holzwege*
ID	*Identität und Differenz*
KM	*Kant und das Problem der Metaphysik*
N I, II	*Nietzsche*, Vols. I and II
PW	*Platons Lehre von der Wahrheit*
SF	*Zur Seinsfrage*
SG	*Der Satz vom Grund*
SZ	*Sein und Zeit*
US	*Unterwegs zur Sprache*
VA	*Vorträge und Aufsätze*
WD	*Was heisst Denken?*
WG	*Vom Wesen des Grundes*
WM	*Was ist Metaphysik?*
WP	*Was ist das—die Philosophie?*
WW	*Vom Wesen der Wahrheit*

WORKS BY HEGEL

Enz.	*Enzyklopädie der philosophischen Wissenschaften* (The abbreviation "add." = "addition" = *Zusatz.*)
Logik	*Wissenschaft der Logik*
PG	*Phänomenologie des Geistes*

[xiii]

Works by Aristotle

An. Post.	*Analytica Posteriora*
Cat.	*Categoriae*
De Gen. et Corr.	*De Generatione et Corruptione*
Meta.	*Metaphysics*
Nic. Eth.	*The Nicomachean Ethics*
Phys.	*Physics*

Foreword

THIS TREATISE is a result of lectures and seminars given at the Graduate Faculty (University in Exile) of the New School for Social Research, New York. Its basic ideas were presented in lectures at the University of Heidelberg during the summer semester of 1958 and developed extensively since. My interest in Heidegger's problematic was awakened by Karl Löwith; to him I owe special thanks. The first half of my introduction to this book appeared under the title "Heidegger and Metaphysics" in the publication in honor of Wilhelm Szilasi, *Beiträge zur Philosophie und Wissenschaft* (Munich: Francke Verlag, 1960).

WERNER MARX

Graduate Faculty
New School of Social Research
New York, July 11, 1960

Translator's Introduction

TEN YEARS HAVE PASSED since this book was first published in Germany. This was before the time that Heidegger began to interpret his own works extensively and before the effort to introduce Heidegger to the English-speaking world developed into landslide proportions. Since then Professor Marx—on the merits of this book—was appointed to become the successor to the chair formerly occupied by Husserl and Heidegger. In an extensive review of the Heideggerian literature from 1953 to 1964, and including works in German, French, and Italian as well as several prominent works in English, Marx's book was held to be "the best and the most philosophical of the more recent publications." [1]

What distinguishes this book from many others is that it does not attempt to merely give an account of Heidegger's philosophy. It rather tries to reflect on the "sense" of the traditional determinations of Being, essence, and of the essence of man in Aristotle and Hegel in order to put into relief the "other" sense of those basic traits of Being, essence, and of the essence of man which Heidegger seeks to develop, in order thereby to initiate a thinking that might carry on beyond Heidegger.

Marx chose Aristotle because his was the most significant formulation of the doctrine of the category of substance at the beginning of our "tradition." Heidegger himself, in a self-interpretation written shortly after this book was first published in 1961, points to his early reflections on the Aristotelian concep-

1. Dieter Sinn, "Heideggers Spätphilosophie," *Philosophische Rundschau*, XIV (1967), 81–182. See pp. 89–90.

tion of *ousia* as crucial to the issue of Being "and" time as he saw it from the very beginning.[2]

Marx chose Hegel because Hegel represents for him the end of the "tradition" under question. For in Hegel, substance—though in a modified sense—came to be subordinated to the category of subject—understood transcendentally. Professor Marx was the first to see that Heidegger's efforts from beginning to end were directed against these traditional categories of substance and subject. Accordingly, while the first part of the book develops the sense of "tradition," the second part shows how the "overcoming" of this tradition was already the objective of Heidegger's early works, even before the task of "overcoming metaphysics" became the explicit aim of his later works (which are examined in Parts III, IV, and V).

The guiding thesis of the following work is that for Heidegger the question of Being is still a question of essence even though essence no longer retains the ousiological traits it had with Aristotle. It is this new and different sense of Being and essence—with its concomitant change in our understanding of the essence of man—that Marx's study tries to put into relief.

At first sight, one might expect any discussion of Heidegger's relationship to the metaphysical tradition in its entirety to turn on the terminal figures of Plato and Nietzsche, if any two figures are to be selected at all. But in another sense, there is a greater kinship of Heidegger to Aristotle and Hegel, making their contrast all the more subtle and significant. It was the reading of Aristotle that first gave Heidegger his basic insight into *alētheia*.[3] And he regards Aristotle as "more Greek than Plato,"[4] insofar as Aristotle's metaphysics makes a "swing back" to the great pre-Socratic beginnings that Heidegger admires so much. The manifest similarities between Hegel and Heidegger have often been noted, particularly after this book was published: the intimate relationship between philosophy and the history of philosophy and the resulting comprehensive historical sweep of their thinking, the interplay between Being and Nothing, the employment of "process" and "field" categories, etc. Marx tries to show that Hegel, while remaining under the dominion of the metaphysical categories of substance and subject, already points to another

2. Preface to William J. Richardson, S.J., *Heidegger: Through Phenomenology to Thought* (The Hague: Martinus Nijhoff, 1963), pp. XII–XIII.

3. *Ibid.*, pp. X–XIII.

4. *N II* 228, 409. (See List of Abbreviations, above.)

realm, a kindred realm which Heidegger—thinking from an opposite direction—is destined to develop further.

Intervening developments serve to accentuate the task: Kierkegaard's existential revolt against the Hegelian system in defense of the uniqueness of the individual; the continuing attack on the tradition of substance and essence, culminating in Nietzsche's pronouncement of the "death of God"; Husserl's call to return to the "things themselves"; under the impetus of world events, the rise of the historical consciousness, with its concomitant hazards of historicism and relativism; the attempt to understand the historicity of "life" by Dilthey and Count von Yorck, which casts further doubt on the suitability of the traditional ontological categories for the task of understanding life historically; [5] the entry of evolutionary philosophy, which poses the problem of time and the emergence of novelty in its own way and helps to shift the locus of creativity away from the subjectivity of the genius, glorified by the romantic age to which Hegel belonged; the emergence of process and field categories in a variety of scientific disciplines, e.g., relativistic and quantum physics, holistic biology, and Gestalt psychology. Consequently, we of the twentieth century are no longer in a position to simply return to the static categories of classical philosophy. For one thing, we have experienced the power of history and therefore find it difficult to accept senses of Being and essence that do not allow for history. Thus, according to Löwith, Heidegger, as a "thinker in a time of need," attempts to think "Being out of time." [6] In Professor Marx's terms—using Hegel's notion from the *Differenzschrift*—the present "need of philosophy" to which Heidegger is responding is to think the essence of essence in a way that allows for the advent of the new, in a creative emergence in which man plays a part without thereby relativizing and historicizing essence (p. 9, below). By contrasting Heidegger with the teleologically closed conception of Being and essence, Marx shows how Heidegger attempts to think Being and essence as a creative occurrence of the new and unprecedented rather than as a noetic and teleologically predetermined order (Aristotle) or as a substantially determined occurrence of the thought of a self-ordering subjectivity (Hegel). For both of these classical formulations are in principle uncreative.

5. *SZ* 397–402.
6. Karl Löwith, *Heidegger: Denker in dürftiger Zeit*, p. 12. (Full publication data for books cited in footnotes will be found in the Bibliography at the end of the book.)

But the task of thinking the historical character of Being is itself historical. If the essence of man is an occurrence rather than a substance, so that human existence is temporal and historical through and through—as *Being and Time* tries to show —then the very human attempt to understand it in its Being is itself subject to the same finitude. Human existence is inescapably situated; it takes place in a historical world of inherited precedents which provides the meaningful context without which we would not understand anything at all. Accordingly, the attempt to surpass the tradition can still be accomplished only from within the tradition.

Therefore, the theme of "overcoming the tradition" (Part II, Chapters 2 and 3, develop Marx's account of the structure of thought of this task for the early and for the later Heidegger, respectively), as I see it, contains an inherent ambivalence. For Heidegger strives to overcome the more immediate tradition of metaphysics by rejuvenating the hidden resources which it retains from a much older and more profound tradition. Overcoming the tradition is therefore not a matter of shaking off the tradition but of appropriating it more originally. Thus, for example, the revival of the question of Being, in turning away from metaphysical categories absolved from history (e.g., substance), still finds suggestions within these very categories (e.g., *ousia* and *parousia* as presence, suggesting an undeveloped relationship between time and Being) which point to other possibilities. It is this creative charge of the unthought which it delivers over to us in order to be thought that makes the authentic tradition more a matter of the future than of the past, as the ordinary "historical" view would have it.[7]

But to view the tradition as a burden of the past is not entirely wrong. Tradition becomes an inhibiting force when it hardens into a dormant deposit that is accepted without question, as "self-evident," so that we forget the primordial and vitalizing experiences invested in it, which first made it a living tradition. Cut off from its creative roots, it becomes de-generate and without fruit. And this tendency to passively understand transmitted meaning is by far the most "natural attitude," as Husserl would put it. And yet, because it still preserves its vital sources in a subliminal way, tradition can also be an emancipat-

7. WD 71 (76). (Numbers in parentheses refer to the pagination of English translations, which are listed in the Bibliography.)

ing force. This is the positive aim of what Heidegger calls "de-struction," which de-structures the hardened sedimentation of tradition in order to explicitly "retrieve" the original experiences concealed in it. Because of the situated character of human exist-ence, the retrieve (*Wiederholung*) is never a simple reiteration of something past but is also a revision and adaptation which explicates the possibilities that are relevant to the new situation. By thus exposing the new and hitherto hidden possibilities of meaning that it offers, the retrieve keeps the tradition alive.

The method is both phenomenological,[8] in its bracketing of the natural attitude and its reductive return to experiential sources, and hermeneutical, in its reading of the transmitted texts of the tradition in order to revive the root experiences de-posited in its basic words and to apply them to the present situa-tion. The fusion of the radical intentions of phenomenology with the hermeneutical procedure of interpreting linguistic works eventually culminates in a radical reading of the texts of the his-tory of philosophy. The epochē or destruction is now seen as the overcoming of the history of metaphysics in its entirety from Plato to Nietzsche, and the re-duction becomes the backtracking from metaphysics into its ground and essence. The retrieve, which draws out new possibilities from old origins, becomes radi-calized into a return to the most incipient beginnings of the Western tradition, to the basic words which have preserved the most basic experiences of Being which the pre-Socratics had. But the retrieve is never a simple return to the past. This initial beginning cannot be preserved precisely as it began; it is neces-sarily left behind. "It can be preserved only by re-trieving it in its originality more originally." [9] It is thus that the first beginning is displaced toward a new and different beginning.

This means nothing less than to *re-trieve* the beginning of our historical-spiritual Dasein in order to transmute it into another beginning. This is possible. It is indeed the crucial form of history, because it takes its start in the ground occurrence. But a beginning is not retrieved by reducing it to something past and now known and merely to be imitated. The beginning must be begun again, more originally, with all the strangeness, darkness, and insecurity

8. Here is where Professor Marx and I clearly diverge, inasmuch as he holds that the method of the later Heidegger is no longer phenomeno-logical. See his review of Richardson's *Heidegger: Through Phenomenology to Thought* in *Man and World*, I (1968), 138–42, and below, p. 117.
9. *EM* 146 (191).

that a true beginning brings with it. Retrieve as we understand it is anything but a better way of continuing the past by the methods of the past.[10]

The retrieve thus radicalized, which displaces the first beginning into a new and different beginning, is now seen to proceed according to a radical historical movement which is guided by what Heidegger variously describes as the ground occurrence, the appropriating event, the mission and history of Being, the profound tradition which is incipience pure and simple,[11] the wellspring of perpetual novelty, the silent power that enables all of man's possibilities. This crucial and rare form of history, in which the very bases of a tradition are shifted onto new ground, is ultimately not a smooth transition from old to new but the deliverance of the unexpectedly new which catches on abruptly as from an abyss, according to a movement that involves ruptures and abrupt new starts, "in which epochs spring up suddenly like shoots." [12] From the side of man, this radical recall that aims at the new and unprecedented is seen as a leap into the abyss of an ineffable movement which takes its own course as it makes way for man. Thus, retrieving thinking, in which man himself explicitly and deliberately transmits the possibilities that he finds in his inherited situation, becomes *seinsgeschichtliches Denken*, thinking according to the history of Being, a process not initiated by man but by the prompting of the mission to which man has been commissioned. This essential thinking can accordingly no longer be construed as a method but is now seen as a "way" that takes its course beyond human control, empowered by the history of Being and not simply by the historicity of human existence (p. 117, below).

A similar reversal takes place in the hermeneutical character of this process. The medium of the hermeneutical process and of the transmission of tradition is and remains language, but now it is no longer the articulate language of man but the silent language of Being (Part V, Chapter 3), which speaks by a withdrawal that draws man forward to new possibilities. The crux of the hermeneutical process is no longer the exposition of hidden meanings, for "before this there is already the bringing of the message and tidings" [13] through the soundless address of mys-

10. *EM* 29–30 (39).
11. *N II* 29.
12. *SG* 154.
13. *US* 122.

tery. The nodal points of this address are the most basic words of our language, the primitive and indefinable terms which have somehow said the unsayable, which, because they open onto the abyss of Being, are bottomless in their possibilities. Such basic words constitute a text which is continually being read in new and different ways according to the demands of different historical contexts. Man's role here is to listen to the soundless saying that speaks to him through his basic words. The preservation of this power of the most elemental words is in the end what philosophy is all about.

The peculiar historical process that philosophy is for Heidegger can—according to Marx—be articulated into three interdependent and contemporaneous tasks (see pp. 120–21, below), following from Heidegger's eschatological presupposition that the Greek beginnings have gathered to a climax in the present consummation of metaphysics, which must accordingly be overcome: (1) recall of the first beginning (Part III); (2) reflection on the essence of metaphysics, which is now coming to an end in technology (Part IV); and (3) anticipation of another beginning (Part V).

The first task, then, is to recall the sense of Being deposited in the tradition in the "great beginning" of Greek thinking, which began great with Anaximander and ended great with Aristotle.[14] Its purpose is not a modern revival of classical antiquity in order to imitate its ways, or an antiquarian interest in reliving the past, but to rethink something which is still very much present and operative in our contemporary world. Specifically, the aim is to recover the exclamatory experiences of the early Greek astonishment with Being that launched the tradition now coming to an end, experiences which are held and preserved in concentrated fashion in their basic words, especially *physis, alētheia,* and *logos.* The sedimented experiences conserved in these words are all governed by the experienced difference between verbal Being (*Sein*) and nominal substantive being (*Seiendes*). The abiding emergence of *physis,* the clearing concealment of *alētheia,* and the polemic gathering of *logos* are convergent and convertible senses of the ongoing presenting process of Being as it was experienced in the first beginning. Aristotle retained a measure of this dynamism in the mobility that he invested in the cosmic order, but this is mitigated by a shift from the comings and goings of an abrupt and intermittent presence to a presence stabilized

14. *EM* 12 (15).

in the recurrence of eternal essences (p. 134, below). The strife of the gathering process thus tends to be stilled, and the dark backdrop essential for any revelation is suppressed in favor of a fixed and permanent order amenable to a totally clairvoyant intelligibility. Nothingness is thereby excluded from Being, and becoming is relegated to the realm of the apparent. Metaphysics is launched toward a static and reified conception of Being within which nothing new is really possible (p. 143, below).

Just how this came about is one of the concerns of the second task, the reflection on the essence of metaphysics, i.e., its occurrence and its profound history, a task which in its entirety includes a reflection on the essence of each of its forms or "stampings," i.e., its various interpretations of "Being" (p. 118, below). The breadth and depth of its concerns counter a possible misunderstanding of Heidegger's intentions toward metaphysics.[15] Overcoming metaphysics does not mean rejecting, much less ignoring, the tradition of metaphysics.

> Precisely because we have embarked on the great and arduous task of demolishing a world that has grown old and rebuilding it truly anew, i.e., historically, we must know the tradition. We must know more, i.e., our knowledge must be stricter and more binding than all the epochs before us, even the most revolutionary. Only the most radical historical knowledge can make us aware of our extraordinary tasks and preserve us from a new wave of mere restoration and uncreative imitation.[16]

Consequently, though the texts that metaphysics has transmitted to us may be interpreted violently, they certainly are not discarded or neglected. They are studied all the more intensively, but now from the vantage of the eschatological consummation of metaphysics. In such a situation, the concealment brought about by the texts of metaphysics is not to be regarded as a lack but as a hidden treasure of something unthought withheld by these texts, and nevertheless held in them.[17] Thus, "Aristotle's *Physics* is the hidden basic book of Western philosophy, and accordingly a book which is never sufficiently thought through."[18]

15. What follows is basically not a paraphrase of Marx's own reflections on this second task but a supplement provoked by them and incorporating Heideggerian texts which appeared after the publication of his book.

16. *EM* 96 (125–26).

17. *HB* 77 (282).

18. "Vom Wesen und Begriff der *Physis*. Aristoteles *Physik* B, 1," in *Wegmarken* (Frankfurt: Vittorio Klostermann, 1967), p. 312. Italicized in the original.

Moreover, even though metaphysics has passed its apogee, its dominion is far from over. The habits of 2,500 years cannot be changed overnight. Our ways of speaking, the very grammar and logic of our language, are metaphysical. Accordingly, the ultimate demise of the dominion of metaphysics may well take longer than the history of its rise and consummation.[19] The reflection on the essence of metaphysics will therefore remain the most worthy of tasks, "as long as thinking does not break off the conversation with its commissioned tradition arbitrarily, thus betraying its mission."[20] "What is metaphysics?" is a question which will be with us for some time to come.

The beginnings of metaphysics are still very much present in the current epoch of science and technology. Plato's *idea* and Aristotle's *energeia* still speak to us today in every scientific concept.[21] And both of these are responses to the Greek problem of *ousia*.[22] How is it that *ousia*, stable and constant presence, became the decisive interpretation of Being at the end of the Greek period? A kind of stasis is already manifest in the pre-Socratic conception of *physis* as abiding emergence. But this standing-in-itself is not a static state but an ec-static process whereby the hidden stands out into unconcealment and nevertheless continues to stand in itself, as the dynamic generating ground of what is made to stand out. Its stand is at once present and absent, perduring and dynamic. Being and becoming remain inextricably together in the standing-back and the standing-forth of *physis*.[23] But it is an easy and even necessary step to regard its standing-out in unconcealment as a standing in the light, as Plato did in terms of the *idea*. What is striking is not so much that this did occur but that *idea* should become the sole and decisive determination of Being.[24] It is thereby detached from its background of the chiaroscuro strife and interplay of the original *physis* and *alētheia*. Emergent reality more and more enters into the stasis of an *eidos*, a fixed and determinate visage which stands before us, the viewers, as an intelligible identity. Truth becomes a matter of correctness of intellectual vision rather than a process of unconcealment, and reality is hypostatized into the standing-in-itself of a substance, which is always there in advance as an underlying substratum. *Physis* more and more becomes a func-

19. VA 71.
20. ID 52 (55).
21. WD 71 (76).
22. WP 25 (55); N II 409.
23. EM 48, 12 (63, 14).
24. EM 138–39 (181–82).

tion and mode of *ousia,* which evolves into the decisive term for Being. Being as permanent presence (the basic trait of "eternalness," in Professor Marx's terms) is distinguished sharply from the realm of becoming. Being as the always identical prototype (selfsameness) is opposed to the vacillations of mere appearance. Being as underlying subject (ground of intelligibility) stands over against its being thought. Being as already given actuality, residing in its *entelecheia* (completeness; literally, "holding itself in its end")²⁵ and therefore constrained within its limits (the basic trait of necessity), is separated from what is not but ought to be.²⁶

Aristotle's *energeia* emphasizes the revelatory work of the particular being standing in its presence; Aristotle thus thinks in a more Greek way, closer to the essence of Being in the first beginning, than Plato, who relegated the individual being to the limbo of the apparent. But between *energeia* and the initially incipient sense of Being stands Plato's *idea.* Aristotle therefore conceives of *energeia* as the stance of the particular being within the vision of the *idea.*²⁷ These two modes of *ousia,* the *idea* common to many and the *energeia* of a this, provide the basis of what later came to be called the real distinction between essence and existence, corresponding to the double stance of *ousia:* the simple standing out into unconcealment of something *that* is (existence), and *what* stands there and appears (essence).²⁸ The onto-theo-logical essence of the meta-physical endeavor springs from this distinction: ontology aims at the supreme universal (*essentia*) of being as such as a whole, and theology strives for the full unique being (*existentia*) which is the ground of all beings.²⁹

Cultivating certain seeds planted by Plato, Descartes launched modern metaphysics by instituting the human subject as the ground of truth, where truth is now interpreted as certainty. The subject is seen as the power of securing the objects that stand before it. Will as the power to secure and control passes through various permutations, beginning with Descartes's will to re-presentation and terminating in Nietzsche's will to will. Metaphysics ends in the absolutizing of the willful subjectivity, in Hegel's metaphysics of the unconditioned subjec-

25. *VA* 50; *Wegmarken* 354; *N I* 77.
26. *EM* 154 (202).
27. *N II* 409.
28. *EM* 138 (181).
29. *N II* 348–49.

tivity of the self-knowing will, i.e., of the absolute spirit, and in Nietzsche's metaphysics of the unconditioned subjectivity of the will to power. Subjectivity is unconditioned because it is not limited by the untruth of error, since for Hegel untruth is elevated to a one-sided kind of truth and for Nietzsche untruth itself becomes the essence of truth.[30]

The fruit of metaphysical thinking is currently ripening in the present dominion of technology, where Hegel's System finds a degenerating counterpart in the organizational complex that Heidegger calls the com-posite (*Ge-stell*) and Nietzsche's will to power manifests itself in the goal of planetary domination. Control and security are the overriding features of the technological network. Its constancy and consistency of function demand the uniformity of stock items, reliability of service, supplies of reserves, back-up "fail-safe" systems for all possible contingencies. The stasis of *ousia* receives its ultimate expression in the functional constant of mathematics, the fixed object (*Gegenstand*) of science, and the positioned stock (*Bestand*) of technology.

Such, in broad strokes, are some of the strands of the Heideggerian reflection on the essence of metaphysics, now coming to an end in the nuclear-space-automated age of technology. The third and most important task—according to the division of tasks set forth by Marx's study—is to think ahead to a new and different beginning on the basis of the rethought traits of Being in the first beginning. Perhaps the most important contribution of Marx's work is his attempt to show how the basic traits of the first beginning as they were deposited in the basic words were transmuted into the fundamental determinants of the new beginning. I would like now to develop a few observations of my own concerning these transmuted traits, once again from the vantage and advantage of ten additional years of Heideggerian publications and scholarship.

First of all, the rethought ontological difference between Being and being gives way to the forethought distinction of world and thing. In *Being and Time* the world was already seen as the meaningful context whose referential network of relations bestows meaning on the things within the world. This process of giving meaning is now emphasized by accenting the verbal character of the world, which now "worlds," i.e., gathers. Moreover, there is not only a distinction but also an "intimacy" [31] between

30. *N II* 196–200.
31. *US* 24 ff.

world and thing, so that the thing in turn manifests the world by "thinging," by gathering the four world neighborhoods of earth, sky, gods, and mortals. This scheme adapted from Hölderlin is the significant new direction by which Heidegger attempts to anticipate the *logos* of the new beginning. Its *physis*, through the interplay of the fourfold, becomes a world play, while its *alētheia* is the mirror play of the neighborhoods reciprocally reflecting one another. But the most significant transmutation of the truth character of the world, its opening and clearing, is the increasingly important role played by its mortals in their speech, which at its best means to let things speak for themselves. For language here is first of all the language of the world, from which it receives all the meaning that it has to convey. Before it is a tool that man uses, language is the medium in which he dwells as in the fabric of his Being, without which he would not be a man. The milieu of truth thus becomes the linguisticality of the historical world, as compared with the intelligibility of the eternal order of onto-theo-logical metaphysics. The world becomes a finite historical auditorium instead of the illuminated realm under Plato's sun, which shone during the reign of light metaphysics. Heidegger now speaks of a historical essence instead of an eternal essence, an indigenous and autochthonous world essence instead of an extramundane essence.

Time is of the essence in the new beginning. Accordingly, certain words usually taken as substantive are given verbal iteration: Nothing nothings; the world worlds; the thing things; speech speaks; essence essences. Central to this linguistic strategy is the new and different notion of verbal essence. "How does the thing essence? The thing things. The thinging gathers." [32] "The world essences by worlding." [33] The essence of speech is to be found in its speaking, in its occurrence, the occurrence of Being. The essence of a thing is to be found in the thing proper, i.e., in its proper activity, its unique style. Essence here is no longer an abstract generality that applies uniformly to all of its particular instances; the same essence in fact always occurs differently, which is the core of the paradox of temporality. Sartre is fond of referring to the Hegelian conception of a fixed and finalized essence: *Wesen ist was gewesen ist:* "Essence is what has been." But for Heidegger *Wesen* is always a *noch wesendes Gewesene,* always suspended in the transition between

32. VA 172.
33. VA 178.

presence (*An-wesen*) and absence (*Ab-wesen*), an "epochal essence," [34] temporal through and through. When Heidegger asks a question of essence, e.g., "What is art?," the operative word is no longer "what," as it has been since Plato, but "is." The most essential essence is always synonymous with the active "is" which is prior to the metaphysical distinction of "what" and "that." The question of essence therefore becomes "How does art essence?," "How does it emerge, reveal, gather, abide, and prevail?," "How does it grant artists and artworks their essence?" Primordial essence is both original upsurge (*Ur-sprung*) and enabling ground, that from which and by which a thing is what it is and as it is.[35] It is that which deploys the essence of particular things and thus lets them be, what Heidegger has called "the essence (verbal) of the essence (nominal) that can be presented tangibly in the form of assertions." [36] It is the essence that gives Being to beings, the essence of Being itself, identical with what Heidegger has called the history and mission of Being.

But the essences that particularly interest Heidegger are generally not of things. Essential essence is not oriented to substance but to the historical world: the essence of metaphysics (oblivion of the difference); of nihilism (oblivion of Being); of technology (com-positing); of poetry (instituting Being in the historical world through the word); of art (fixing truth in a work); of truth (concealing clearing).

Central to these is the essence of man (Part VI), the essence which Heidegger has elaborated in numerous convergent ways and relationships: ex-sistence, Being-in-the-world, concern, temporality, opening given by Being itself, respondent to the call of Being. After the turn, the issue is to understand how Being bestows man's essence, i.e., his unique historical abode and dwelling, his way of Being. What Husserl called the functioning intentionality, what the early Heidegger described in terms of man's concern for Being, is now viewed from the vantage of how Being approaches and therefore concerns (*angeht*) man in his essence. The consideration of this crucial relationship ultimately spans two key words in the Heideggerian meditation: *Brauch* and *Ereignis*. *Brauch* is Heidegger's unique translation of the very first word for Being in the Western tradition, found in Anaximander's fragment: *to chrēon*. It is the first documented attempt to think the genitive relationship in the Being *of* being.

34. *HW* 311.
35. *HW* 7 (649).
36. *SF* 30 (81).

In the metaphysics of grammar, "of" is the genitive of possession; rethought by Heidegger, it becomes the genesis of the
proper, the process whereby beings come into their own according to a certain propriety (*Brauch* also means custom). *To
chrēon* or *Brauch* as this befitting process is then forethought as
Ereignis (p. 226, below), the appropriating event in which man
and Being belong together in an immediate and ineffable identity. There is therefore a close correlation between the West's
first word for Being and Heidegger's word for the future. Just as
to chrēon is *to apeiron*,[37] the indeterminate, so the event of appropriation is the indeterminate "there is" of a giving. Just as *to
chrēon* is *Moira*,[38] the dispensation of lots, so the event of appropriation is the sending of the mission of Being. Just as the
Greeks saw in *to chrēon* the handing-down of their mores and
customs, so Heidegger tries in his formulation of *Ereignis* to
think the proper character of the transmission of the profound
tradition of Being, whereby man comes into his own through his
response to the needs and demands of the historical situation in
which he finds himself. For Being "speaks" precisely through the
claim that our unique historical situation makes on us to dis-
cover what is truly meet and just, right and proper, as a response
to it. The response is ours, but the situation in its needs and demands is both the provocation making the response possible to
begin with and that toward which this response is directed.
Thus, Being as need, claim, and demand (*Brauch*) is both behind and ahead of thought, the alpha and omega of the thinking
of Being. "This genitive accordingly says that Being as such
shows itself simultaneously as that which is to be thought and as
that which behooves (*braucht*) a thought to correspond to it." [39]
     Being as empowering want is therefore the enabling element
which is conducive to thinking, not as a wanting lack but as an
inexhaustible source of possibilities. Outside this element, like a
fish out of water, man could not function as a man. And since
the element in which man lives, moves, and has his Being is
linguistic through and through, *Brauch* is called the hermeneutic
relation.[40] Because language preserves the unthought possibilities that are to be thought, like a shelter or hold, *Ereignis* is the
holding relationship par excellence, "appropriating-holding-hold-

37. *HW* 339.
38. *HW* 340.
39. Richardson, *Heidegger: Through Phenomenology to Thought*, p.
XVII. See the translator's note on pages 126–27 for more on *Brauch*.
40. *US* 122–28. "This behooving implies a command, a calling" (*WD*
119 [196]).

ing to itself, the relationship of all relationships, the hold of all holds." [41] Being and man meet and are held together in the medium of language, which itself points to something immediate. For Being and man are not related as two substances but belong together and appropriate each other in a unique occurrence which is simplicity itself, in which Being is nothing but the claim that addresses man, and man is nothing but the response to this appeal.[42] This abrupt plunge into the experiential abyss of identity is the new "principle" of identity by which Heidegger seeks to overcome metaphysics, by means of a backtracking into its essence and ground. All the paths of Heidegger's thinking ultimately lead back to the unique simplicity of the occurrence whose appropriation is expressed in many ways: presenting, essencing, commissioning, clearing, empowering, wanting, claiming, behooving. To put it simply, the backtrack that attempts to get to the bottom of things ultimately reaches a point where the bottom falls out, and all that can be said is *es gibt*: "there is a giving." Even here, the substantive "it" of the "it gives" gives way to the pure and simple giving which is the essence of Being.

But "it" gives by withdrawing, and it is this withdrawal that continually gives rise to thought, as a Nothing which gives, which gives Being a history. The reticent giving points to a reserve of Being charged with possibilities that exceed the actuality of any of its particular revelations of being. "Being withdraws itself insofar as it reveals itself in being." [43] Withdrawal is what makes the difference between Being and being, and the oblivion of this difference is why metaphysics overlooked the surplus of possibilities which constitute the ongoing history of a Being that is radically creative. Being reveals itself in being, but there is always something more, something new and different yet to be said in what is already said. But what does it mean to read the unsaid in the already said, to uncover the unthought to be thought? The course of hermeneutic differentiation is such that it is not a matter of understanding the Greeks better than they understood themselves, as Schleiermacher's hermeneutic would have us do, but of understanding them differently,[44] appropriating from their suggestive unsaid something that demands saying in one's own time, something which previous thinkers could not see. The reticent giving of withdrawal thereby articulates it-

41. *US* 267.
42. *ID* 22–23 (31).
43. *HW* 310, 311.
44. *US* 134; *HW* 197.

xxxii / HEIDEGGER AND THE TRADITION

self according to epochs, and "the epochal essence of Being belongs to the hidden time character of Being."[45] In a conscious break with the metaphysical time sense which stressed the standing presence of *ousia,* Heidegger describes this time in terms of a "con-temporaneity" in which the three dimensions of time are mutually implicated in a reciprocal play whereby they pass into one another and at once hold one another apart, thus yielding an opening, a clearing, the contemporary world in which the unthought to be thought in what is already thought yields new and unsuspected possibilities. But the creative occurrence of the new and unprecedented is at once always what Gadamer has called the "occurrence of tradition." " 'Being' always speaks by way of a historical mission and is therefore always permeated by tradition."[46] And yet the unity and movement of this tradition open onto the abyss of the mystery of Being, so that surprises, new directions, creative bursts are always possible, disrupting all that has gone before, bringing forth radical new ways of questioning and therefore revolutions in the very problems of philosophy, let alone solutions. But when all is said and done, the only access to the mystery that lures the philosopher on is precisely in and through the tradition which somehow preserves it in all of its ineffability. The unsayable is somehow said and preserved—such is the mystery of language. "In one great moment, language once said something unique which remains inexhaustible, because it is always incipient and thus beyond the reach of any kind of leveling."[47]

These are but a few of the reflections that Professor Marx's theme of "Heidegger and the tradition" prompts in me and lays before us for further cultivation, in a "thinking that carries on" (see below, the "Conclusion," for Marx's own list of tasks).

Murray Greene translated the Introduction and Part I, and I the remainder. Our translations were then collated to iron out the inevitable differences between translators working independently. Professor Marx has generously given of his time to check the translation at various stages of its development and to make numerous suggestions that have materially improved the accuracy of its intent. Discussions with Professor Marx, Zygmunt Adamczewski, William Richardson, and Robert Jordan have aided me in coming to terms with the translation of the critical

45. *HW* 311.
46. *ID* 47 (51).
47. *WD* 168 (191–92).

Heideggerian terms, though more often than not I have eventually gone my own way (see the translator's notes).[48] References to Hegel's and Heidegger's works include in parentheses the corresponding pages of extant English translations (see the Bibliography), except for the *Encyclopaedia,* which is referred to only by section number, and *Being and Time,* which is already cross-paginated with the German editions. These translations have often provided helpful insights into our reading of Heidegger and Hegel. However, translations here of direct quotations from the German are for the most part our own, in accord with the specific needs and direction of this treatise. References to the main works of Heidegger, Hegel, and Aristotle have been abbreviated (see the List of Abbreviations preceding this introduction). In the interests of further brevity, publication data have in general been left out of the footnotes and will be found in the Bibliography. Finally, special thanks are due to Mrs. Virginia Seidman of Northwestern University Press for her excellent editing, especially in purging the errata from the Greek.

THEODORE KISIEL

DeKalb, Illinois
January 26, 1970

48. Translator's notes are indicated by asterisks in the text.

A Reappraisal of
Heidegger and the Tradition

by WERNER MARX

THE PRIMARY CONCERN of *Heidegger and the Tradition* was to find an answer to the question: wherein lies for Heidegger the *other* meaning of Being and essence, and the *other* meaning of the essence of man?[1] It is a question posed not merely out of historical interest, but out of a desire to stimulate further thinking concerning the basic terms which Heidegger presents in his later philosophy.[2] That this further thinking has not taken place in Germany since the book's publication may perhaps be attributed to the fact that interest in Heidegger has receded in the face of interest in other philosophical movements. Some efforts in this direction have been made, however. There have been attempts to combine analytic philosophies of language with Heidegger's thought; and efforts, on the part of "critical theory" in particular, have also been made to integrate elements of Heidegger's basic conception with a revisionist Marxism. Philosophical hermeneutics represents a further productive continuation of Heidegger's thought, though it is concerned only with a concept of understanding as interpretation such as found in *Being and Time*.[3] Philosophy in Germany, even where it has not striven toward a renaissance of practical philosophy, has taken refuge in preserving the tradition: it has remained "between tradition and a new beginning."[4] Further thinking, therefore, remains a desideratum. Its fulfillment would be — in accordance with Heidegger's sense of practice[5] — of great "practical" importance.

Heidegger's publications since this book's appearance should have facilitated further thinking. This is especially true of the two volumes on Nietzsche, whose basic thought had already been dealt with in an appendix to the first edition of this book; the collection of essays and lectures entitled *On the Way to Language*; and, above all, his last publication, *On the Issue of Thought*, which contains the lectures *Time and Being* and *The End of Philosophy and the Task of Thought*. In these writings, the key word *Ereignis*, translated in this book as "the event of appropriation," was introduced more resolutely than in previous writings, and from this vantage point the fundamental term *aletheia* was also given a different emphasis. Though these developments had already been presaged in the publications available at the time of the first edition of this book, they could not be precisely recognized at that point.

An important thesis of this book was that Heidegger "rethinks" (*andenken*) experiences made in the first beginning of the early Greeks, experiences whose sedimentations were to be found in the basic words *physis*, *logos*, and *aletheia*, in order to "forethink" (*vordenken*) them in "basic terms of another beginning."[6] We set as our task the critical investigation of the question whether or not these forethought basic terms of another beginning may be truly "legitimized" through those basic terms of the first beginning. We asked, therefore, whether one might now acknowledge them to be "binding." We came to the conclusion that such is not the case. The terms seemed to rest not only upon experiences which the early Greeks had had,[7] but rather upon those which Heidegger himself had had with Being.[8] And, in our opinion, this judgment has been further confirmed. For, in his last publication, Heidegger declared that he "awoke"[9] to another experience within the bearing of thought which he termed "a step back"[10] in the experience of the "obliviousness to Being" (i.e., the concealment of the meaning of Being). This experience was had within the modern technical world, within the "essencing of technology," whose definition as "com-posite" (*Gestell*) this book depicted extensively.[11] The non-creative interplay in the "positing" (*Stellen*) of Being and man was for Heidegger a "preliminary form of the *Ereignis*."[12] Within this form of withdrawal (*Entzugsgestalt*) of all creative Being, the attention of thinking "in withdrawal"[13] experiences the essencing of technology as a "preliminary appearance of the *Ereignis*."[14]

What is meant by "*Ereignis*"? For Heidegger, this word has a very different meaning from the usual senses conveyed in common speech, i.e., "something that happens" or a "mere event." For him, in the meaning of "*Ereignis*" there lies the sense of a "giving." He attempted to think of Being, presence without recurrence to a foundation of presence in that which is present.[15] In this attempt, there showed itself to him a presence in letting be (*Anwesenlassen*) which alone made possible the letting be of all that which is present. A basic trait of such presence in letting be is that it brings every being which is present into the "own" (*Eigenes*) which belongs to it. This, above all, constitutes the meaning of the key word "*Ereignis*."

Thus one could say that *Ereignis* has the function that the universal traditionally had — with the important difference that the latter was meant to bring forth only something "general" and precisely not that which is in each case "appropriate" (*eigen*), in the sense of that which is "own." The traditional concept of essence or nature was always directed toward the grounding of a being in a ground. Metaphysics thought of Being in various manners as this ground. *Ereignis*, on the other hand, implies a groundless bringing forth of beings present and absent.

The words with which Heidegger tries to fathom the *Ereignis* are all words that are supposed to ward off notions of a "grounding" as it is conceived of in metaphysics — words such as "playing," "sending," "presenting an offering." They all denote the groundless occurrence which, for Heidegger, is expressed in the German *es gibt* and in the French *il y a*. The meaning of this *es*, however, is that it is precisely not a *hypokeimenon*, a substance — for it is meant to name something which, in giving, withdraws itself in favor of that which it offers.[16] It is the indisposable letting be of that which is present. That which gives in *Ereignis* is also termed "that which grants" (*das Gewährende*). In deviation from the traditional notion of essence, this granting *Ereignis* is precisely not "that which lasts."[17]

We are thus able to say with certainty that, on the basis of Heidegger's later publications, the *other* Being and essence for Heidegger which was sought in this book, is the event of appropriation that grants. It would be even more correct not to speak of Being at all any more. Heidegger writes: "The *Ereignis* is by its very nature different, much fuller than any metaphysical determination of Being."[18] And in his final publication, he speaks of a "disappearance of Being"[19] and of "Being turning into *Ereignis*."[20]

We were convinced in this book that Heidegger has an increasing tendency to overcome (*überwinden*) Being by thinking of it as the essencing of the world (*Weltwesen*).[21] It can be clearly seen that his intention was to take leave of the "ontological difference" as thought of in metaphysical thinking, and to allow it to change into the relationship between world and thinking.[22] We can now clearly see that this took place in the world neighborhoods (*Weltgegenden*) of the world fourfold (*Weltgeviert*) which presents itself in the "thing" (*Ding*), a theme dealt with in this book.[23] These were thought of in terms of *Ereignis* such that each of the world neighborhoods was conceived of as "brought into its own" ("*ins Eigene geborgen*")[24] both for itself and in interplay with its counterparts.

What is perhaps most important about the key term "*Ereignis*" was pointed out in this book. "This key word of forethinking," we wrote, "is now called upon to determine the distribution of power and impotence between Being and the essence of man. It is intended to indicate how, corresponding to the original sense of the word, the 'focused' (*er-äugte*) essence of man as 'glimpsed' can only 'respond' to that which addressed itself to him in the realm of language, in an address that comes soundlessly as a claim and appeal of Being and the world."[25]

Thus we emphasized the following connotation of the word "*Ereignis*": Being and man, as belonging to each other, are "appropriated" to each other (*einander zugeeignet*). What is proper, own (*eigen*) to man, is that he is able to respond to that which appeals to him in the granting event of *Ereignis*.[26] In *On the Way to Language* the ability of man to respond to the appeal of that which grants was similarly determined by Heidegger from the perspective of the "essence" of language — which in turn was thought of in view of *Ereignis*.[27]

The significance of "that which grants" as *Ereignis* also becomes clearer in the later publications because there, in a similar manner, Heidegger tries to think of *aletheia* in terms of *Ereignis*.[28] Aletheia's structure is thus altered in an important manner. Up until this last publication, he had termed *aletheia* "truth" or "the truth of Being."[29] In his last work, Heidegger recognized that he should have more clearly distinguished between the "natural concept of truth" as assimilation – in the sense of agreement between ideas and entities present – and the occurrence experienced in *aletheia* which makes this correspondence at all possible. He goes on to call this occurrence a "clearing" (*Lichten*), and sees it as a "making free and open" that results in "the free area of the clearing" (*Lichtung*) or "openness."[30]

Now, however, it becomes even more distinct that only in and owing to the clearing can truth be that which it was traditionally conceived of to be: the evidence, and the certainty of propositions.[31] Clearing here has the same meaning for him as "unconcealedness" (*Unverborgenheit*) of the presence (Being) of that which is present (beings).

It was, furthermore, a central thesis in this book that Heidegger's importance lies above all in his attempt to overcome the traditional "metaphysics of light." We saw the historical beginnings of this tradition in Aristotle, who through the determinations of *nous* and *noesis* conceived of all that is as being luminous, i.e., intelligible. He thus also recognized in man the capacity for knowledge free of error, at least potentially.[32] For us, there already lay in Hegel's concept of truth at the end of the tradition – to express it metaphorically – the recognition of a "realm of darkness" which is overcome, however, through the power of *logos*, through concept and spirit, or – to express it metaphorically – through the "realm of light."

It was our conviction that Heidegger had thus tried to overcome this tradition of a "metaphysics of light" by thinking of the "realm of light" and the "realm of darkness" as "equal partners."[33] This relationship of equal status between the realms of light and darkness was demonstrated by us in the basic traits rethought in the first beginning and in those forethought in the other beginning. This especially holds for the relationship between unconcealment and concealment which Heidegger thought of in *aletheia*. We therefore considered *aletheia* to be a concept in opposition to the traditional metaphysics of light, insofar as it implies that concealment, self-concealing, and obliviousness to Being belong to Being according to its very essence.

In his last publication, Heidegger expressly warns against the confusion of clear*ing* in a verbal sense with light or luminousness, even though, as he also declares, "the possibility of a real connection between them" does exist.[34] So an objection to the above-mentioned thesis of this book could perhaps be raised on this account. Our reply, however, would be that, wherever a "realm of light" was spoken of in this book, this was done metaphorically. We certainly did not mean a "beam of light": concerning such a beam, Heidegger correctly observes that it is not created by the clearing, but rather that it traverses the clearing.[35] The term "realm of light" was supposed to indicate what Heidegger conceived of in the determinations of "clearing" and "unconcealment" of the particular presencing valid for that which is present. The clearing and unconcealedness of the presence of that which is present is the result of clearing, a clearing which produces the "shining forth" of that which is present, its appearing. Appearing is, seen positively, luminous.

For precisely this reason, in the *Introduction to Metaphysics*, Heidegger had termed the opening of Being as "stepping into the light,"[36] and the appearance of Being as a "standing in the light."[37] In the essay "Aletheia" he had admittedly defined the clearing as a granting that brings forth not only the free area, but also lucidity, appearance, luminating, and illumination. There it is stated: "The pure clearing brings not only the lucidity but at the same time the free area."[38] The decisive basic trait of clearing and disclosedness of the presence of that which is present was for him their unapparent shining (*unscheinbares Scheinen*).

The metaphor which we used, "the realm of light," retains its justification especially when we consider its relationship to the "realm of darkness." We also spoke of a "realm of darkness" in order to illustrate Heidegger's determinations "concealment," self-concealing, and obliviousness to Being. Heidegger's decisive position, counter to the traditional metaphysics of light, lies in these determinations. Though we defined the relationship between the "realm of light" and the "realm of darkness" as that of "equal partners" in this book, we must now point out, however, that with the structure of *aletheia* Heidegger ascribes a more important role to concealment—to the *lethe* as thought of from the vantage of the *Ereignis*—than to disclosedness.[39]

The essay "Aletheia," to which we referred in this book, already showed this tendency. However, it is only in the later publications that *lethe* "gains the upper hand" over disclosedness by being termed "the place of stillness" and by being determined as the "heart" of *aletheia*.[40] The heart and place of stillness is that which gathers in itself, *which first grants disclosedness*. In this power of *lethe* there lies a new determination of *aletheia*, in particular of the history of Being prevailing as *aletheia*.

As to the history of Being: up until now, the clearing of presence has concealed itself to thought. Even the occurrence of presence has concealed itself till now, just as everything coming holds itself concealed in *lethe's* concealing. Heidegger, at the same time takes the view, however, that the history of Being has reached its end in his thought, because for the first time he was able to conceive of and bring forth into language the self-concealing clearing of presence, as well as the clearing of the self-concealment in presence, and the clearing of the self-concealing concealment. Therefore, there is now an "awakening to *Ereignis*."[41] "Concealment conceals itself no longer; thought is rather also attentive to it."[42]

The fact that, for Heidegger, metaphysics, as the obliviousness of Being, as the history of the concealment and withdrawal of that which Being gives, has reached its end confirms a supposition which we had already expressed in this book.[43] This does not imply that the abrupt turn of another commission of Being has already arrived, or that humans have become "mortals," or that thought has made a turn under the lasting dominance of "that which essences in technology." But to be sure, in contrast to the tradition, a "changed essence" has become visible through Heidegger's "insight."[44] For Heidegger, the *other* essencing of Being which we sought has shown itself to be that "granting" which proceeds from *lethe* and makes the prevailing unconcealment of the presence of that which is present at all possible.

NOTES

1. Werner Marx, *Heidegger and the Tradition*, trans. T. Kisiel/M. Greene (Evanston, 1971), pp. 10-11.

2. *Ibid.*, pp. 243 ff.

3. Hans-Georg Gadamer, *Wahrheit und Methode* (Tübingen, 1960), pp. 240 ff.

4. Cf. Werner Marx, *Reason and World*, trans. T. Yates/R. Geuss (The Hague, 1971), pp. xi-xii.

5. Cf. Martin Heidegger, "Letter on Humanism," in *Martin Heidegger: Basic Writings*, ed. David Krell (New York, 1977), pp. 239 ff.

6. *Heidegger and the Tradition*, pp. 172 ff., 177.

7. *Ibid.*, pp. 225-26.

8. *Ibid.*, p. 179.

9. Martin Heidegger: *On Time and Being*, trans. J. Stambaugh (New York, 1972), pp. 30 ff.

10. *Ibid.*, pp. 27 ff.

11. *Heidegger and the Tradition*, pp. 172 ff.

12. *On Time and Being*, p. 53.

13. *Ibid.*, p. 53.

14. *Ibid.*, p. 32.

15. *Ibid.*, p. 2.

16. *Ibid.*, p. 40.

17. Martin Heidegger, "The Question Concerning Technology," in *The Question Concerning Technology and Other Essays*, trans. W. Lovitt (New York, 1977), pp. 30-31.

18. Martin Heidegger, *On the Way to Language*, trans. P. Hertz (New York, 1971), p. 129.

19. *On Time and Being*, p. 43.

20. *Ibid.*, p. 53.

21. *Heidegger and the Tradition*, p. 226.

22. *On Time and Being*, p. 37.

23. *Heidegger and the Tradition*, pp. 187 ff., 197 ff.

24. *On Time and Being*, p. 37.

25. *Heidegger and the Tradition*, p. 226.

26. Werner Marx, "Das Denken und seine Sache," in *Heidegger: Freiburger Universitätsvorträge zu seinem Gedenken* (Freiburg, 1977), p. 35.

27. *Reason and World*, pp. 90 ff., 97 ff.

28. *On Time and Being*, p. 41.

29. *Heidegger and the Tradition*, pp. 145 ff.

30. *On Time and Being*, p. 65.

31. *Ibid.*

32. *Heidegger and the Tradition*, p. 147 ff.

33. *Ibid.*

34. *On Time and Being*, p. 65.

35. *Ibid.*, p. 66.

36. Martin Heidegger, *An Introduction to Metaphysics*, trans. R. Manheim (New York, 1961), p. 88.

37. *Ibid.*, p. 92.

38. Martin Heidegger, "Aletheia" in *Early Greek Thinking*, trans. D. Krell/F. Capuzzi (New York, 1975), p. 118.

39. *On Time and Being*, p. 41.

40. *Ibid.*, p. 68.

41. *Ibid.*, pp. 30 ff.

42. *Ibid.*, p. 41.

43. *Heidegger and the Tradition*, p. 173.

44. Martin Heidegger, "The Turning," in *The Question Concerning Technology*, pp. 45 ff.

Heidegger and
the Tradition

Introduction

THE QUESTION RAISED OF OLD, says Aristotle, the question that is raised today, that will be raised in all eternity and will ever baffle us, the question: *ti to on*—what is the Being of a being—is just the question: *tis hē ousia*—what is the *essence* of a particular being.

In this famous passage from Book VII of the *Metaphysics* Aristotle thus declares: The question as to the *Being* of a being is the question as to its *essence*.* And he predicts that the question of *Being* will eternally be posed as a question of *essence*, which implies that essence will eternally retain the meaning of *ousia*.[1]

---

* A distinction may be made between essence as a general category and essence answering to the more specific "what is" question. The same distinction applies to other Hegelian terms, e.g., concept (*Begriff*, frequently translated "notion" in the past). The old approach was to capitalize the categorical sense; but to avoid the excesses of "Teutonic" capitalization, this orthography will be avoided here as much as possible; the context usually makes clear which of the senses is intended. In only a relatively few instances did the translator feel compelled to bow to custom and retain the capitals of "Idea" and "Absolute," for example. With regard to Heideggerian terms, "Being" and "Nothing" will be capitalized, for the following reasons: "Being," in order to stress the all-important distinction of the "ontological difference" between "Being" (*Sein*) and "being" (*Seiendes*), inasmuch as the latter will also be usually translated in the singular; and the category of "Nothing" will be capitalized to distinguish it immediately from the numerous English idiomatic uses of "nothing."

1. *Meta.* 1028b3 ff. This reading best renders the particular interpretation of the meaning of *ousia* that became decisive historically. With what follows cf. the author's *The Meaning of Aristotle's "Ontology."* [Full publication data for all books cited will be found in the Bibliography at the back of the book.—Translator.] With reference to the more radical interpretation of the manifold ways in which Being can be expressed—the

[3]

Aristotle proved amazingly correct in these two predictions. Western philosophy has continued to philosophize predominantly from the assumption that the question of Being amounts to the question of essence. In considering the ways of Being of a being, philosophy first of all paid attention to the essential constitution of the being. And that, generally speaking, meant that philosophy asked in the first place about the what-is, or the what-ness, of a being. In this regard the effect of Aristotle has been truly decisive and far-reaching. It extends into contemporary philosophy. Whether accepted or rejected, this influence determines the contemporary question about Being and essence. Hence we who wish to deal with the question of Being and essence in contemporary philosophy must ask with amazement: How it is that after almost two and a half millennia we still feel the force of this Aristotelian thinking? How is it that Aristotle proved right to so great a degree in his prediction that the question of Being will eternally be asked as a question of essence? A really convincing explanation would have to show that the phenomena themselves require referring the question of Being to the question of essence; that it is therefore appropriate to the subject matter—and hence necessary—to philosophize in this way.

It may be claimed that, within the framework of the traditional meaning of Being and essence, Aristotle has indeed shown this in Book IV of the *Metaphysics*.[2] The Being of a being is articulated in many ways and therefore is expressible in many ways (*legetai pollachōs*), e.g., in its being a magnitude, according to the category of quantity; or in its being heavy, according to the category of quality. But these and all other ways-to-be[3] of a being are permeated by a specific relationship, a relating movement that refers the various ways-to-be of a being back to "one certain *physis*," which determines and unifies them all; to the *ousia*, the essence. This occurs, Aristotle explains, in the same way that a healthy complexion or a healthy medicine or a healthy march relate of themselves to the one signification *health*, which determines them all as its ways or modes.[4] Only

---

on legetai pollachōs—cf. *Meta.* 1026a33 ff., 1045b35 ff.; and, with reference to the interpretation of *ousia* that leads to the Scholastic doctrine of the transcendentals, cf. *Meta.* 1053b10 ff.

2. *Meta.* 1003a33 ff.

3. It should be mentioned that, according to another reading, these "other ways" do not relate to the *ousia*.

4. This is only a brief reference to the difficult problem of how the manifold ways-to-be were ascribed to the *pros hen* unity that is not generic.

because the Being of a being is itself permeated by this relating movement back to essence, only because the subject matter itself so requires, does Aristotle [5] demand of every philosopher that he ask first of all about the principles and ultimate grounds of *ousia*, of essence; that he raise the question about essence whenever he raises the question about Being. That Western philosophy after Aristotle, apart from certain exceptions, met this demand is further explained, however, by the fact that Aristotle profoundly thought out the essence of *ousia* and was able to demonstrate its great effectiveness with respect to an understanding of the particular being.

Can it also be maintained, however, that Aristotle's prediction was confirmed in its claim that the essence of essence would eternally be thought as *ousia*? Did essence in this signification determine the history of Western thought, and does it still so determine contemporary thinking? There can be no doubt that *ousia*, in its translation as *substantia*, underwent many transformations in the history of Western thought. And nevertheless, with few exceptions, the variant doctrines of substantiality remained at least oriented toward the fundamental meanings of Aristotelian *ousia*. Thus, categories authoritative for the final great "Doctrine of Being and Essence" of the Hegelian *Logic*, for example, derive from certain basic features of Aristotelian *ousia*, despite incisive changes in the history of thought.

Hence if Aristotle proved essentially correct in those two predictions, if in the history of Western thought the question of Being remained predominantly understood as a question of essence, if essence retained many telling traits of *ousia*, and if the influence of Aristotelian thinking reaches down into our time— then when, in our day, a philosopher expressly poses the question of Being *no longer* as such a question of essence and expressly thinks *no longer* in the sense of *ousia* or substance, we must regard this attempt as a veritable revolution.

Regardless of Aristotle's prediction—and in the face of the Western tradition—Martin Heidegger holds himself no longer bound to that strict Aristotelian demand: in the question as to Being, to inquire in the first place about the grounds and principles of the essence of a being. While Heidegger's thinking, as Aristotle had also predicted, is still disturbed by the question about Being and essence, it is not disturbed by the question about

---

Cf. J. Owens, *The Doctrine of Being in the Aristotelian Metaphysics,* pp. 49 ff.

5. *Meta.* 1003b18.

Being that asks about the *ti*, the "what," of a particular being—whereby this "what" has the meaning of essence, and essence has the meaning of *ousia* or substance. The task of the present exposition will be to demonstrate how Heidegger's question as to Being and essence, turning away from the Aristotelian, gains access to another realm, attains another dimension. And it will be shown how in this other realm the basic words "Being" and "essence" obtain a meaning so altered and opposed to the traditional as to render pointless that basic Aristotelian demand that the question of Being be formulated as a question of essence.

Even in his early writings Heidegger attempted to show that traditional philosophy completely overestimated the efficacy of essence in the meaning of substantiality. In *Being and Time* he sought to break the sovereignty of substance by proving that this category can properly grasp neither the essence of man nor the essence of those things that man cares for in his world. Though the main attack in *Being and Time* is directed against substance in its Cartesian formulation, it is also aimed against the Aristotelian *ousia*.

For a time it appeared that Heidegger altogether denied that there was something like "the essence." Or certain paradoxical turns of thought in *Being and Time* were misunderstood, so that Heidegger seemed to have affirmed the pre-eminence of a Scholastically understood existence of man over a Scholastically understood essence of man, in much the same way that Sartre later did. Meanwhile, however, it was generally recognized that Heidegger's analyses of structures of Being—whether of Being-there [*Dasein*], Being-with (others) [*Mitsein*], the being of things, or the question as to the "idea of Being in general"—were somehow "questions about essence," though it did not become clear how the concept of essence underlying these analyses was distinguished from the traditional concept of essence. Perhaps the tendency of Heidegger to think the meaning of Being and essence in *another* way could already have been recognized in the inaugural lecture, *What Is Metaphysics?* For there [6] he tried to show why, contrary to the traditional conception, the "Nothing" in its "nihilating ways" belongs to Being. A clear indication of Heidegger's main endeavor, however, was first given in the final section of the treatise published in 1943, *On the Essence of Truth*. There Heidegger stated: "The present essay leads the question as to the essence of truth beyond the accustomed con-

6. Cf. especially, WM 32, 36.

fines of the usual concept of essence and helps toward a recon-
sideration of whether the question as to the essence of truth must
not at the same time be in the first place the question as to the
truth of essence"; and to this Heidegger adds: "In the concept of
essence, however, philosophy thinks Being." Here one can recognize the endeavor to part with the Aristotelian comprehension
of Being as essence, as well as with the traditional concept of essence. It becomes clear only from his later writings, however,
that Heidegger's efforts center around this single goal: to experience the meaning of Being and essence in *another way* and to
bring this experience to speech.

To be able to evaluate the meaning of these efforts toward
another experience of Being, one must ever keep in mind that
for Heidegger this goal was not a matter of solving an academic
problem. His is not the task of a philosophical enterprise that still
regards itself as a contemplative *theōria* in the sense of Plato or
Aristotle, or as a conceptual science in Hegel's sense, or as an ob-
serving and descriptive science in Husserl's sense. Though Heidegger does not conceive his thinking as some sort of "product"
of his human "faculty," he nevertheless sees in it a highest "doing and achieving."

On the meanings of *ousia* and substance attacked by Heidegger obviously rest the traditional ontologies, anthropologies, cos-
mologies, and theologies that have strongly influenced the development of the Western spiritual tradition. Heidegger himself,
however, apparently does not so much view the "doing and
achieving" power of his thinking as directed toward a revolutionary overthrow. He sees it rather as a transforming and "building"
power, capable of preparing the way toward a different meaning
of Being and essence. The thinking of another meaning of Being
and essence may prepare its coming and make possible a helping
toward the "saving of the essence of mankind." [7]

The terrible dangers that threaten the essence of man by the
essence of technology are described by Heidegger particularly in
the essay "The Question of Technology." Man for once stands in
peril of completely forgetting that he alone is essentially singled
out to experience the meaning of Being, that he alone can respond to this meaning and therefore plays a definite role in the
occurrence of Being [*Seinsgeschehen*]. Man stands in danger of
comprehending himself only as a material, as stock. And in
nearly opposite manner, man at the same time finds himself in

7. Cf. the author's "Heidegger's New Conception of Philosophy," *Social
Research*, XXII, no. 4 (1955), 451 ff.

a second and even greater danger: that he take himself as sole lord of the universe, believing that everything he encounters subsists only insofar as it is of his "making."

According to Heidegger, however, precisely this imperiling essence of technology necessitates our thinking "what is ordinarily understood by essence in *another* sense."[8] And the experience of an "other sense" of Being and essence thereby necessitated has the power "to let saving grow"[9] or, as stated in the introduction to *What Is Metaphysics?*:[10] "to help bring about [co-occasion] a change of the essence of man." Similarly, Heidegger already had explained in the lectures of 1935, which appeared under the title *Introduction to Metaphysics*, that it is a matter "of experiencing Being from the ground up in a new way";[11] for "the word 'Being' and its meaning," as he remarks earlier,[12] "contains the spiritual destiny of the West."

On such questions as: in what meaning of essence can the "essence of technology" be at one and the same time the "highest danger" and the promise of "deliverance"; whether the spiritual destiny of the West really depends on the experience of another meaning of essence; whether a thinking experience of Being has in fact the "doing and achieving power"—these and similar questions obviously can be argued intelligently only after a certain clarity has been attained on the question: "In what, then, really consists the other meaning of Being and essence in Heidegger, as departing from the tradition?"—a question that always includes the question as to the essence of man.

We believe that an answer to this question must for once be sought in a "systematic" fashion secured by the historical structure of Heidegger's thinking. First of all, it is central for the understanding of Heidegger; the "discussions" and "reflections" during the second phase of his thinking already move within another "locus" and "sense" of Being and essence, while the reader often remains under the impression that the discussion is still within the traditional realm and meaning.

Second, an answer to our question could serve a critical interest above and beyond the interpretive. For Heidegger's work itself must be the final proof as to whether it really demonstrates another sense of Being and essence in accord with its intention.

8. *VA* 38.
9. *VA* 36 ff.
10. *WM* 9 (209).
11. *EM* 155 (203).
12. *EM* 28, 32 (37, 42).

The third reason for concentrating on the question of Being and essence in Heidegger goes beyond an interpretive or critical interest in Heidegger. We are convinced that it is the present-day "need of philosophy" to keep alive the question of the essence of essence. To be sure, the philosophical consciousness of our time has already to a great extent found its way back from the historicist, relativist, and positivist tendencies of the most recent past to the realization of the necessity of "essence" and possibly of an "essential order." But philosophy has been influenced so basically by the repercussions of "historical" or "epochal" thinking since Hegel's death, pre-eminently through the effects of Kierkegaard, Marx, and Nietzsche, by the insights of the natural sciences, and by the shattering experiences of the past century, that it cannot simply return to the traditional doctrine of essence, to Aristotelian *ousia* or the conceptions of substantiality based thereon. Awakened, moreover, by the transcendental turning point, especially, however, by Hegel's insights in the *Phenomenology of Spirit*, philosophy has seen itself ever more strongly forced to think the essence of man as a *doer*, if not indeed as a creator or cocreator, who not only can alter his world but even fashion the new. If philosophy today wants to go back to a "doctrine of essence," then it must try to think an "other" essence, not an essence that, like the Aristotelian *ousia*, is "eternal," and, as the "same," is the ground of every change, of all coming to be and passing away. The immense difficulty of the task consists rather in so comprehending the essence of essence that the *new* can arrive and the essence of man play a role in such a transformation—without the essence again becoming "historicized" and "humanized" through such arrival of the new and participation by man. The essence to be thought must also reveal the essence of our "things" in such a manner that they are not submerged in an utter inessentiality of meaning. An answer to the question of wherein properly lies the other sense of Being and essence in Heidegger will perhaps then lead to a judgment on whether Heidegger's contribution does justice to this "need of philosophy."

It might seem strange in a thinker with such an extraordinary command of expression and force of construction, who has repeatedly interpreted himself, that a clarity free of doubt does not exist on this central question which we are posing. Heidegger himself has given us an explanation for this in his essay *The Question of Being*. Concerning the essence of essence, no information can be imparted ready-made in the form of vouchsafed propositions. The sense of Being and essence in Heidegger is in fact not a concept that lends itself to being apprehended and handed back in the form of a *horismos* or definition, nor is it a concept in the Hegelian sense. It also does not permit itself to be expressed in the Aristotelian way of a referring-back to a basic meaning, nor in the Hegelian manner as a speculative proposition. Heidegger has often stressed that the "yield" of his thinking should not be "answers" but rather remain "questions," questions regarding subject matters worth thinking and worthy to be tasks for further thinking.

If this is the case, then only an attitude that *asks-along [Mit-fragen]* has the prospect of understanding the meaning of Being and essence that departs from the tradition. Such an asking-along must make sure that it directs itself to the same matter that Heidegger has under regard. So long as it concerns itself only with understanding the subject matter thought by Heidegger, it will "re-experience the experiences" that have led him to another sense of Being and essence.

Every asking-along, however, must attain to a thinking-along, which thinks-along the problematic that Heidegger's questions have opened for its own sake. Such a thinking-along, however, can succeed only if it holds itself open in a relationship of *krisis*, or separation, from its thought content, but of course in such a manner that it still remains close to it and does not sacrifice the purpose of a thinking-along.

We believe that traditional thought affords the desired separation. We cannot, of course, be concerned here with demonstrating the traditional problematic of "Being and essence" and the "essence of man" in its total development. What is required, rather, is to grasp the tradition where it first shaped its guiding thought conceptually, the thought of substance, and then again where it begins to dissolve this thought. On the foundation of Platonic thought, Aristotle for the first time comprehensively apprehended substance; and specifically he unfolded it in the direction of the question as to the *on hēi on*. This question, guided by his interest in the constitution of the Being of individual beings, remained exemplary for all subsequent philosophy. The *ousia* of Aristotle remained the prototype; as "that which underlies," that is, as "substance" or as "subject," *ousia* comprised the constitution of a being.

Hegel, on the other hand, represents for us the "end" of this Aristotelian tradition, since his thinking was still determined by the initial starting point of Being as substance and subject. To that extent he still belongs to this tradition. But he thinks it "to the end," since as a consequence of *another turn of the question* he attains to *another realm* in which substance and subject not only signify the constitution of the Being of a being but rather in the first place constitute categories of "Being" itself. This "realm" will be identified more closely, since despite all differences it is the realm in which Heidegger's thinking also moves. Herein lies the justification for the view that Hegel's *Science of Logic* can mediate to us an understanding of the radically *other* meaning of Being in Heidegger.

In the first main section of this work we shall elaborate the form and meaning of the Aristotelian *ousia*. Then we shall reflect on four of its *basic traits:* its "eternalness," its necessity, its self-sameness, and its intelligibility. It is these same basic traits that we shall again encounter, within a radically altered problem situation, in Hegel's "Being." This is essentially why we regard ourselves as justified in terming the thinking from Plato and Aristotle to Hegel simply as "the tradition" and viewing, on the other hand, Heidegger's thinking as the attempt toward a "turning-away" from this tradition. From this we derive the justification for the title of the present work.

After these basic traits of Hegel's "Being" are developed, the essence of man in Aristotle as well as in Hegel will be treated. All this, however, serves only as an introduction to Heidegger's problematic. Therefore, we can take up only those questions that announce this problematic, even if from a distance.

In the subsequent main sections, the *other* basic traits of Being and essence and the *other* essence of man in Heidegger will be set in relief in the light of the traditional basic traits. This comparative presentation, however, will neither follow the development of Heidegger's thinking in its individual stages, nor will it cite the various interpretations [13] of pre-Socratic and other philosophical texts from which Heidegger obtained those other basic traits of Being and the essence of man and from which he made them understandable. We see our task as consisting rather in exhibiting the basic determinations now present *in toto* as though they were "categories." The reader will be introduced immediately to the "ground plan" of the "comprehensive blueprint." This will afford him the opportunity to look over and examine the total nexus of determinations hitherto put forward by Heidegger. This "instrumental method" contains a conscious

13. Cf. below, pp. 109, 120.

offense against the historical—and also in a definite sense "poetical"—thinking of Heidegger. We are, however, convinced that this price has to be paid. A "thinking-further" can be prepared only by soberly laying bare the historical and poetic structure on its "scaffolding." Only then can we become open for what is perhaps still unfinished, neglected, or even unsuitable in Heidegger's work and what in a pregnant sense is for our generation "the task to be thought." Only in this way will we come to those key areas from which interrogations of Heidegger must proceed, such as whence his thinking and thought are really "legitimated," whether his thought is really "binding," and other questions so disturbing to contemporary philosophy. We shall in the course of our "reconstructive" presentation and in the concluding chapter refer to problems that can become the task of a "thinking-further."

In this way the second main section will show how Heidegger in *Being and Time* sought to "overcome" the traditional meaning of Being and essence, substance and subject, and how, in the next step, out of the insight into the temporality and historicity of man, he developed the structures for an interpretive thinking.

Our interest, however, is above all in the later work of Heidegger that seeks the "other" meaning of Being and essence. Therefore we shall first of all have to clarify the essence—the method as well as the range of tasks—of the thinking that unfolds it and which Heidegger calls "rethinking" and "forethinking." The range of tasks of this rethinking and forethinking prescribes the course of the subsequent main parts of this investigation.

By way of rethinking, the third main part determines the "other sense of Being and essence" in the direction of the "first beginning" of the Western experience of Being. The next main part seeks it in the direction of a "history of Being" that rests on these experiences (as rethought) and, above all, in the final form of this "history" which Heidegger sees in the now sovereign "Being" or "essence" of technology. And by way of forethinking, the presentation in a further main section finally determines the meaning of Being and essence of that which, in the proper sense of "other," is the meaning of Being and essence of "another beginning"; whereby the real goal of this work is reached.

The final main section deals with the "essence of man" and, specifically, first of all, the essence of man at the "first beginning" according to the rethinking, and then the essence of man of the period of "another beginning" according to the forethinking. It may already be emphasized here that the separate treatment of the essence of man is followed only for purposes of a better presentation and that such a separation, properly speaking, is contrary to the subject matter itself and to Heidegger's intentions.

The present work, an introduction to Heidegger, treats only of the Heideggerian problematic and not of Heidegger's person. Therefore, biographical facts are not taken into account even when they are in themselves important for the development and closer determination of philosophical problems.[14] Insofar as this comparative presentation is guided exclusively by definite traditional problems in Aristotle and Hegel, other philosophers are treated in passing or not at all, even when they have perhaps directly influenced Heidegger considerably. Hence Augustine, Kant, Schelling, Kierkegaard, and even Husserl[15] remain unconsidered, and only a little is said about Nietzsche,[16] who had a particularly strong influence on Heidegger's later thinking.

Our approach to Heidegger is not through a reflection on the history of ideas. It is much rather a comparative demonstration and reconstructive investigation of the interconnection of the ground determinations of Being. These determinations, therefore, are not transcribed descriptively but are cited in the course of the text. This method seems the only reliable one in this particular case. For Heidegger, proceeding as no one before him from a very definite insight into the essence of speech, has so intrinsically bound up his thinking with the special way in which he has formulated his terms that every attempt at transcription must in fact lead to difficulties. If for this reason the treatment

14. Here also belong the avowals, ever most profoundly dismaying, of Heidegger to National Socialism during the first years of the regime. With reference to his speech *Die Selbstbehauptung der deutschen Universität* and the "Verlautbarungen des Rektors" (*Freiburger Studentenzeitung*), see, especially, Karl Löwith, "Les implications politiques de la philosophie de l'existence" in *Les Temps Modernes*, November, 1946, and August, 1948; *Heidegger: Denker in dürftiger Zeit*, pp. 50 ff.; and *Gesammelte Abhandlungen*, pp. 117 ff. See also below, p. 251.

15. Cf. here of late particularly H. G. Gadamer, *Wahrheit und Methode*, pp. 240 ff.

16. Heidegger's latest publication, *Nietzsche* (2 vols.), appeared during the printing of this work (1961) and therefore could not be taken account of within the text. Nevertheless, the Appendix (see below, p. 257) deals with the "method" and range of the Nietzsche interpretations and provides reference to thoughts which further clarify what is here presented and make understandable the development of Heidegger's thinking. The Appendix especially draws attention to a number of considerations made public for the first time which confirm the interpretation of Heidegger's concept of Being represented in the present work.

adheres closely to Heidegger's text, this does not mean that it wants to give up the "distance" from which it investigates Heidegger's work in a way that keeps "thinking-along" with him.

In conclusion, we might offer a hint to the reader interested mainly in the problematic of Heidegger's work. Since our treatment desires not only to investigate but also to "introduce," it frequently repeats for didactic reasons the traditional determinations that are developed more elaborately in the first main section on the history of the problem. Therefore it is possible for the reader to begin with the second main part and then go back to the chapters on the history of the problem.[17]

17. The reader is also referred to two articles by the author complementing sections V and VI which have recently appeared in a selection of his essays, *Vernumft und Welt, Phaenomenologica* 36 (The Hague: Martinus Nijhoff, 1970), English translation, *Reason and World,* to be published by Nijhoff in 1971.

PART I
The Tradition

1 / The Form and Meaning of the Aristotelian *Ousia*

HEIDEGGER WANTS TO THINK THE ESSENCE of Being and essence differently from the tradition. Since almost all variants of the doctrine of substance in Western philosophy have remained oriented to the Aristotelian *ousia,* it seems proper for us to reflect on the form and meaning of Aristotle's *ousia,* in order in its light to be able to think along with him the problem of the form and meaning of Being and essence in Heidegger as inimical to *ousia.*

Such a reflection on the *meaning* of essence is in itself wholly "un-Aristotelian." For Aristotle's question is addressed precisely *not* to the meaning of Being and essence. The *direction* of his question is toward the particular being as such. He wanted to know, as he explained in the first chapter of Book IV of the *Metaphysics,* what a being is insofar as it *is—on hēi on.* He focused only on this particular being and then turned from it toward its Being and essence.

Heidegger characterized this Aristotelian direction of the question as "metaphysical," for in order to apprehend the particular being *as* a being, it strode over and beyond [1] the particular being—*meta ta physika*—toward "Being," for which reason Heidegger termed the "being-ness," [2] as Aristotle viewed it, "the going-beyond" [*Überstieg*] or "the transcendence." [3] We are convinced with Heidegger that Aristotle, as a consequence of this direction of his question, was able to see only one particular

1. WD 135 (223). Cf. also WM 35 (370).
2. HW 163.
3. WD 135 (223); SF 33 (87).

[17]

"side" of Being. The question cited before—*ti to on*—what is "Being," was concerned only with the constitution of the Being of the divine, human, and nonhuman being. It did not ask about the occurrence of Being itself. It did not ask in the first place about the "essence" and not at all about the "sense" of Being; it asked rather about the "what" of "that which had been enabled" by Being and essence, the "what" of the particular being. In the present chapter the *meaning* of *ousia* will be considered by way of an elaboration of some of its standard basic traits, against which those basic traits of the *other* meaning of "Being and essence," which Heidegger seeks to unfold, will then be set off. The basic traits of *ousia*—"eternalness," necessity, selfsameness, and intelligibility—will be treated. We shall again recognize these fundamental traits in Hegel's "Being," albeit in altered form after a two-thousand-year history of thought.

In the course of this reflection on the meaning of *ousia*, however, we shall develop only such problems as have remained significant for Heidegger in a radically altered problem situation. Our discussion of the Aristotelian "answers" to these problems will seek to prepare the way for an understanding of those other kinds of "answers" in Heidegger.

Aristotelian *ousia* can obtain the living form necessary for an active thinking-along with Heidegger only when the presentation is restricted to sketching the contours of *ousia* in a few strokes, while expressly forsaking any attempt at justification of the viewpoints here brought forward.[4] In so doing, we shall treat only those structures that are alive in the concept of essence still current for us today.

I. The Form of *Ousia*

LET US BRIEFLY RECALL the form of *ousia*—the essential constitution of the particular being in the sublunary sphere —as Aristotle conceived it in the particular light of his question. While he kept the particular being in view, he asked, proceeding from it, about its essential constitution.

In the treatise *Categories* a distinction is made between a "first *ousia*" and a "second *ousia*."[5] As instances of the second

4. Cf. the treatment in detail by the author in *The Meaning of Aristotle's "Ontology."*
5. *Cat.* 2a13 ff.

ousia, Aristotle cites genus and species.[6] From them derives the "concept of the universal," whereby Scholasticism determined the quiddity or "what-ness" of a being. The quiddity of any man is his *genus,* the universal concept "living being," under which animals are also included; his *species* is his determination as "two-legged living being"; and every man indiscriminately falls under this determination. The genus of a jug is "container," under which cups and cans are also included; and under the species "jug" are likewise included water jugs, wine jugs, and such jugs as were once employed for sacrificial purposes and stand in museums. Or the species "bridge" includes every water overpass, whether a bridge of modern technology or some bridge over the Neckar in Heidelberg celebrated in song by the poets.

Heidegger rightly pointed out [7] that this universal concept, the *quidditas* or the *essentia,* lies at the ground of the current concept of essence. Even if we do not proceed syllogistically, and even if we do not in definition derive the species out of the genus, this conception of "essence" nevertheless determines our everyday as well as our scientific understanding. This does not exclude the fact that the insufficiency of these determinations that refer to essence has often been noticed, since they name a universal indifferently applicable to all things. For this reason it might be assumed that Aristotle had already developed the "essence" more deeply in the sense of the first *ousia.* The "philosopher," unlike the "scientist," was not satisfied with compartmentalizing and ordering the "classes" *kath' hen,*[8] "according to the one," the universally applicable. He would far rather apprehend in a philosophical orientation [9] another kind of "essence" in a relating way *pros hen.*[10] He wants to apprehend the *"certain physis"* [11] which determines all ways which can be spoken of relative to a being and which determines all categories as relating to that *physis.* This "nature" of a being, that which is its "enabling power," the *archē* [12] or "first ground of its Being," the *aition prōton tou einai,*[13] is *ousia.* It is the mysterious oneness of the "this-somewhat" or *tode ti,*[14] of the sheer "to be" [*Seiendseins*] of a being and its

6. *Cat.* 2b7 ff.
7. *VA* 37; *HW* 39 (676).
8. *Meta.* 1003b12.
9. Cf. Marx, *op. cit.,* pp. 8 ff.
10. *Meta.* 1003a33; 1003b16.
11. *Meta.* 1003a34.
12. *Meta.* 1003b6; 1041b32.
13. *Meta.* 1041b29.
14. *Meta.* 1028a12.

"what-is" or *ti estin*,[15] more exactly its "what it is as ever having been," its *ti ēn einai*.[16] In the doctrine of the categories,[17] Aristotle names "this man" or "this horse" as examples of the first *ousia*. "This man" or "this horse" is a *"physis"* [18] which "enables" that, not some sum of "elements," some flesh and bones "is," but a particular man or a particular horse.[19]

Only because this *physis* is "present" (*hyparchein*)[20] is there a meaningful being; only because there is this "simple thing," this *haploun* [21] or *asyntheton* [22] that determines the "something" in *its* "to be as being" and its "what-is." This "first *ousia*," this enabling unity, can therefore also be called a "whole." This term could be of use especially with regard to that "wholeness," understood quite differently, from which Heidegger determines the essence of "things." Let us keep it firmly in mind that in the *ousia* of Aristotle the term concerns a "whole" that "from inside out"—from its central core—makes possible the meaningful particular being.

It proved decisive for the history of the problem that Aristotle comprehended this whole-like *physis* as the *hypokeimenon*, that which *lies at the ground* of something. Thereby the phenomenally experienceable fact—namely, that sensible beings, mainly things of use and natural things, lie before us as self-subsisting and independent unities—became capable of being grasped thinkingly.[23] The "first *ousia*" is presented as lying at the ground [24] of all that is merely contingent and merely possible, all the alterable, all the accidental. Or, expressed grammatically, all predicates can be predicated of it, while it can never itself be a predicate.[25] The first essence in this sense is Being as "lying at the ground of" and "being present for," the "bearer of attributes" or the "core" of the particular being.

From the following discussions it will emerge that this ability to bear attributes and qualifications as well as to be a core of

15. *Ibid.*
16. *Meta.* 1028b34.
17. *Cat.* 2a13.
18. *Meta.* 1041b31.
19. *Meta.* 1041b11 ff.
20. *Meta.* 1041b7.
21. *Meta.* 1041b10.
22. *Meta.* 1051b18.
23. Cf. Marx, *op. cit.*, p. 41.
24 *Meta.* 1025a13 ff.; cf. the important study by E. Tugendhat, *TI KATA TINOS*, pp. 13 ff., which develops the structural interconnection of the occurrence of coming-to-presence in Aristotle by means of a close exegesis of the pertinent textual passages.
25. *Cat.* 2a12; *Meta.* 1029a22.

a being was by no means understood statically or rigidly by Aristotle but as a highest moving *referential relationship.* The *hypokeisthai* of the *hypokeimenon* was later translated by *substare* and *subicere;* and, under the influence of Cartesian thinking, "substance" and "subject" came to be understood no longer "referringly" but rigidly, with each standing in itself as a *res*—a transformation that purportedly contributed to the increasing "reification" of man and his things. When we keep in mind that, in later times, not only lifeless natural things or things of use but also things of art as well as animated beings and, above all, the essence of man came to be comprehended by categories reified in this manner, then we can begin to understand the course Heidegger followed in his early work *Being and Time.* He wanted to "overcome" these comprehensions of substance and subject from a more "primordial" level, insofar as they determined the essence of man and those things with which man concerned himself meaningfully. In a later chapter we shall treat in detail of this effort of Heidegger, and it will be shown that his attack is directed above all against the "reified" meaning of Being that lay at the basis of the categories of substance and subject in their Cartesian mold. Some passages in *Being and Time* [26] give rise to the impression that for Heidegger at that time the *hypokeimenon* of Aristotle also had a "reified" sense of Being.[27] The following fundamental ways of *ousia* prove, however, that Aristotle conceived it as a highly mobile power.

The way whereby the "first *ousia*" "enables" the essential being was determined by Aristotle from manifold viewpoints. Each of these determinations is the expression of a highest "movement" —and by this we do not mean movement or *kinēsis* in the narrow Aristotelian sense. Even the determinant *eidos-(morphē)-hylē,*[28] most often interpreted statically, is a concept of movement. For the form must "form" the matter; it forms a material suitable, for example, for sawing, in that it emerges in the material as the figure (*morphē*) of a saw and shows itself in the semblance of its what-being as the *eidos* of a saw.

This movement, in which form and matter grow together into a *synholon,* does not end in a static being. The *synholon,* on account of its individual matter of *hylē,* remains perishable and alterable. Further, its figure and form, which is at the time "present," remains related to the "absent" figure and form from which

26. SZ 46 ff., 319; cf. below, p. 87.
27. Cf., however, SZ 25, 26.
28. Cf., here, Marx, *op. cit.,* p. 45.

it arose and into which it can again change back. In the meaning of this relation, something warm that is now present "is" also the "absent" something cold from which it, as something warm, derived and into which it again changes back. This tension between *eidos* and its privation, *sterēsis*, especially attests to the mobile character of "first *ousia*." [29] Aristotle made this even more plain, however, in that he determined the *eidos* as *energeia* and the *hylē* as *dynamis*.[30]

Within the framework of this sketch of the form of *ousia* it is not necessary to demonstrate more closely how "first *ousia*" as *energeia* "effectually and actually" engenders the unity of its being-as-particularity and its what-being and thereby actualizes its *dynamis*, its "potentialities" and "potencies" and "forces," within the free play of its possibilities. As *entelecheia*,[31] *ousia* is further conceived by Aristotle as the movement that contains within itself its "products" (*telē*) in such a wise that these, as renewed potencies, always lead to renewed actualizations. Through these determinations, "first *ousia*" was in fact conceived as moving so strongly within itself that it really ought to be spoken of not nominally but "verbally."

The particular course of the inner movement of "first *ousia*" was further determined as *telos*.[32] *Ousia* in realized phases brings its natural capacities to ful-fillment [*Voll-endung*], in cyclical form actualizes this "beginning" (*archē*) through its end—the fulfillment taking place like the "history" of a relation that "turns back to itself." This form of the "first *ousia*" will be more closely determined in connection with the following demonstration of the fundamental traits of *ousia*.

The form of the "first *ousia*".of a *synholon* is delineated along the aforesaid lines in the following way: it is *power* as enabling, the unitary "whole" of the "to be" [*Seiendsein*] and what-is; it is independent; it is that which, resting in itself, *lies at the ground of* and is *present for* [*Zugrundeliegendes und Vorliegendes*] all determinations and accidents. *Ousia* is the form moving within itself—the form, both absent and present, of the matter which belongs to it; it is the moving unity of *energeia* and *dynamis;* it is *entelecheia* and the ful-fillment (*telos*) that realizes itself in the course of its phases.

29. *Ibid.*, p. 49.
30. *Ibid.*, pp. 50 ff.
31. *Ibid.*, pp. 52 ff.
32. *Ibid.*, pp. 57 ff.

The inner motility of *ousia* is further evidenced in that the determinations designated are essentially unfolded in the *genesis* of *ousia*. For this reason, form, matter, and ful-fillment are "grounds," or *aitiai*, which, each for itself or together with the *causa efficiens*, the *archē tēs metabolēs*, determines that and how a real particular being emerges.[33]

It is really due to this interest of Aristotle in the *genesis* of *ousia* that so many aspects of the single being were most thoroughly comprehended. Of special relevance in this connection is the schematism of the categories, which the book *Categories* sets forth in a manner that proved fundamental for the whole tradition. In this book the first *ousia*, as the first category, lies at the ground of the other categories in the "logical" buildup of the particular being therein developed.[34] The predominance of the genetic aspect might account for the insufficient treatment of the question of how the being "is" in its Being *after* it has come into being. The special *direction* of the Aristotelian question did not permit the problem to arise as to whether the real being that has emerged—this "whole," this unity of the "to be" [*Seiendsein*] and the what-is—is not also meaningfully determined out of that great "totality" to which it belongs, which envelops it and flows beneath it—out of that collectivity that Aristotle comprehended (in a broad sense)[35] as *physis* and, with an eye to preceding thinkers, designated as the *kosmos* or *world*.[36]

In his published commentaries on Aristotle, Heidegger did not make mention of the lack of this aspect;[37] to be sure, he himself will seek to determine the being, insofar as it is a "thing," from the vantage point of a world that envelops it.

In what follows, four fundamental traits of *ousia* will be developed, which admittedly by no means exhaust the rich problematic of *ousia*. They are intended merely to serve the purposes of a historical introduction to the problematic in Heidegger. In line with our specific intent, only the *ousia* of a *synholon* in the sublunary realm will be treated, and many important thoughts of the *corpus aristotelicum* on *prōtē ousia* in general and on unmoved *ousia*, as well as *ousia* that does not arise but is moved, will be left undiscussed. For this same reason, in the

---

33. *Ibid.*, pp. 54 ff.
34. *Ibid.*, pp. 39 ff.
35. *Meta.* 1072b14.
36. *Meta.* 984b16.
37. The author is not familiar with Heidegger's lectures on Aristotle.

following demonstration of the fundamental traits of *ousia* more weight is laid on *ousia* as *ti ēn einai* [38] than as *hypokeimenon*.

2. THE MEANING OF THE "ETERNALNESS" OF *Ousia*

AMONG THE MOST IMPORTANT FEATURES of Aristotelian philosophy is its acknowledgment that all bodies in the sublunary realm are perishable. The fact that terrestrial beings, men, animals, things, "come to be and pass away" (*genesis kai phthora*) was a basic experience of which Aristotle sought to take account. This is the reason for his asking questions about the essence of movement, matter, and, especially, time.

His thinking, however, was motivated by the second, even more powerful, basic experience, that, despite all perishability, chaos does not prevail but rather that Being is ordered (*taxis*) and there exists a beautiful structuredness, the *kosmos*, the world. This experience presumably came to him from the awesome sight of *ouranos*, the starry heaven's dome that arches over the islands of Greece. It offers itself to the eye as fixed in its limit (*peras*), as ungenerated and imperishable (*aïdion, aei*), as a true image of order. And, even more important, this order that presents itself to the senses is no rigid order resting in itself but manifestly a *moving* order. The great planets, the sun, the moon, and the stars reveal themselves in their regular rhythmic rotation, the periodic revolution that produces on earth the cycle of the great solar year, the return of the seasons, and the change from day to night and night to day.

In the light of this image of a *unity* of order and movement, Aristotle conceived the idea of reality as a synthesis of Being and becoming.[39] The accepted fact of such a kind of cosmic order remained a starting point for his thinking. We shall see how each problematic shows itself differently to a way of thinking that can no longer orient itself to a cosmic image of a "moving order" given to the senses.

Aristotle conceived the synthesis of Being and becoming in many areas. Of particular import for Western thinking, however, were his efforts to think this very synthesis for that realm which,

38. Insofar as the other categories and the essential attributes or *propria* also have a *ti ēn einai*, many aspects of the following "basic traits" will apply also to them.
39. This assumption of a pre-eminently phenomenal determination of Aristotelian thinking does not contradict the fact that Aristotle was influenced by the doctrines of Eudoxus.

in accordance with his own basic experience, is ruled by perishability, the realm of the particular being on earth. It is a mark
of the greatness of his thought that he determined the moved
perishable being, the *on gignomenon,* not, like Plato, as a not-
being, a *mē on,* or even as an *ouk on;* rather, Aristotle beheld and
thought in the perishable being an imperishable Being and essence and thereby reclaimed the perishable particular for the
"eternal" reality of Being of a "moved order." The basic Aristotelian insight thus consists in the thought that *ousia* itself neither
"comes nor passes"; it is not subject to coming to be (*genesis*)
and passing away (*phthora*). It would be absurd to suppose that
the artist who produces a bronze figure also begets the form of
the spherical or the round. For that would imply that the process
of production would never come to an end.[40] According to Aristotle, however, not only are such forms ungenerated and imperishable, but also the essence "house," for example. "A house
always comes to be from a house,"[41] "health always from
health,"[42] or, in general, "a like-named from a like-named."[43]

In the sphere of natural beings the imperishability of the
essence is indicated, for example, in that "a human being always
begets a human being."[44] Through the chain of generations and
births, the essence "man" remains beyond all becoming and
passing away, although the individual man, by virtue of his
matter,[45] "comes and passes," is born and dies.

However, the decisive thought of Aristotle, which was finally
to overcome the Platonic dualism (*chōrismos*) of the imperishable Idea and the perishable particular being, is the thought that
in the sublunary realm the "eternal" essence, which does not
come to be and pass away, is present only in the concrete being,
the perishable *synholon.* Hence the question arises as to the
meaning of the "eternalness" * of the *ousia* of a *synholon.* How
was the "eternal" essence to be thought, insofar as it "is" in
the realm of things that "come to be and pass away"? What is the
meaning of its "eternalness"? Since what is involved here is the
relationship to the realm of things coming to be and passing

---

* *Ewigkeit,* ordinarily translated "eternity," has the sense of an attribute here; accordingly, "eternalness."
40. *Meta.* 1033b5; 1033b23 ff.; cf., also, *Meta.* 1043b17, 1051b30, and
1069b35 ff.
41. *Meta.* 1034a24.
42. *Meta.* 1034a29.
43. *Meta.* 1034a22.
44. *Meta.* 1032a25; 1033b33.
45. *Meta.* 1033b19.

away, and thus of things in movement, it is germane to seek the meaning of eternalness by reflecting on the Aristotelian determination of "unmoved Being." We shall not follow up the question in this direction, however, but rather seek to answer it within a problematic that leads us close to the realm of the decisive question in Heidegger, to the problematic of *Being and Time*.

In the discussion of the essence of time in the *Physics*,[46] the "eternalness" of the *aei onta*, to which the *ousiai* belong, is determined from the vantage point of "time." In contrast to "beings in time," [47] the "beings not in time" [48] are determined by a twofold consideration. The "eternal beings" are not "encompassed by time" (*periechetai*)[49] and their Being is "not measured by time." [50]

In order to understand the meaning of these delimitations, we must examine more closely how Aristotle comprehended "beings-in-time." This will clarify Aristotle's conception of the essence of time, which occasioned Heidegger to understand the essence of time differently.

Beings-in-time are "encompassed by time." [51] This potency to encompass is a sign of the destroying character of time. "Things suffer (*paschein*) through it"; time "wastes things away, and . . . all things grow old through time, and . . . there is oblivion owing to the lapse of time." [52]

Thus time is comprehended in the first place as a "power." At the same time, however, this power is understood as limited, since Being and essence, the first *ousia*, is not as such subjected to it. Here we encounter that fundamental conception that took its rise in Plato and Aristotle and has since dominated Western thinking. Thus Hegel at the end of the tradition still writes: "the concept [i.e., fulfilled 'Being'] is the power of time." It is precisely this fundamental position of the tradition that Heidegger will seek to overcome. He will attain to the view that, conversely, "time is the power of Being," wherein, to be sure, the meaning of Being (essence), as of time, has been radically altered.

Aristotle comprehended the essence of time, however, not only as a "power" but also as a "number"; and it was this time conception that remained definitive for the "natural understanding" and characterized philosophical thinking up to Hegel. The

46. *Phys.* 217b29 ff.
47. *Phys.* 221a27 ff.
48. *Phys.* 221b3.
49. *Phys.* 221a29.
50. *Phys.* 221b7.
51. *Phys.* 221a29.
52. *Phys.* 221a30 ff.

many questions connected with this conception will be treated here only insofar as they point to problems that Heidegger treated in another way.

According to this fundamental Aristotelian definition, time is "the number (*arithmos*) of motion (*kinēsis*) in respect of 'before' and 'after' (*kata to proteron kai hysteron*)." [53] Aristotle himself further explicated this definition as meaning that number here signified "what is counted," a quantity of enumerable units that are counted on a determinate course of motion. The motion, in its before and after, must be unequivocal, ordered, unlimited (*apeiron*), continuous (*syneches*), and divisible. It must run its course through discrete (*stigmai*) magnitudes (*megethē*). More exactly, this is the motion of the celestial rotation, the *periphora*.

The essence of time is thus understood from a definite original linking with divisible locomotion, magnitude, and the point, hence with *space*. It thus falls into a certain dependence on space. In contrast, Heidegger will try to understand space as dependent on time and, later, as of equal rank with time, whereby of course the essence of time is comprehended in non-Aristotelian fashion.

If, in the ordered motion, something that is moved passes through two successive points of magnitude, the being of time becomes experienceable. The former point is then understood as the "earlier-being," the succeeding point as the "later-being," and the stretch through which what is moved ran its course obtains the meaning of a "duration" or a "while." This duration or while in the Aristotelian comprehension of time presents a stretch of time, a quantum, that is measurable. The numbered or measured "how long" of the duration or while comprises the essence of Aristotelian time. Heidegger will direct his attack against this comprehension of time as a measurable quantum and will seek to show that it is only the "vulgar" derivative of an originary understanding of time that is to be thought qualitatively. In *Being and Time* he will develop this "originary" time as a condition for the possibility of Dasein as that which understands Being. In his late writings Heidegger understood a "qualitative" meaning of time as a basic trait of Being, or more exactly of the world, and thereby sought to "overcome" this Aristotelian "quantitative" meaning.

The Aristotelian comprehension of time as a measurable quantum signifies above all that it is *indifferent* toward any and

53. *Phys.* 219b1 ff.

every "content"; whether ten minutes by measure are eventful or empty has nothing to do with the essence of time. This trait of the indifference of time determined the entire tradition up to Hegel, for whom time was an indifferent "simple something," [54] the category of immediate Being.

It is important to explicate the deeper reason for this indifference of time, since with few exceptions it determined the traditional comprehension of time. The reason lies in the essential structure of that point in the ordered motion which Aristotle understood as "time-point" and termed "now-point." The essence of a now, a *nyn* or *nunc*, and of a point consists in its being a "very same" that is at the same time an "other" and "again another." [55] Every now-point in the motion has the character of the same now and yet as such is always "another now-point." In this lies the indifference with which a now-point follows another and with which every now-here is always already again another. It is within the meaning of such an indifference that we speak of the "flow of time."

Heidegger will attempt to overcome this indifference of time by abandoning the orientation of the time conception to the point and the now. Thus "time-space" obtains a different meaning from the Aristotelian now-here, which abstracts from all content.

The now designates the time dimension of the *present*. The present, for Aristotle, is the criterion that offers the standard. From this present the "past" is the now that "was" and the future the now that "will be." The now as present is the limit (*peras*) [56] that divides the present from the past and the future, and at the same time it serves as the boundary in the transition wherein everything future must come to the now, in the same way that everything past was once a now. This predominance of the time dimension of the present remained a determining force for Western thought. In contradistinction to it, Heidegger in *Being and Time* will attempt to show up this present as a derivative "inauthentic" mode of an "authentic present" of the "moment." In addition he will move the future to a pre-eminent position over the present, whereby the future will of course not be comprehended as the "not-yet-now." Moreover, he will think this future as linked in definite connection with the "having-been" [*Gewesenheit*], which for him is not the "no-longer-now." Finally, in his

54. PG 81, 86 (151–52, 156).
55. *Phys.* 219b12–15.
56. *Phys.* 222a12.

late writings he will determine this differently understood present as "contemporaneous" with the other time dimensions.

Heidegger in *Being and Time* achieved this renewed awareness of an originary essence of time only from the standpoint of the essence of man, Dasein. In this respect he moved within the Aristotelian tradition, in that for Aristotle too the essence of man had essentially to do with the full determination of the essence of time. The *"nous* of the soul" [57] must hold apart the two points of magnitude in the motion of what moves and measure the how-long of the motion's duration, so that "time" is. The holding-apart of the points from one another and the measuring are therefore "conditions for the possibility" of Aristotelian time. For Heidegger, such a mensurative holding-apart will constitute just the opposite of man's "authentic" way of fulfillment, which relates to the "primordial time."

In the passage from the *Physics* already discussed, [58] Aristotle divides off the region of "beings not in time"—"eternal" beings, the *aei onta,* to which *ousia* belongs—from the region of "beings in time." The meaning of the eternalness of *ousia* is thereby determined as "atemporal" or "outside time." In this way, however, the matter involves only a nonbelonging to determinate time, whose essence was explicated in the manner we saw. Thus the eternalness of *ousia* permits of identification negatively: it neither underlies the destructive power of time nor is it measurable as number in a spatial movement, and it is especially not to be comprehended from the now, the present. When post-Aristotelian philosophy nevertheless always determined the eternalness of the essence from the standpoint of the "now" and the "present," this was due to the Christian desire to give expression to the "omnipresence" of God the creator. For this reason this eternalness of essence was comprehended as the "standing now" or *nunc stans* and as the "eternal present." For the Greeks, however, there was no God who *ex nihilo creat.* Neither the cosmos nor the order of essence is "created." The Greeks were not confronted with the task of assuring the eternalness of the highest particular Being in the face of his transitory creation.

The quest for a positive determination of the meaning of the eternalness of *ousia* must be variously pursued, depending on whether it deals with unmoved *ousia,* or *ousia* that is not generated but is moved, or *ousia* in the sublunary realm that is generated; and in these last instances attention can be directed to

57. *Phys.* 223a25.
58. See above, p. 26.

the *prōtē ousia* [59] or solely to the *synholon*. We are interested here only in the question of how the meaning of the eternalness of the *ousia* of a *synholon* lends itself to positive determination within the particular Aristotelian distinction of the two regions of atemporality and temporality. Aristotle, however, did not expressly ask how the "synthesis" in the *synholon* of the particular being "not-in-time" and the particular being "in time" is to be understood. He did not explain whether that "eternalness" is somehow "temporalized" by virtue of this "being-in," and he did not determine the "kind of time" that would rule here. We do no more than broach the question here, since it serves as a case in point that the subject matter itself can give rise to a thinking that seeks a "kind of time" beyond the Aristotelian time determinations and since our answer leads us into the neighborhood of an important problem in Heidegger.

In technical production something comes into "Being or essence" when the four causes are present together. Then the *synholon*, the *technēi on,* and this *ousia* is in this way there. It has "arrived." And after successful production, this essence remains; it "lasts" until the concrete being passes away. That it arrives again in a renewed technical production and again lasts, further signifies that the *ousia* "returns" and in this sense "endures." In the genesis of the *physei onta* is shown the same arriving, lasting, and returning-enduring of the *ousia*. The *ousia* "human being" arrives with the birth of this particular human being, lasts until "this man" dies, always returns through the chain of procreation and births, and endures through the generations. While for Aristotle the individual, as a being "in time," is "transitory," the *ousia* human being returns and endures.

A common meaning underlies the arriving, lasting, and returning-enduring. These are three ways in which *ousia* makes itself *present* in its "to be" and its "what-is" as the "same." It may perhaps be maintained that in this "self-presenting" lies the "temporal meaning" of a kind of "presence." [60] This presence, to be sure, is not identical with the Aristotelian time dimension, since in these ways that *ousia* presents itself there is no question of a *nyn*, a "now," as "boundary" or "transition" in relation to a "no-longer-now" and a "not-yet-now." Nevertheless, this "presence" which underlies the arriving, lasting, and returning-endur-

59. *Meta.* 1035a29 ff., 1039b23 ff., 1043b14 ff.
60. SZ 25, 26, 19. Cf. E. Tugendhat, *TI KATA TINOS,* who discusses the "presence" in most precise fashion. The question of its temporal meaning is not treated.

ing is obviously not a form of "extratemporal" eternalness. The essence of the kind of "time" prevailing here remains unclarified, but for our purposes there is proof enough that the Aristotelian time determination does not suffice for a grasping of the relationship of "Being and Time" even within the Aristotelian problematic.

Heidegger in *Being and Time* did not ask about the meaning of the "eternalness" of the *ousia* of the *synholon*. He sought rather to determine the temporality of the viewpoint within which Aristotle understood *ousia*. From there Heidegger specified the first *ousia*, above all, temporally, as a "presence," whose meaning at the same time lies outside the Aristotelian time determinations. It is worthy of note that Heidegger, in a recent publication that interprets the Aristotelian concept of *physis* [61] without reference to the temporality of the understanding of Being, seeks to determine the meaning of the "eternalness" of *prōtē ousia* from the phenomenon that as a *hypokeimenon* it offers or "presents itself by itself at a given time," i.e., "temporalizes" itself in a way that likewise does not allow itself to be grasped by means of the Aristotelian time dimensions. [62]

3. The Meaning of the Necessity of *Ousia*

THE COSMIC PATTERN of a "moved order," which predetermined the meaning of "eternalness" as a basic trait of *ousia*, presumably also imparted its stamp to the meaning of the second basic trait of *ousia*, its *necessity*. External evidence for this is provided in the numerous textual passages where Aristotle links the phrase *ex anankēs* with *aei*. [63]

In the fifth section of Book V of the *Metaphysics*, the general meaning of necessity is first determined as follows: [64] "We say of that which cannot be otherwise that it is necessary." In the same section it is then explained that the "necessary" in the strict sense (*anankaion*) is the "simple" (*to haploun*). [65] The simple is the indivisible what-is of a being, the *ousia*. *Ousia* is thus "necessary," since it "does not admit of more states than one," so that it "cannot be in one way and in another." [66]

61. *Il Pensiero I* 155.
62. See below, pp. 131 ff.
63. E.g., *De Gen. et Corr.* 338a20.
64. *Meta.* 1015a32 ff.
65. *Meta.* 1015b12 ff.
66. *Meta.* 1015b14.

Relevant to the understanding of this characterization of the necessity [67] of *ousia* is the consideration that the way to be of the "in-one-way-and-in-another-being," i.e., "alterability," is dealt with in its own right and as complementary to the former. Alterable beings, the *endechomena allōs echein*, have ways to be that we today designate categorially as "possibility," "contingency," and especially "accidentalness." [68] Thus the meaning of the necessity of *ousia* is first of all determined in *contradistinction* to alterability and its ways to be. Necessity of essence signifies unalterability.

It must be noted, however, that alterability is understood here as a "becoming other and other," wherein an other interminably passes over into an other. In addition to this, however, Aristotle identified a kind of "alteration" whereby the movement "turns back to itself." [69] Such a turning back to itself is an alteration wherein a condition already predetermined in its what-is is realized. It is a course that runs its way through ordered phases and leads to a completion predetermined by this beginning. This kind of "alteration" is present in the essence, in the *ousia* itself. [70] It is there as *telos,* the "end" firmly circumscribed, limited, and predetermined in its what-is, the "end" of this movement and at the same time its "beginning." It is the "cause" for the sake of which the predetermined condition realizes itself in a course of stages. *Ousia* as the *telos* of a being at the same time realizes itself in the sense that it is the "purpose" of another being and its *telos,* and thus in this relation of "the one and its other" it turns back to itself. This relationship constitutes the structure of the inner connectedness, of the "teleological" order. In this movement of the relating of the *telos* to itself and its phases, as well as to "the other," there is a specific mode of "obligation" [*Müssen*] and "constraint." In this "obligation" lies the positive meaning of the basic trait of the necessity of *ousia.*

That this positive meaning of necessity is to be understood as deriving from *telos* is evidenced in the concept of the "necessity

---

67. Cf. Karl Ulmer, *Wahrheit, Kunst und Natur bei Aristoteles,* pp. 91 ff.

68. It should be mentioned that Aristotle also noted the "necessary" accidentals, "the attributes of an essentially coincident character," the *symbebēkota kath' hauta.* The questions pertaining hereto, however, are not relevant for the determination of the fundamental meaning of necessity.

69. *De Gen. et Corr.* 338b14.

70. Even the heavenly bodies move within themselves; this is the *kinēsis kata topon.*

from hypothesis" (*ex anankēs ex hypotheseōs*).[71] In order that a natural being, or *physei on,* and a being of human manufacture, or *technēi on,* be able to come into Being and essence, all four causes must be present. This occurrence, however, is "necessary" only on the "hypothesis" of, or in consideration of the presence of, one of the four causes, *telos.* Only on the "hypothesis" that in human manufacture, for example, the *telos* of a completed house-as-it-is [*Hausseins*] determines and guides the other three causes does this manufacture occur "necessarily." The boards or bricks (*hylē*), the beginning of the work (*archē*), and the shape (*morphē*) and form (*eidos*) are "necessary" causes of the production of a house, because the *telos,* the completed house-as-it-is, is related to them. This relationship of the *telos* to the other three causes also has the character of a "must."

The constraint of *telos,* however, does not have the sort of severity of the "must" as in that "type" of necessity which later denoted for natural science the connection of "cause and effect" as well as "ground and consequence." For in the teleological relating of the *physis,* the possibility of failures (*hamartēmata*) [72] and hindrances [73] was recognized. In the kind of necessity ruling here, it suffices that all natural things either always or "for the most part" [74] attain their predetermined fulfillment.

Natural occurrence, no less than human production, was a *poiēsis.* It is of great importance for the understanding of "the other meaning of Being and essence" in Heidegger to emphasize that Aristotle comprehended the "creative," the "poetic," element in the occurrences of *physis* and *technē* as thus bound up with the demonstrated constraint of necessity. In natural occurrence there is the *poiein* that lets the particular being "beginning from itself" [75] come forth to its *telos* "from hypothesis, necessarily," just as there is the *poiein* that operates on another particular being and lets it come along forward to its own essence.[76]

Aristotle's fundamental teleology and the "kind" of necessity grounded on it determined Western thinking in many areas up to our own time. Even after the natural scientific outlook, through Galileo and Descartes, won a complete victory for the *causa efficiens* over the teleological cause, or *causa finalis,* and the Aristotelian view of a teleological order had been reduced *ad*

---

71. *Phys.* 199b33 ff.; cf. Ulmer, *op. cit.,* pp. 105 ff.
72. *Phys.* 199b4.
73. *Phys.* 199b26.
74. *Phys.* 199a33 ff.
75. *Phys.* 192b15.
76. *De Gen. et Corr.* I. 6–9; cf. Ulmer, *op. cit.,* pp. 101 ff.

absurdum, the structure of *telos* remained alive in eschatological thinking. It continued to be decisive, at least formally, for Christian eschatology, in the same way that it lies at the basis of the atheistic Marxist eschatology of historical materialism.

It is indicative of the "present-day need of philosophy" that numerous contemporary philosophers consciously take the road back to Aristotelian teleology and the "kind" of necessity that rests on it. This arises out of an antirelativist and antihistoricist impulse and out of the desire toward a new "order of essences." It may be questioned, however, whether it is really possible simply to turn back to the Aristotelian ousiology, after its cosmic model has been completely discredited. Heidegger, on the other hand, tries to take another path and hence seeks "another sense of Being and essence." He therefore strives first of all to "overcome" all interpretations of essence and substance that rest on Aristotelian *ousia.* Hence this "other sense of Being and essence" cannot sustain the basic traits that characterized *ousia.* The question we shall face, therefore, is whether this sense of Being is really determined by a "necessity" or, rather, which "kind" of necessity governs.

The referential structure of *telos,* from which the meaning of necessity was determined for us, refers to a third basic trait of *ousia,* its selfsameness.

4. The Meaning of the Selfsameness of *Ousia*

THE MEANING OF THE BASIC TRAIT of the selfsameness (*hē tautotēs*) of *ousia* must be determined either from the "opposite of" or from the "relation to" nonselfsameness, i.e., to manifoldness, to change, and to transformation. In Plato, in accordance with his question about the "one and the many" (*hen kai polla*), the meaning is determined from the "opposite" of the many; in Aristotle, on the other hand, from the "relation" to the many, the incidental attributes, the *symbebēkota.*

This relationship obtains its decisive expression in Aristotle in the problematic of the "change in essence" and the "coming to be of essence" (*genesis haplōs*). This problematic makes clear how a thinking predetermined by a cosmic guiding image transformed into a "moving order" the chaos of restless change and coming to be, and it indicates once more why a kind of thinking that is no longer determined by a cosmic idea of reality must break with these conceptions.

Aristotle comprehended the change in the essence of a determinate concrete being from the standpoint of three categories.[77] The qualitative determinations of the essence can alter; this is the case in alteration taken in the narrow sense of an *alloiōsis*. Or the quantitative determinations can alter in the way of increase or decrease (*auxēsis-phthisis*). Or the concrete particular being can change its place, the alteration here consisting in change of place (*phora*). An example of the first case is the change in a man from "uneducated" to "educated." Here the alteration, as one incidental attribute's turning into (*metabolē*) an "other" (*allo*), takes place in such manner that the disappearing of the one means the rising of the other. This way to be of "unselfsameness," however, stands in close reference to selfsameness, from which it obtains the form of an "ordered movement." For in the first place the "turning-into" takes its course according to "that which lies at the ground," the first *ousia*, as in "this man." "This man" as such endures. He perdures as "selfsame" in his relation to or connection with the changing determinations.[78] He remains—in Hegel's words—"with himself in otherness." He remains the same whether walking or sitting, young or old. The qualitative change is therefore not capable of making inroads against the fundamentally self-preserving order of the essence as a what-is. From this self-preserving order the fundamental essence in its selfsameness also bestows an order on the "unselfsame" changing determinations. The "turning-into" takes place only between contraries lying opposite each other, *enantia* and *antikeimena*, whose potentialities are predetermined by *ousia*, the ground of both. Hence a man can certainly turn from a state of being uneducated into a state of being educated, but never—as though he were the leaf of a plant—from being green to being yellow.

Aristotle, however, also conceived a kind of change in respect of the first category, the *ousia* itself. This is the grave problem of the coming to be of the essence qua *synholon* (*genesis haplōs*). In this emergence into Being or emergence into essence of a man, an animal, a thing, or a work of art lies the real problem of *genesis*.

It must be noted that Aristotle, despite deep research and measured judgment, conceived this problematic in *De Generatione et Corruptione* on the model of the *alloiōsis*, although it was an entirely different problematic from that of mere alteration in

77. *De Gen. et Corr.* 319b32 ff.
78. *Phys.* 190a14.

the essence. And it is also understandable why he was obliged to do so in order to preserve his conception of the meaning of Being. He wanted to remain faithful to the Eleatic principle without, however, denying the possibility of the movement and becoming from "determinate Being" to "determinate Being." In the first place, it is true also for this case that there must be a substratum, a something always already present, a *hypokeimenon*, so that something can become at all. In the *Physics*,[79] reference is made to a "perceptible" substrate, like the seed, which is always already present in plants and animals before an actual new being can arise. Or the bronze is the substrate insofar as it is also always there already, before the statue can emerge.[80] Looked at in this way, all coming to be would be only a remodeling, an augmenting, or a compounding of this substrate, which as such perdures. The treatise *De Generatione et Corruptione* goes beyond this crass position; in this work it is acknowledged that the substrate need not at all be only something perceivable by the senses.[81] Rather, the substrate is understood as that which is always already present in potentiality and perdures, as, for example, the Being of the living being in the animal-human *genesis*. This Being is consistent with the Eleatic principle "beyond all coming to be and passing away." [82] It is that which, in relation to the many qua a sequence of generations, remains the same. But insofar as, in the *genesis haplōs*, the matter has to do with the becoming of "determinate Being" into "determinate Being," two additional structural elements belong to the occurrence as a whole: the form (*eidos*), the whereto of the movement of the *genesis;* and the privative form or *sterēsis,* the wherefrom of the movement.[83] These interrelated determinations, together with the substrate as *hypokeimenon,* have always extensively prestructured the process of genesis, so that the Aristotelian ideal of an "order" moving within itself is in no way endangered by the possibility of a "transformation." Herein lies the consequence, so decisive for the history of the problem, that even the transforming of the essence does not permit the origin of something really *new,* something never there before. This essential consequence of the basic trait of the self-sameness of *ousia* determined the course of subsequent philosophy and ever entangled it afresh in great difficulties whenever

79. *Phys.* 190b3.
80. *Phys.* 190b5 ff.
81. *De Gen. et Corr.* 318b21–27.
82. *Phys.* 192a29; *Meta.* 1009a37.
83. *Phys.* 191b15 ff.

the arrival of something new had to be accounted for. It has set into contradiction all attempts at "historical" or "epochal" thinking; it left unexplained the results of natural science, such as the insights into the emergence of "new species" and mutations; and again and again it barred philosophical access to the secret of the work of art, which creates something radically new. Above all, however, the basic trait of the selfsameness of *ousia,* conceived in this fashion, decided the role of man in a way that left no room for the fact that he is a participant in the coming to be of the new, as in art or technology.

5. The Meaning of the Intelligibility of *Ousia*

Only what "presents" itself in the temporal and the transient and in this sense is "eternal"; only what in its course is predetermined from its aim on, forcibly reined in, and in this sense "necessary"; only what in all change and alteration remains with itself and in this sense is "selfsame"—only this is also wholly and completely knowable, is "intelligible." The meaning of the fourth basic trait of *ousia* lies in the meaning of the three already discussed. And to the extent that those three were ultimately understood according to the pattern of the cosmic "moving order," the fourth basic trait of *ousia* likewise rests on this Aristotelian world view.

The Greeks early conceived knowability as the *logos,* which at one and the same time signifies the order itself and the knowing of the order. And today, too, the "logical" means the "knowable" and the "ordered," although the kind of order is no longer oriented to the Greek cosmos but to a recent meaning of *ratio* and has acquired the significance of the "rational." Heidegger's thinking is directed pre-eminently against the "rational." Insofar, however, as the "rational" for him has its origin historically in the *logos* and in the "logical" of Aristotle, Heidegger as early as *Being and Time* considered it his task to "destroy" the history of meanings which begins with Aristotle, i.e., to prove that the *"logos"* and the *"legein,"* even freed of all the "covering-up" of traditional interpretations, lack an "originary methodological basis." [84] This "primordial basis," in *Being and Time,* is the existential analytic of Dasein. Heidegger later regards the meaning of *logos* understood in the Aristotelian way as a decisive

84. *SZ* 160.

expression of "metaphysics," which is based on the early Greek comprehension of the word *"logos"* as a "basic word" [*Grundwort*]. Out of this "ground of metaphysics," Heidegger will seek to unfold "another" meaning of Being and essence.

In order to be able to think along with Heidegger the "otherness" of the meaning of Being and essence developed by him, let us now take up briefly how, for Aristotle, the Being and essence of the particular being was in principle unconditionally and unobstructedly intelligible. This intelligibility resulted for Aristotle from the supposition of an unconditional sovereignty of the principle of complete transparence. The early Greeks had already termed this principle the *nous*. Thus Aristotle, expressly referring to this insight of Anaxagoras,[85] declares that *"nous* governs." Aristotle conceived this sovereignty of the *nous* in the likeness of the light (*phōs*). The *energeia* of the *nous poiētikos* is like the effectiveness of the light, which, through its shining, confers "transparency"[86] on everything and transforms the "potential" colors into "actual" colors.[87] With regard to the particular being as a whole, this effectiveness of the *nous* ought perhaps to be expressed as follows: owing to the *nous*, *ousia* is luminous, transparent, "noetic," i.e., "thinkable."[88] Only because *ousia* is thinkable, because it is ready for thinking, man, through the intuitive beholding *noēsis*, is able to think it. The "gnosiology" follows the "ontology"; the basic trait of the intelligibility of *ousia* "establishes" its thinkability by human thinking. Transcendental philosophy will later start out in reverse fashion from the conditions of the possibility of knowing—from the subject—and will conceive the thinkability, i.e., experienceability, of the "objects of experience" (in Kant) and the conceivability of Being, essence, and concept (in Hegel) as "object for a subject." These "objects" are in principle wholly and completely knowable, accessible, "lucid," and in this sense "true" for the "subject." In this respect the entire Western traditional metaphysics, apart from a few exceptions, is identified correctly as a "metaphysics of light," which, in Scholastic terminology, sets out from the proposition that *omne ens verum est*, that every particular being is "true." In the next chapter we shall see that in Hegel, through a change in the meaning of *truth*, the way is prepared for a departure from this

85. *De Anima* 429a19.
86. *De Anima* 418b13.
87. *De Anima* 430a15.
88. *De Anima* 432a10.

"optimistic" outlook. And later it will be shown how, likewise through an altered meaning of the essence of truth, Heidegger attempts a complete "overcoming" of the "metaphysics of light." In Aristotle the basic trait of the intelligibility of *ousia* is also connected with the truth (*alētheia*) in the sense that every obstruction of this intelligibility, whether through error or semblance, is excluded. To *noēsis*, to the intuitive beholding comprehension of the "simple," of the *ousia*, the latter shows itself in its truth.[89] "Neither semblance nor error is here possible," Aristotle expressly remarks at the end of Book IX of the *Metaphysics*.[90] This cryptic passage [91] must be interpreted to mean that the essence must be completely and wholly intelligible, completely undisguised, "lucid, and transparent"; otherwise the *noēsis* cannot grasp it unerringly through a simple "contact" (*thigein*).

If one agrees to regard the cited passage on the Aristotelian concept of truth as an evidence of the total intelligibility of *ousia*, then one must immediately point out that another concept of truth applies to the *legein*. The kind of knowing and stating (in judgment form) of science—of *epistēmē* as such—the knowing that refers to the "attributes of an essentially coincident character" (the *symbebēkota kath' hauta*) and determines a something in relation to another "something" (*ti kata tinos*), brings the thought either "truly" (*alēthes*) or "falsely" (*pseudes*) into correspondence (*homoiōsis*) with the "subject matter itself." [92] This conception of truth as *homoiōsis* entered into Western thinking in the form of the *adaequatio intellectus ad rem* and the *adaequatio rei ad intellectum* and was not basically altered until Hegel.

The possibility that human *legein* is subject to error does not mean that these necessary connections of being are not in themselves manifest and completely comprehensible through knowledge. For the particular being, for Aristotle, is an *epistēton*. Human error can be "corrected" and through practice and perseverance man can succeed in knowing the particular being as it is.

Convinced of the complete intelligibility of *ousia* and of the

89. *Meta.* 1051b17 ff.
90. *Meta.* 1051b25.
91. The author, in his treatise on the Aristotelian "Ontology" (Marx, *op. cit.*, p. 16), had tended toward an interpretation at variance from the above.
92. Cf. *De Interpretatione* 16a6; cf. here E. Tugendhat, *op. cit.*, pp. 20 ff.

"attributes of an essentially coincident character" as lending themselves to human beholding and knowing, Aristotle outlined that proud picture of man that remained fundamental for the self-understanding of the West: of the man who has the power of knowledge, the *zōion logon echon*,[93] who by nature strives for more and more insight[94] and cultivates this yearning to see (*orexis tou eidenai*) step by step above mere experience (*empeiria*) and practical competence (*technē*), to science, to *epistēmē* as such, and from there is able to attain to the *epistēmē* inspired by mind (*nous*), *epistēmē* in the wider sense of "love for science," *philo-sophia*.[95]

A look at the essence, scope, and aim of *epistēmē* affords additional evidence that Aristotle understood *ousia*, the object of *epistēmē* in the wider sense, as equally intelligible in principle as the objects of *epistēmē* in the narrower sense and that he therefore regarded its complete knowability through human "science" as possible. The various essential determinations of *epistēmē*, above all in the *Analytics* and the *Nicomachean Ethics*, are grounded especially on the basic traits of *ousia*: its "eternalness," necessity, and selfsameness. Guided by the *noēsis*, which has already apprehended *ousia* and the first principles,[96] *epistēmē* in the narrower sense—in contrast to practice (technical, ethical, and political action)[97]—is directed only to the "necessary," "eternal," and "selfsame" universals[98] (*ta katholou*), which stand in an order ruled by laws[99] and in fundamental connections.[100] This order, as a "logical" one, is so established that it can be wholly and completely grasped by the scientist's *legein* through the exhibiting of causes, syl-logism, demonstration (*apodeixis*), and definition (*horismos*). For this reason, knowledge itself can be characterized as "necessary"; it is valid "forever and everywhere" and in this sense is "universal."[101]

We have carried out this interpretation, which leads to an understanding of the inherent intelligibility of *ousia* and of the "attributes of an essentially coincident character," also because

93. *Nic. Eth.* 1102a30, 1139a5.
94. *Meta.* 980a22 ff.
95. *Meta.* 980a22 ff. and *An. Post.* 99b30 ff.
96. *An. Post.* 71a1 ff., 100b10.
97. *Nic. Eth.* 1140a25 ff., 1141a1.
98. *An. Post.* 87b30 ff., 88b30 ff., 73a34 ff., 73b27. These universals, as is well known, deal with the "attributes of an essentially coincident character."
99. E.g., the law of excluded contradiction, *An. Post.* 77a10.
100. *An. Post.* 90a5, 90a32.
101. *An. Post.* 87b28 ff., 88b30 ff.

Heidegger in *Being and Time* takes up this problematic from his point of view.

Heidegger [102] sees the fundamental meaning of *logos* in articulation [*Rede*]. He understands articulation on the basis of the Aristotelian text in the treatise *De Interpretatione* as a making-manifest, an *apophansis*, of that which the articulation is about. The *logos* has the function of a "letting-see" by pointing out; and the *synthesis*, together with the *diairesis* through which the *legein* simultaneously sets together and sets apart a "something as something," has the same "apophantic" meaning. It is for this reason that the *legein*, for Heidegger, is an "uncovering" and has the meaning of a "being-true" [*Wahrsein*] understood as an "uncovering," an *alētheuein*. Therefore Heidegger can write: [103] "The 'being-true' of the *logos* as *alētheuein* means that in *legein* as *apophainesthai* the entities *of which* one is talking must be taken out of their concealedness; one must let them be seen as something unconcealed (*alēthes*); that is, they must be *discovered*." Since *legein* can also go astray, Heidegger adds as an essential determination of the *logos* that it is a way "which can also conceal."

With this interpretation of the *logos* [104] Heidegger intends to lead the analysis back to the primordial essence of truth as an uncovering by Dasein. Dasein, for reasons to be explained later, must always first "wrest" from the particular being its "unconcealment," must always tear away the concealment of error and semblance. The unconcealedness of particular being that at times occurs is understood as a robbery [*Raub*], and therefore it is no accident that the Greeks expressed themselves on the essence of truth by way of a *privative* (*a-lētheia*). If *legein* is seen in this way, which tries to establish it on an originary basis, Aristotle would have had a concept of truth in which unconcealment and concealment reigned together in a specific relationship. In this comprehension of the essence of truth lies the "pessimistic" consequence that man, through the *legein* and the possibilities for the cultivation of his knowing based upon the *legein*, is *never* able fully and completely to grasp the particular being in its necessary determinations and connections. This denial of an intrinsic intelligibility stands in contradiction to the interpretation of the ancient problematic that we have just presented.

102. With what follows compare SZ 32, 159, 160, 219, 226, and below, p. 153.
103. SZ 33.
104. SZ 222.

This is an example of how the traditional problems concern Heidegger and how he takes them up for his own purposes. In *Being and Time* the intent is a working-out of the existential structure of Dasein, in which Dasein understands itself in the ambivalence of being authentic and being immersed [*Verfallensein*], being unconcealed and being concealed. These structures were to be viewed as the primordial basis of ancient ontology.[105] On this ground, perhaps, one may explain why Heidegger concentrated his analysis on the *legein*, which in fact can just as well express right as wrong judgments. One wonders what understanding of truth Heidegger would have arrived at in *Being and Time* had he not discussed the *noēsis* so briefly there [106] and had not placed the whole burden of his analysis on the *legein*. Heidegger's *over-all* concern in *Being and Time*, however, was to gain *an other* concept of truth opposed to that of the metaphysical tradition. The essence of truth had in fact a determinate structure in the tradition. This structure begins to change in Hegel, as should appear from the following chapter.

105. *SZ* 160.
106. *SZ* 33.

2 / The Meaning of Being, Essence, and Concept in Hegel†

THE MEANING OF THE ARISTOTELIAN *ousia* of a *syn-holon* was arrived at through a reflection on its basic traits. This reflection was "un-Aristotelian," since the direction of Aristotle's question was not toward the meaning of Being and essence but toward the being's essential constitution. If, with the purpose of clarifying this constitution of the being, Aristotle investigated its ways of Being and essence, his thinking nevertheless tran-scended the being and proceeded away *from* it to its ways of Being and essence. As a consequence of this direction of the question, which transcended the being and therefore became identified in this sense as the "meta-physical" direction of in-quiry, these ways of Being and essence came to view only within a restricted perspective. One sector alone of the sphere of Being

† The jump from Aristotle to Hegel, certainly inadmissible from the viewpoint of the history of thought, is justified by the aim of our work, which is to obtain Heidegger's "other" understanding of Being, particu-larly by contrasting it with the "traditional" notion of substance (see above, p. 28, and below, p. 70). Our presentation of the most important doctrine of substance dating from its initial formation at the beginning of the "tradition" is now to be followed directly by the most significant ver-sion of substance in the period of its final demise, the end of the "tradi-tion." The long history of the development of the notion of substance, including the attempt toward its devaluation in Locke, Berkeley, and Hume, cannot be dealt with here; nor can we pursue the radical change in meaning that began with Kant's turn toward transcendental finite sub-jectivity and that was further developed by German Idealism to absolute subjectivity. As regards an important aspect of this development, how-ever, see below, p. 71, n. 171. The following presentation of the meanings of Being, essence, and concept in Hegel will show their decisive distinc-tion from the Aristotelian *ousia*, although the problem of this distinction cannot here be treated as a theme in its own right. [Author's note.]

[43]

and essence was illuminated by the Aristotelian type of thinking, the sector that was of importance for Aristotle's interest in the constitution of the being.

As compared with this Aristotelian thinking, the direction of Hegel's "absolute" "conceptualizing" [begreifendes] thinking is not in a similar manner transcending or "metaphysical." In his demonstration of Being in the *Science of Logic* the issue is not the restricted theme of the constitution of the Being of the being but with "Being" as such, as thought in speculative self-knowing. This may be briefly explained, since our view that the meaning of Being in Hegel can mediate to us the entirely different meaning of Being in Heidegger is based on the fact that both thinkers deal with the problem of Being and essence and in this sense move within the same *realm*.

Absolute thinking is the "last embodiment of spirit" [1] in the road of the natural consciousness. Here, as a consequence of the dialectical movement that consciousness executed "on its knowledge as well as on its object," [2] consciousness has sublated [aufgehoben] its "untrue" or "unreal" knowing [3] to the true, real knowing that knows "itself as concept" [4] and is thereby spirit that knows itself as spirit. [5] When self-consciousness has developed to this form that it knows that all Being-in-itself [Ansichsein] of the object is sublated in the transparent Being-for-itself [Fürsichsein] of the concept—i.e., is sublated in the unifying oneness of the "self" [6]—then it "descends into the depths of its own being" [7] and brings forth science. [8] For now it knows that this "self" is the place in which the Absolute in and for itself [an und für sich] is and wants to be with us "from the start." [9] It knows that here "in this self-form" [10] it finds all the "powers" that have always had us "in their possession" [11]—the categories of Being, essence, concept, and Idea. Therefore, in order to be able to grasp and demonstrate these notions in their systematic unfolding, thinking really does not direct itself toward being, nor does it transcend it, but rather it bends back toward its own self.

1. PG 556 (797).
2. PG 73 (142).
3. PG 66, 67, 75 (135, 145).
4. PG 558 (800).
5. PG 557 and 564 (798 and 808).
6. PG 558 ff., 562 (800 ff., 805).
7. PG 184 (282).
8. PG 556 (798).
9. PG 64 (132).
10. PG 562 (805).
11. Logik I 14 (35).

It comes to know that what it requires to attain to the categories that are "with us from the start" is precisely not a "transcendence." It has reached the insight that it always already resides within the "realm of Being," so that the task really lies only in the unfolding of Being.

Thus absolute thinking does not think the essence of "Being" from a perspective already limited by the "metaphysical direction of inquiry." Nor does it, in the first instance, concern itself to determine the "constitition" of being. "Being," developed for its own sake and in its categorial determinations, proves itself to be far more than only the constitution of Being of the being. Being, essence, and concept, the "conceived concepts" [*die begriffenen Begriffe*] in the *Science of Logic*, are for Hegel in fact nothing less than the demonstration of God "as he is in his eternal essence before the creation of nature and finite mind." [12] It is no contradiction to this that, in the second place, the categories known in knowing's knowing itself determine being. For Hegel conceived the "Absolute" precisely not as a "beyond" but as the movement of infinity that dwells in finite things.

Heidegger overcomes the Aristotelian direction of inquiry differently from Hegel. Heidegger too attains to a thinking that interrogates the occurrence of Being [*Seinsgeschehen*] itself. For Heidegger, to be sure, the Hegelian way of thinking, no less than the content of Hegel's thought, is so characteristically "metaphysical" that, in Heidegger's words, "the consummation of metaphysics" [13] begins with Hegel. Since both thinkers ask about Being, there is sufficient "kinship" here for us to venture to understand the radically different meaning of Being in Heidegger by way of elucidating the meaning of Being, essence, and concept in Hegel.

Hegel identified the proper province of the *Science of Logic* as the "examination of the truth" of the "living spirit," since "the truth" of its forms "has never been considered or examined on their own account." [14] In the *Logic* the "living spirit" in "its forms" is Being—from the categories of immediacy [*Unmittelbarkeit*] up to the categories of fulfilledness [*Erfülltheit*]. And hence in numerous passages Hegel speaks of the "truth of Being." If, with Heidegger, we proceed on the basis that the words of thinking are not fortuitous terminologies but "words that have grown," we must pay heed to the meaning of Hegel's words on

12. *Logik I* 31 (50).
13. VA 76.
14. *Enz.* § 162.

the "truth" and especially the "truth of Being," particularly so because Heidegger has posed the question concerning the sense of Being as a question concerning the "truth of Being."

1. THE OCCURRENCE OF BEING AS THE OCCURRENCE OF TRUTH

WHAT MEANING DO THE WORDS "truth" and the "truth of Being" have in Hegel? Truth is—or, stated more correctly, "occurs"—as a *process*.[15] It is the process in which the opposition between "reality" and "concept,"[16] or between "objectivity" and "concept,"[17] or between "content" and "concept"[18] is sublated to unity. This "unity of the ideal and the real"[19] is the Idea, and this is the "adequate concept: the objectively true or the true as such."[20]

In this sense, notes Hegel, "something has truth only insofar as it is Idea."[21] For example, one speaks of that state [*Staat*] which measures up to its idea as the "true state."[22] Here the objectivity, or the reality, or the object is identical with its concept.[23] The Idea has completely "worked through [*durchgearbeitet*] its reality."[24]

Two conceptions are to be avoided if the uniting process of the Idea is to be understood properly as a truth process. What is at issue here is not truth in the usual meaning of *adaequatio*, the result of a "coincidence" of knowledge and its "object." This kind of truth, which involves the "formal coincidence of our representation [*Vorstellung*] and its content"[25] and therefore only a "reference to consciousness," Hegel expressly terms "mere correctness," as distinct from the actual truth, wherein a "coincidence of the object with itself, that is, with its concept," must be forthcoming.

The second incorrect conception consists in the view that this "coincidence" is to be regarded "as a dead repose or bare pic-

15. *Enz.* § 215; *Logik II* 412 (759).
16. *Logik II* 496 (835).
17. *Enz.* § 213.
18. *Logik II* 231 (592).
19. *Enz.* § 214.
20. *Logik II* 407 (755).
21. *Ibid.*
22. *Enz.* § 213; cf. also *Logik II* 410 (757).
23. *Enz.* § 213.
24. *Logik II* 410 (757).
25. *Enz.* § 172, add.

ture, spent and without impulse or motion." [26] Idea and concept must rather be thought as a unifying occurrence, as the process that unites both sides in such a way that the one side—the concept—"generates from within itself," [27] as its very own, the other side—the "reality" or "objectivity"—in that the concept sublates it to itself as "adequate content" and thereby posits it as "pure truth." [28]

The entire *Phenomenology of Spirit* can be regarded as an example of such a process of the Idea, or an occurrence of truth. For it is the process of the uniting of the object, Being-in-itself, substance, with the concept, Being-for-itself, subject. There is, however, a particular way of such an occurrence of truth that we wish to exhibit here, since it helps make clear the "sense" of Being in Hegel. It concerns the case where the "other side" is likewise "concept"—with the consequence that the uniting process is between "concept and concept" and is in this sense a "self-conceiving of the concept." This is the case of the *Science of Logic* itself. Here the Idea is "its own object." [29] The concept or Idea unites to itself a totality of concepts and in this sense brings them to their "truth." This uniting process is expressly termed "the self-knowing truth" and "all truth." [30] However, it is also termed briefly "Being," since "Being" for Hegel has the meaning of the "pure concept" which "is related only to itself" or is "simple self-relation." [31] In this unmistakable sense, therefore, the *Science of Logic* is the "occurrence of Being as occurrence of truth."

The closer meaning of this "occurrence of Being as occurrence of truth" becomes evident from Hegel's definition of the "beginning of science"—Being—as the "indeterminate immediate," as a "concept that is only implicit [*nur an sich*]." [32] This means in the first place that even the very beginning has not to do with an "immediate of sensuous intuition or of representation, but of thinking," [33] of a "determination of thought," [34] of "conceptual thought," [35] a category. This shows that Being, for Hegel, is from the beginning "identical" with thinking, that Be-

26. *Logik II* 412 (759).
27. *Logik II* 230, 231 (592, 593).
28. *Logik II* 231 (593).
29. *Logik II* 406, 505 (753, 843); *Enz.* § 236, add.
30. *Logik II* 484 (824).
31. *Logik II* 504, 488 (842, 828).
32. *Enz.* § 84.
33. *Logik II* 488 (827).
34. *Logik II* 493 (833).
35. *Logik II* 488 (828).

ing is always "in the medium of thought," [36] retained in thinking
—in short, that Being is *thought.*

The "concept in itself" is also termed "the simple" and "the
universal," [37] with "simple" signifying the "one in the manifold,"
and "universal" the "one in the many." This entails that the "concept in itself" must explicate itself into the "many" thought determinations, for it is "endowed with the urge to carry itself further" [38] and contains within itself "the beginning of the advance
and development." [39] Hence, that Being is an occurring is in the
second place implicit in the formulation of Being as the "concept
in itself."

That the concept of Being is only a concept "in itself" signifies that this occurrence is consummated in a specific direction
and way—on the model of the Aristotelian relationship of *dynamis* and *energeia.*[40] This way in which the "in itself" comes to
its "fulfillment" was understood by Hegel as a "process." The
particular movement of advancing and returning to its source,
whereby "immediate Being" unfolds itself to "fulfilled Being," [41]
was demonstrated by Hegel as a dialectical process. The meaning of Being as thinking is thus determined, in the third place, as
an occurrence that has the structure of a *dialectical process.*

In this "course" [42] of the dialectical process, immediate Being, the "concept in itself," becomes "posited" concept,[43] essence,
substance; and it fulfills itself as "concept for itself," as subject.
In the *Phenomenology of Spirit* Hegel characterized the particular aim of his efforts as "grasping and expressing the ultimate
truth not as substance but as subject as well." [44] That the "concept in itself" and all the thought determinations deduced and
posited therefrom attain to the clarity and transparency of the
"concept for itself" constitutes what is decisively new in Hegel's
conception of the occurrence of Being. "Conceiving Being" "unfolds itself" in its subject character into the determinations of
the "Subjective Logic." It shows itself (since Hegel expressly ad-

36. *Enz.* § 19.
37. *Logik II* 488 (829).
38. *Logik II* 489 (829).
39. *Logik II* 490 (830).
40. Cf. Hegel, *Lectures on the History of Philosophy,* trans. E. S. Haldane, II, 138 ff., where these concepts are interpreted from Hegel's particular viewpoint.
41. *Logik II* 504 (842).
42. *Logik II* 3 (389).
43. *Enz.* § 112.
44. *PG* 19 (80).

hered to the insights of transcendental philosophy) as the "nature of self-consciouness," the "transcendental apperception of the ego." [45] This "self" posits itself in the moments of "universality," "particularity," and "individuality"—thus divides [*urteilt*] and "closes" [*schliesst*], i.e., judges and concludes. In its course through the determinations of "objectivity" the subject develops itself to the "Idea," the "unity of the concept and objectivity." [46] The Idea is the "subject-object"; [47] the totality of objectivity and of the concept is *for* it. In its fulfilled form it is self-knowingly and absolutely an "acting knowing" that knows itself as the condition of all objectivity and of its own self and thereby speculatively "brings forth" itself. It is the "absolute activity," [48] the "necessary doing," and the "method" [49] which produces the entire thought-like dialectical process of the occurring of Being in the *Logic* and thereby brings immediate Being, the beginning, the "concept in itself," to fulfillment. In subjectivity thus understood lies the fourth trait of Being in Hegel. This subjectivity, this method, however, is nothing other than the aforementioned "process" [50] through which the Idea brings the totality of concepts to themselves and in this sense to their truth—the "uniting-occurring" [*Einigungsgeschehen*] that Hegel called the "self-knowing truth" and the "whole truth." Hereby, in the fifth place, the occurrence of Being is characterized as an occurrence of truth.

The process of truth accomplishes itself as dialectic. Hence a closer definition of the "dialectical method" can explain more exactly the meaning of the occurrence of Being as an occurrence of truth. The first stage, the thesis, is an identity, but an identity that already has "implicitly" [*an sich*] within it the nonidentical, the different, the other, thus the "negative"—in the present case the concrete totality of thought determinations. From this potentiality grows the movement to "posit" this nonidentical expressly as a second stage, as antithesis. This second stage is the explicated "negativity"; it is the posited "relation" [*Verhältnis*] wherein the negative is the "negative *of* the positive," the "other *of* an other." [51] Inasmuch as the distinction which the concept

45. *Logik II* 220, 221 (583, 584).
46. *Enz.* § 213.
47. *Enz.* § 214; *Logik II* 411 (758).
48. *Logik II* 486 (826).
49. *Logik II* 485 (825).
50. See above, p. 48.
51. *Logik II* 496 (835).

contains "in itself" emerges as a "determinate" distinction, the *contradiction* shows itself. Contradiction, however, is "the principle of all self-movement," [52] "the root of all movement and life," [53] and therefore speculative thinking has to drive the manifold entities "onto the sharp point of contradiction." [54] This stage of negativity thus understood constitutes the turning point of the movement of the concept [55] and the innermost source of all activity, of all living and spiritual self-movement—the dialectical soul.[56] On this stage, as the most important form of "subjectivity," of "method," rests "the sublation [*Aufhebung*] of the opposition between the concept and reality," the "unity which is the truth." [57]

In the third stage to which this occurrence presses on, the "truth" has the form of "result." [58] This result "mediates" the movement and activity of the subjectivity itself, in that the contradiction sublates itself to a new identity, to the synthesis of the antithesis, while the negativity of the preceding stage is in its turn negated. This new immediacy, however, distinguishes itself from the immediacy of the first stage precisely because it is the "result" of the two preceding stages: it bears within itself "the entire mass of its preceding content" [59] and "inwardly enriches and consolidates itself." It is "sublation" [*Aufhebung*] in the threefold sense of *tollere, conservare,* and *elevare.* In this sense the third stage, synthesis, is indeed "a progress to itself from contradiction" but thus at the same time a "return." A progress which in this sense is also always a return to self presents a *moving order* that has the structure of a circle. The *Science of Logic,* in the dialectically ascending steps of its stage-by-stage movement, contains many circles. Further, the *Science of Logic* itself, in the structure of its total occurring, is a "circle returning upon itself, the end being wound back into the beginning, the simple ground, by the mediation." [60] For the Absolute Idea, in which the *Logic* ends, is nothing other than the occurrence through which the "concept for itself" grasps the "concept in itself," the immediate categories or "the beginning." Thus the

52. *Ibid.*
53. *Logik II* 58 ff. (439 ff.)
54. *Logik II* 61 (442).
55. *Logik II* 496 (835).
56. *Ibid.*
57. *Ibid.*
58. *Logik II* 499 (837).
59. *Logik II* 502 (840).
60. *Logik II* 504 (842).

occurrence of Being demonstrated as a science of logic—the "moving order" of the occurrence of truth conceived as such a logic—has the structure of a "circle of circles." [61]

This interpretation of the structure of the dialectical process could be seen as evidence that Hegel remained within the tradition deriving from the Aristotelian *ousiology*. Aristotle conceived *ousia*, understood as *telos*, as a movement circling within itself. In the *Phenomenology of Spirit* Hegel, with express reference to Aristotle, recognized *telos* as a model for his own thinking and as describing a circle "which presupposes its end as its purpose and has its end for its beginning; it becomes concrete and actual only by being carried out, and by the end it involves." [62] Certainly Hegel was no longer influenced phenomenally by the cyclically rotating order of *ouranos*. But one can nevertheless say that the circle-figure, conceived on the Aristotelian model, of the occurrence of Being as a dialectically ordered return to self, represented the final expression of the Greek yearning to comprehend a synthesis of movement and order, becoming and Being. In modern times, to be sure, this took the form of the "method" of the "absolute activity" of the "subjectivity," whose "necessary act" produces itself as this dialectical process of the "occurrence of Being" in the manner of thought. Much has been said about the dialectical nature of the meaning of Being in Heidegger. Heidegger's efforts in his early works, however, are directed toward an "overcoming" of substance and subject,[63] i.e., the categories from which alone the structure of this dialectical movement is determined. Although the sense of Being in Heidegger will no doubt also prove to be an "occurrence," it is, nevertheless, neither an occurrence that is predetermined by Aristotelian substance qua *telos* nor an occurrence of pure thought—an occurrence that, as "subjectivity," produces itself. And nevertheless it is, as in Hegel, an occurrence of truth. A closer characterization of the meaning of truth in Hegel is therefore necessary.

Hegel terms "the truth" the synthesis that is reached each time in the dialectical process through thesis and antithesis. This definition implies that the preceding stages, thesis and antithesis, represent the "untruth." Since, in the stage-by-stage movement of the *Logic*, each synthesis reached is again the basis of a new movement leading to the antithesis, this means also that the truth is the "untruth" of a succeeding stage. For example,

61. *Logik II* 504 (842).
62. PG 22, 20 (83, 81).
63. See below, p. 85.

Hegel terms essence "the truth of Being," [64] but on the stage of the concept in the Subjective Logic, this truth is an untruth, for "the concept is the truth of essence." [65] The same holds true for the entire process of the *Logic*. No doubt the Absolute Idea is expressly termed "all truth." [66] But while it is the end of the *Logic*, it is also the beginning, i.e., immediacy and untruth. Out of the dialectical process-structure of the logical occurrence of Being, therefore, the meaning of truth is characterized as a particular relationship to untruth.

In "The Spirit of Christianity and Its Fate," in his *Early Theological Writings*, Hegel understood the truth in the likeness of the light. [67] He called it here *phōs;* life, as "comprehended" [*aufgefasstes*] living, is light. Even at that time, presumably, "life" for Hegel was an expression for "Being," just as later, in the *Logic*, "life" is an "immediate" category of the idea of "fulfilled" Being. Instances can be found showing that Hegel, along the lines of this light metaphor, experienced the *Science of Logic* as an "occurrence of truth" in which Being increasingly "emerges into the light" and finally attains to the fullness of light. It is important that we go into this more fully, since here again is an "element of kinship" that leads to the essence of truth in Heidegger. As far as Heidegger himself is concerned, Hegel's concept of truth is determined exclusively from the Cartesian position, whereby truth signifies "certainty." [68] The true is what is known in the unconditional knowing of self. Truth is no longer said to be the correspondence of the representation with the being; rather, it is said to consist only in the representing [*Vorstellen*] through which the subject conveys or "represents" to himself that which is certain for him and at the same time in and through this representation becomes certain of himself. [69] This representing is said to have "absolved" itself of every one-sided tie to what is objective [*das Gegenständliche*] and therein has found its "security." Such a kind of "absolved" knowing, i.e., "absolute" knowing, as a "representing" freed from the objective,

64. *Logik II* 3 (389).
65. *Enz.* § 159; *Logik II* 214 (577).
66. *Logik II* 484 (824).
67. *Early Theological Writings,* trans. T. M. Knox, p. 258; cf. also H. Marcuse, *Hegels Ontologie und die Grundlegung einer Theorie der Geschichtlichkeit,* pp. 231 ff.
68. Recently in the treatise "Hegel und die Griechen," in *Festschrift für Hans-Georg Gadamer,* Heidegger indicated that even Hegel's philosophy could not escape the rule of *alētheia.*
69. HW 122, 124.

is the "absolute presenting" of the absolute, i.e., of the true.[70] In this sense, the truth according to Hegel consists only in the "absolute certainty of the self-knowing absolute subject." [71]

Heidegger obtained this version of Hegel's conception of truth exclusively from the *Phenomenology of Spirit*. It is open to question whether the Absolute, in the form of the "self" that is the known or the "certain" as such, can be understood as a derivative of the "certainty" [*Gewissen*] that the Cartesian self-certain representing knows. For the decisive determination of absolute knowledge in Hegel is that Being and knowing are no longer "distinguished" from each other. In absolute knowledge this distinction has been "sublated," while every "representation" as such must essentially contain this distinction. Furthermore, the "subject," which makes itself present in the representation, is no longer the *ego cogito*, for which it is important only that the guarantee of the *me esse* is contained in its *me cogitare*.[72] The "self" of absolute knowing is precisely that which no longer wants to "assure" itself but only the Absolute, which "wants to be with us." It knows that the thought determinations of the Absolute "have us in their possession." [73] The crucial objection against Heidegger's determination of the essence of truth in Hegel, however, is that the essence of truth is shown in its pure form not in the *Phenomenology* but only in the *Science of Logic*. Not when the truth is "with us" but when it is "with itself" does its essence let itself be grasped in a valid way. And even the fundamental *meaning* of this essence of truth permits of access only from the *Logic*. The following analysis will attempt to determine the meaning of the essence of truth in Hegel from the fact that he experienced the total unfolding of the *Logic* in the guiding image of the "light."

The sphere of immediate Being sublates itself to the sphere of essence as "its truth" in that it "reflects" itself as essential "shine" or "show" (i.e., as the unessential in the essence).[74] The reflection-determinations are doubled in intro-reflection, wherein, "at first, essence shines or shows within itself." [75] This doubling was explained by Hegel himself as the way a ray of light doubles through reflection. Being brings itself forward to a

70. *HW* 125 ff.
71. "Hegel und die Griechen," p. 52.
72. *HW* 100.
73. *Logik I* 14 (35).
74. *Logik II* 7 ff. (393 ff.)
75. *Logik II* 6 (391); for the explanation of the expression "reflection," cf. *Enz.* § 112, add.

further stage more fully in the light, inasmuch as "the show perfects itself" and the essence "appears." [76] The words "shine" or "show" [Schein] and "appearance" [Erscheinung] are expressions of a self-augmenting intensity of the illumination of the light. The appearing essence steps "forth" as the subject matter [Sache] [77] and posits itself as the "truth of Being," [78] as "existence" [Existenz],[79] in order finally to "reveal" and to "manifest" itself as actuality [Wirklichkeit] so as "to shine" or "to show" [scheinen] [80] as the relationship of substance to its accidents. Hegel writes: "Light in nature is not something, nor thing, but its being is only its showing or shining [Scheinen]; and similarly manifestation is self-identical absolute actuality." [81]

The sphere of the concept "unveils" [82] the sphere of essence of its still "blind" necessity.[83] In its complete development to Idea, the concept comes fully into the light. The Absolute Idea is the light. For Plato [84] the Idea was like the light of the sun, and for Aristotle the noēsis noēseōs was the utmost degree of transparency of the nous thought in the likeness of the light.[85] Hegel, too, understood the Absolute Idea as a noēsis noēseōs. The final section of the Encyclopaedia quotes the Greek text of that famous passage of Book Lambda in the Metaphysics in which Aristotle deals with the way of Being [Seinsweise] of the divine and the way of Being of the philosopher as akin to that of the divine.[86]

Precisely when we take note of the light metaphor and tend to interpret the ascending emergence into the light, demonstrated in the Logic, as the meaning of the "truth of Being" in Hegel— precisely then does the crucial distinction emerge which separates Hegel's thinking from the tradition and leads into Heidegger's thinking. For then it becomes evident that Hegel, to put it metaphorically, knows not only the "realm of light" but also the "realm of darkness" and that the essence of the truth in Hegel is

76. Logik II 101 (479).
77. Logik II 99 (477).
78. Logik II 102 (481).
79. Ibid.; cf. also Enz. § 213, add., where Hegel explains the literal meaning of "existence" as a having-proceeded from something [Hervorgegangensein].
80. Logik II 185, 186 (554, 555).
81. Ibid.
82. Enz. § 157.
83. Logik II 183 (552).
84. Republic 508b–f.
85. De Anima 430a15.
86. Enz. § 577.

thereby defined in terms of a specific "relationship" of light and darkness.

The history of the light-and-darkness metaphor reaches back to the early period of Western thinking. The various metaphysical positions were developed in the image of light and darkness, which often stood for "archetypal powers." In some positions the darkness ruled first, and in others light and darkness reigned "dualistically." The influential positions for the history of Western thought, however, were those in which the light possessed complete mastery over the darkness. The Aristotelian vision, which proved so significant for the Western tradition, has already been identified as a "metaphysics of light"; the basic trait of the total intelligibility of *ousia* was an expression of his "optimistic" world view. Its noetic character, its luminousness, guaranteed its thinkableness. The "moving order" conceived on the image of the visible cosmos, the vision of Being as "hale" [*heil*] and unbroken, notwithstanding all mobility, was consistent only with the supposition of a rule of the light, of the *nous*, which is unclouded by any "alien admixture." [87]

By contrast, Hegel's intellectual world from the time of his youth was stirred by the basic conviction that reality in itself is in the deepest sense rent, sundered, estranged, full of contradiction. Thus in the early writings already cited, after he had called life the light, he expressly says: "These finite entities have opposites; for the light there is darkness." [88] That there is "darkness" Hegel brought out again and again in all his subsequent works. There is darkness in the form of "untruth," [89] "error," [90] "evil," [91] and death. [92] That Being is in principle a brokenness is evident in his thinking, for which "everything is inherently contradictory" [93] and "pain is the prerogative of living natures." [94]

Together with this conception, however, there goes another, implanted within him from youth through the study of antiquity as well as the two late critiques of Kant. This is the even stronger basic conviction that the *nous*, reason, has the power to heal and to reconcile every breach and sundering of Being, every estrange-

87. *De Anima* 429a20.
88. *Early Theological Writings*, p. 258.
89. *Logik II* 486 (826).
90. *Logik II* 56 (437).
91. *Logik II* 55, 56 (437).
92. *PG* 29, 69 (93, 138).
93. *Logik II* 58 (439).
94. *Logik II* 424 (770).

ment and diremption. In all his penetrating into the "realm of darkness," the young Hegel is already certain that reason can lead out of the darkness into the light because it is itself the light.

One is tempted to say that, with this second insight of Hegel's, the Aristotelian outlook again won the victory and that Hegel therefore was also a "metaphysician of light." But then one overlooks the essential distinction that for Hegel, unlike Aristotle, Being and essence are *not* purely and simply disclosed. For this reason there is not in Hegel the *noēsis*, the intuitive inspection [*Schau*] which, on sheer contact, is able without possibility of error to grasp the truth of Being and essence unobstructedly showing themselves in their manifestness. And the "absolute intuition" of Schelling is likewise not in Hegel; [95] rather there is only the "strenuous toil of rational reflection," [96] which can only grasp the true as the "whole," i.e., as "the essence reaching its completeness through the process of its own development." [97] For the essence ever anew drives the manifold entities "to the sharp point of contradiction," [98] in order to win the truth that can be won only circuitously through this "absolute sunderance." [99]

The "thought determinations," the determinations of reflection that pervade "reality" and relate to one another, are the "conflict" [100] of the light with the "darkness," [101] of virtue with vice and evil, of truth with error. They effect the "positive negativity" [102] of evil or of error, the "opposition" which, as the relation to virtue, to the good, and to the truth, comes to its showing [*Scheinen*] or reflection. When Hegel remarks that, "without the knowledge" that the truth of the determinations of reflection consist only in their relation to one another, "not a single step can be taken in philosophy," [103] he is not referring to a "method in the theory of knowledge" but to the "method" of the Absolute Idea itself. Of this "Idea in its process" he expressly declares [104] that it "creates that illusion" itself "by setting an other to confront" itself and that its doing consists in sublating this illusion. Only out of such error is truth said to emerge. And otherness or error, sublated, is

95. Cf. here *PG* 20 (80).
96. *PG* 48 (116).
97. *PG* 21 (81).
98. *Logik II* 61 (442).
99. *PG* 30 (93).
100. *Logik II* 55 (437).
101. *Ibid.*
102. *Ibid.*
103. *Logik II* 56 (438).
104. *Enz.* § 212, add.

itself said to be a necessary moment of the truth, which only "is" in that it constitutes itself its own result.

It is implicit in these determinations that the way to the light, to the truth, is always a roundabout way through the "realm of darkness." Though reason is stronger than the sundering of Being, the light of reason does not come in one burst. This is shown in the *Science of Logic,* inasmuch as "activity," i.e., the subjectivity, must "bring itself forth"; it has to unveil [105] the "blindness" [106] of the categories of the "objective logic." Since this "unfolding" [107] (understood in a nontemporal sense) of the truth is consummated as a "coming forth into the light," it must take place in a relation to the not yet luminous. The light metaphor thus indicates that Hegel experienced the occurrence of the truth as a "relationship" of "light" and "darkness," as a pathway on which each lighted station arrived at results from the overcoming of the hitherto prevailing darkness, until the goal of this path is attained. If each of the stations in the darkness to be overcome is called an "untruth," then a glance at the light metaphor confirms the conclusion that in Hegel the essence of the truth determines itself from its relationship to the "untruth."

It is important to keep in mind, however, that, in this relationship of the "light" to the "darkness," the light retains predominance. This is evident also in the way Hegel thought "order" and "movement" together. The already noted dialectical process and structure of subjectivity determine the way that "light" and "darkness," truth and untruth, belong together. Though each stage of truth attained in the dialectical process again becomes an untruth, each synthesis taken for itself is nevertheless "higher" than its antithesis and thesis. And within the total process of the *Logic* each succeeding synthesis is understood as the "higher" stage of the preceding syntheses, the final synthesis being the "highest" stage. Although this highest stage, the Absolute Idea, the full truth, contains, in Hegel's words, "even the harshest opposition," it nevertheless "eternally overcomes" it.[108] The dialectical order thereby guarantees the conclusive victory to the light, to the truth undisguised by the untruth.

But just because the Absolute Idea "always produces anew

the highest opposition" and because it is the "whole truth" that, ever again circling the categories of immediacy to comprehend the "beginning," must thereby become "untruth"—precisely here lies a motif that directs the historical destiny of the problem beyond Hegel's position and leads to a problematic that obtains expression in Heidegger's understanding of truth.[109] It is not difficult to see that this motif presses toward an order connecting truth and untruth, an order in which both become "equal partners," in which "light" and "darkness" play an equally significant role *in* the essence of truth. Paradoxically, it is the self-knowing Idea that endangers its own victory. For only in the light of the self-knowing Idea do the realms of "alienation" [*Entfremdung*] and "exteriorization" [*Entäusserung*] dealt with by Hegel in the *Phenomenology of Spirit* first become clearly and plainly visible. These insights so strongly motivated post-Hegelian thinking that it was soon found necessary to understand these realms in their own right and to call them up as witnesses that the occurrence of Being cannot be an occurrence of "pure thought" and that the essentially nonluminous, the essentially concealed, as well as semblance and error—the "realm of darkness"—is of equal rank with and belongs to the "truth of Being."

If a visible cosmic order is no longer pregiven to thinking and if faith has been lost in the power of thought to produce an orderedness out of itself, if the idea of Being as a "moving order" no longer serves as guide, and if inquiry is directed only to the meaning of the phenomena that offer themselves to experience—then the essence of truth as such and the essence of the truth of Being in particular become problematical in a new and radical way. And this new problematic will trace its origins, not only in the sobering experiences of the history of the past century and in the anti-idealistic thought-motifs in Kierkegaard, Marx, and Nietzsche, but pre-eminently in the consequences of the last great "doctrine of Being and essence," the doctrine of Hegel. No doubt it may be shown that Heidegger was influenced much more strongly in his early period by Augustine and Kierkegaard, and later by Nietzsche, than by Hegel. As regards the history of the problem, however, there is a "kinship" with Hegel in that for both thinkers the essence of truth is determined from its relationship to untruth and from the relationship of "light" and "darkness," regardless of the fact that the two thinkers un-

109. See below, pp. 145 ff.

derstand this relationship differently and that in many respects "light" and "darkness" signify different things to each.

In Heidegger the question concerning the "essence of truth" is linked with the question concerning the "truth of essence." [110] In Hegel the sphere of essence is the mean in which the sphere of immediate Being is sublated so as to be mediated into the sphere of concept. If we wish to determine the "truth" or the meaning of essence in Hegel, the basic traits of essence, we cannot isolate the sphere of essence; on the contrary, both of the other spheres must be kept in view. The basic traits of "essence" in Hegel will henceforward be demonstrated in this fashion. The demonstration will involve the same basic traits that characterized the Aristotelian *ousia:* selfsameness, necessity, eternalness, and intelligibility. The meaning of intelligibility has in large part already become clear to us from Hegel's conception of the essence of truth. However, while in Aristotle these basic traits are valid in respect to the constitution of the Being of a being, in Hegel they are valid for "Being" speculatively thought. Though Hegel's model of thought remains oriented to the ousiology that, for Aristotle, determined the constitution of the particular being, Hegel nevertheless thinks within the realm of enabling [*ermöglichend*] Being, the realm in which Heidegger's thinking, hostile to *ousia,* also moves.

2. THE BASIC TRAIT OF THE SELFSAMENESS OF BEING

HEGEL CONFRONTS THE TASK of grasping Being, known speculatively through a knowledge knowing itself, in the manner of a self-moving order moving toward itself. This movement must recognize the contradictoriness of Being and at the same time heal and reconcile it. The principle of this order and movement, for Hegel, lies in that "relationship" already seen by the ancients and understood as the "other of the one" (*heteron*) and from which the basic trait of the selfsameness of the Aristotelian *ousia* was also determined. Hegel endowed this order-relationship with movement in the highest sense in that he conceived it in the element of thought as a dialectical process. The relationship, which Hegel explicated and posited as the contradiction of "the other *and* the one," becomes the categorial ex-

110. WW 27 (348).

pression of the sundering of Being and at the same time the motivating force for the restoration of the order, the "return." But it is a "return" that is also an "advance" and an "enrichment" and, in this sense, the "concrete" synthesis of the one and *its* other. Understood in this way, the principle of selfsameness lies at the basis of the entire movement of the *Logic*.

In Aristotle, too,[111] this basic trait of selfsameness assured the ousiological order and guaranteed that in all alteration and change a "fundament" endures as a "selfsame." In Hegel this basic trait guarantees not only the order of the constitution of Being of the being but in the first instance the order of Being itself. It is the guiding clue whereby not only the Objective Logic determines itself to the category of the relation of substantiality, but also whereby the Subjective Logic determines itself to the category of the Absolute Idea. Further, the basic trait of selfsameness determines the categories involving change and alteration. Above all, however, it determines the meaning of the other basic traits of Being.

For Aristotle the basic trait of selfsameness was the conceptual expression of his experiences of the phenomenon of the cosmos. The cosmos bore witness to the return and endurance of the same. Everything that did not permit of being grasped in thought through the basic trait of selfsameness, everything new and unprecedented [*Niedagewesene*], was consequently for Aristotle an exception that lacked essence.

Hegel's era presented him with a radically different problematical situation. The cosmological conceptions of the Greeks were discredited, and the ideas of Christianity, as well as the experiences of history, testified to the possibility of the arrival of the new. Hegel's insights into the "power of history" have often been regarded as the beginning of that historicism and relativism which widely dominated the intellectual outlook of the succeeding period. In the *Science of Logic*, however, Hegel had made a last great effort to "save" the notion of the occurrence of Being as an occurrence of an order by determining the occurrence of Being from the basic trait of selfsameness. This basic trait, however, excluded an understanding of the "course of Being" as "poietically creative" in a radical way. This will be shown in detail, since the view of such a constraint on Being must be disturbing to the kind of thinking that wants to prepare for the arrival of the new and to present Being as radically creative. Actually

111. See above, p. 34.

Heidegger has taken issue with "selfsameness" only in one of his later writings, and there very briefly. But perhaps one would not go amiss in supposing that he had long since desired, through a "primordial" comprehension, to "overcome" this traditional basic trait of selfsameness, which gained its highest expression in Hegel. Heidegger took a position as regards "selfsameness" in a publication entitled *Identity and Difference*. "Identity" and "difference" are the standard categories wherein the particular trait of selfsameness obtained expression in Hegel. They are the "reflection-determinations" of essence wherein "otherhood" [*Andersheit*] is recognized in Being and at the same time taken into the order of essence as "essential." Hegel conceived "difference" as so properly a part of "identity" that he treats of both these categories as one, the category of nonidentical identity.[112]

The particular conception of these categories is of importance problematically in two respects. The categories, in greatest movement, are interconnectedly ordered. Identity is an "internal repulsion" toward difference, which at the same time is "repulsion which immediately recalls itself into itself." [113] All other categories of essence, the categories of "appearance" [*Erscheinung*] and of "actuality" [*Wirklichkeit*], were developed on the pattern of movement of identity and difference. One can perhaps say that the traditional meaning of essence was thereby thought through "to the end." No doubt the Aristotelian *ousia* as *hypokeimenon* was also a "selfsameness" or an identity which stood in connection with the "accidentals," the different properties, but here there was no suggestion of a "repulsion." Rather, the relationship based on this connection gave to Being the repose of a moved "order." Presumably the radical movement of the "categories of essence" in Hegel's *Logic* contributed to the development in later thinking wherein the thought of an essence enduring through all change was forgotten and the gate was opened to the avalanche of radical historicism and relativism. It was in this situation in the history of thought that philosophy found itself, until in our time the "need" awakened anew to ask about "essence" and perhaps an "order of essence."

Hegel's particular understanding of the categories of identity and difference are in the second place significant problematically

and historically inasmuch as the movement from identity to difference and back to identity is not a matter of a "return" to the
"same" identity. Rather, the movement [114] proceeds dialectically
to an "identity" that is enriched through the "progress" of the
thesis via the antithesis. What is involved here, therefore, is not
a "returning-enduring" of the "same." In this possibility of "progress" in the dialectic, we might be tempted to see an unlimited
"historicity," which would therefore make room for the arrival
of the new. In that case, however, we would overlook the fact
that each synthesis, each new and enriched identity in the sphere
of essence, contains within itself the preceding stages as "sublated" and results only from them, the "pregiven" and the "having
been" [Gewesenen].[115] For this reason Hegel conceives this "progress" as a "return" [116] and regards the whole movement on the
model of the Aristotelian telos as the revolving of a circle.

That Hegel determined Being from the basic trait of selfsameness and therefore excluded the possibility of the arrival of
the new is even more plainly evident from the categories of "actuality." After essence has already constituted itself as the "doing
of the subject matter" [Tun der Sache], after it has already "appeared" as "existence," and after it has exhibited itself in the "infinite connection of grounds and grounded," of "world," and has
essentially penetrated "immediate actuality," there yet remains a
further categorial "process." Only through the "process of actuality," through a development from "immediate" to "essential"
actuality, does essence "come forth as such," "reveal" and "manifest" itself. The Encyclopaedia demonstrates this process in language of a "revolutionary" and "historical" ring. Thus we hear:
"Immediate actuality is in general as such never what it ought to
be; it is a finite actuality with an inherent flaw, and its vocation
is to be consumed." [117] Out of the immediate actuality there comes
"quite another shape of things," [118] from which a "new" [119] actuality emerges. Immediate actuality is in truth only the collectivity of "conditions which are sacrificed, which fall to the ground
and are spent." [120]

But these high-sounding revolutionary and historical determinations should not serve to conceal the fact that they were

114. See above, p. 49.
115. Logik II 3 (389).
116. Logik II 15 (401).
117. Enz. § 146, add.
118. Ibid.
119. Enz. § 146, add., and 147, add.
120. Enz. § 146, add.

ultimately meant within the "conservative" and "timeless" principle of selfsameness, of Being-with-itself in otherness. "Immediate" actuality, in the words of the *Encyclopaedia*,[121] already has within itself the "possibility" of the "new" actuality as its "other" in the form of the "inner." In this sense the "immediate" actuality is the "condition" and the "germ of the other." Thereby the "new" actuality that "emerges" from this process is not all "new" in the sense of what has never been there before; on the contrary, it is nothing else than the "inner of the immediate actuality." This is explicitly stated: "Thus there comes into being quite an other shape of things, and yet it is not an other: for the first actuality is only put as what it in essence was. The conditions which are sacrificed, which fall to the ground and are spent, only unite with themselves in the other actuality." [122]

From the basic trait of the selfsameness of Being, as it obtains expression in this "process of actuality," the basic trait of the "necessity" of Being is also determined. Hegel developed the "process of actuality" *modally* and exhibited it as the "process of necessity." [123] Conceived modally, the "immediate actual" is a "contingent" or—on a developed stage—a "possible that *is*" [*ein seiendes Mögliches*]. The contingent "as such" is defined as that "whose being or not-being, and whose being in this way or otherwise, depends not upon itself but on something else." [124] The "possible that *is*" is the "possibility of an other." [125] The "other," into which the "contingent" and the "possible that *is*" develop in the "process of actuality," is the "essential" actuality. Thus this development occurs only because there is an order that is grounded in the relationship of the "one" and *its* "other." Since there is this relationship of selfsameness in otherness, the categories of contingency and possibility *must* so determine actuality that this development takes place. In the compulsion of this "must" lies the meaning of the category of necessity, in which the two other modal categories are "sublated." Only because the "process of actuality," modally conceived, is the expression of this compulsion does this process constitute a "process of necessity."

Hegel on the whole understood the category of necessity as a manifestation of the principle of selfsameness. For this reason he called it the "absolute relationship." [126] It posits itself, first of

121. *Ibid.*
122. *Ibid.*
123. *Enz.* § 147, add.
124. *Enz.* § 145, add.; cf. also *Enz.* § 193.
125. *Enz.* § 146.
126. *Enz.* § 150.

all, as the relationship in which the "power" of substance is with itself in its otherness: the totality of accidents; then as the "causality relationship" of cause and effect: this reflection-within-itself; and finally as the relationship of reciprocity.[127] That the basic trait of necessity is an expression of the basic trait of selfsameness is shown most concretely in this final category of the Objective Logic, in which all preceding categories are sublated. For "reciprocal determination" means precisely that "the members, linked to one another, are not really foreign to one another but are only elements of one whole, each of them, in its connection with the other, being, as it were, at home, and combining with itself."[128]

The basic trait of the *eternalness* of essence, concept, and Idea is the most profoundly conceived expression of the basic trait of selfsameness. Hegel contested the "perishability" of terrestrial beings as little as did Aristotle. In contrast to Aristotle, however, he understood this perishability not as an essential consequence of their "temporality" but of their "finitude." Not because the concrete particular beings are "in time," as in a "receptacle,"[129] are they perishable and temporal, but rather because, by virtue of their ontological structure, they must alter, and, as alterable, perish, go "to their end." "Finite things are temporal, however, because they are subject to alteration, whether brief or long."[130] Only "because things are finite are they therefore in time."[131] For "the process itself of actual things makes time."[132]

Taking his point of departure from "ontology" has guarded Hegel against remaining within the supposition of two regions of Being, like Aristotle, and has induced him to look for the "truth" of this finitude. When finitude is thought dialectically in that which it is in "truth," it unveils itself as in-finity [*Un-endlichkeit*], as the process of selfsameness in otherness which Hegel terms "affirmative infinity." This conception of "infinity" will later serve to bring out the meaning of "finitude" in Heidegger and therefore warrants some expansion. Every determinate being [*Daseiende*] is determined, conditioned, and "qualitatively limited" as a

127. *Enz.* § 153 ff.
128. *Enz.* § 158, add.
129. *Enz.* § 258, add.
130. *Ibid.*
131. *Ibid.*
132. *Ibid.*

"something." Hegel offers the following example: [133] a piece of ground having a meadow is *not* a wood or a pond. This delimiting or limit constitutes the reality of this something and is at the same time its negativity. The something is this something because it is *not* an other. Precisely as a something it is not the other, but in order to be a something it must itself be so structured that it can relate itself to an other. Its own Being or Being-in-itself [*Ansichsein*] is its Being-for-other [*Sein-für-Anderes*]. Thereby a something is at the same time not an other and yet is in itself [*an sich*] an other. Herein lies a "contradiction of its self" and the impulse to "send itself on beyond" [134] its former Being and determine itself to that which it already is in itself, to become an other or "to alter itself." This process of alteration [*Veränderung*, "becoming other"] appears to be in-finite in the sense of a "perennial continuing," since every other of the something opposite it is likewise a something, and the first something is an other to the other opposite it. Understanding [*Verstand*] clings to this insight, since understanding does not raise itself to speculative thinking; and, in this process of alteration, understanding does not grasp the meaning of the concrete being's "finitude," which, as such a being, leads to the "true infinity."

Since every something must become an other, the Being of the something is properly its non-Being. And that it must, by virtue of its inner contradiction, always project itself beyond its Being signifies that its Being also is always already its "end" (as a something). Thus Hegel writes:

> They *are*, but the truth of this being is their *end*. The finite not only alters, like something in general, but it *ceases to be;* and its ceasing to be is not merely a possibility, so that it could be without ceasing to be, but the being as such of finite things is to have the germ of decease as their Being-within-self [*Insichsein*]: the hour of their birth is the hour of their death.[135]

It is in this way that the process of finitude or perishability determines itself, and it is also by virtue of this process that finite things are also "temporal." "Time is only time of the finite." [136]

Important for this problem is the fact that the finitude of the

133. *Enz.* § 92, add.
134. *Logik I* 117 (129).
135. *Ibid.*
136. *Enz.* § 247, add.

being is not determined here from the Christian theological viewpoint; the particular being is not "finite" because it was *created* but because it bears the ontological determination of "finitude." Heidegger too will proceed "ontologically" in determining the "finitude" of the Being of man, and for him, too, this finitude is not determined out of creaturehood. Heidegger, however, will understand finitude above all as an essential consequence of temporality thought in a particular way.

Thinking reason, according to Hegel, does not persist in "this sorrow of finitude" but rather thinks how "transitoriness and the ceasing-to-be cease to be." [137] It does not remain in the contradiction contained in the finite; it ponders the fact that, in the contradiction of a something and the other, it is implicit that the something relate itself to the other and thereby, as something, not indifferently stand over against the other.[138] If a something is always already a Being-for-other—thus always already has the other in itself [*an sich*]—then the alteration or "transition into other" is in "truth" a fulfilling of its own Being-in-itself [*Ansichseins*] as a Being-for-other [*Sein-für-Anderes*]. Thereby the movement to otherness is not at all a movement to an other as a stranger but is rather a movement to self, a remaining-with-self [*Beisichbleiben*]. Such a return to self is witness to the power of self-determination which the something has over itself, for it is the fulfillment and completion of the Being-in-itself of the something. The something does not come to its end, does not pass away, but rather maintains itself, in that it determines itself, or is Being-for-itself [*Fürsichsein*]. Precisely in the movement that determines the something as finite in relation to limit (and barrier), and in passing beyond the limit, consists its "truth" as "infinity," speculatively understood. The finite is in truth the infinite, not through an "alien force" [139] but by reason of its own "nature." [140]

Infinity in general does not come about by the sublation of finitude in general: the truth is rather that the finite is only this, through its own nature to become itself the infinite. The infinite is its *affirmative determination*, that which it truly is in itself. Thus

137. *Logik I* 118 (130).
138. *Enz.* 92, add.
139. *Logik I* 126 (138).
140. *Ibid.*

the finite has disappeared in the infinite, and what is, is nothing
but the infinite.[141]

The movement of selfsameness in otherness of a something
in the sphere of the immediacy of Being is the weakest evidence
of the power of affirmative infinity. The "readiest instance" is the
"I" as an expression of the "reference-to-self which is infinite." [142]
Affirmative infinity, however, is above all the way in which infinite spirit moves; and in the *Logic* this infinity is the fundamental structure of the "subjectivity" of the whole occurrence of
Being that has the character of an occurrence of self ["*selbst*"-
haftes Seinsgeschehen], of the "method" of ideality. Only because
thought is this movement of selfsameness in otherness does it
have the power to heal, to reconcile, to "idealize" the "brokenness
of reality" and thereby, in the movement to itself, give order to
itself. In this movement of affirmative infinity lies the power of
the concept and the Idea.

In the same way that "temporality" is an essential consequence of "finitude," "atemporality" is an essential consequence
of infinity. This "absolute timelessness" Hegel calls *eternalness*.[143]
The meaning of the eternalness of Being is determined from the
power of the affirmative infinity, i.e., from the basic trait of the
selfsameness of Being, from the process of Being-with-itself in
otherness.

But Hegel also called eternalness the "absolute present." [144]
It signifies "the now without before and after." More exactly, Hegel writes: "Eternalness will not be, nor was it, rather it *is*." [145]
This "is," however, will be conceived expressly as "the activity of
the Absolute Idea," the process of its "accomplished return upon
itself," i.e., as affirmative infinity in its movement. Hegel says of
it: "It is and is there, it is present and before us." [146] It would
seem mistaken to view in this characterization a "temporalizing"
of eternalness or the affirmative infinity.[147]

141. *Ibid.*
142. *Enz.* § 258, add.
143. *Enz.* § 258, add.; cf. also *Enz.* § 247, add.
144. *Enz.* § 258, add., and § 247, add.
145. *Enz.* § 258, add.
146. *Logik I* 138 (149); *Enz.* § 213, add.
147. Though Marcuse recognized the "nontemporality" of the movement of the Idea, he nevertheless is of the view that it "in no way has the
character of the extra- or supratemporal" (see Marcuse, *Hegels Ontologie,*

The "pure" concept, in this timeless sense, is the "eternal" process of selfsameness in otherness, and even time is "eternal" insofar as it is grasped as pure concept.[148] As "pure" concept it is "becoming," [149] which, as the *Logic* shows, is the unity that results dialectically from abstract Being and Nothing. It is a becoming that "posits" itself, then, only with respect to the dimension of time when "natural time" [150] and the relation to the "intuiting" [*Anschauen*] of finite mind (of pure self-consciousness) [151] are involved. This time is then "intuited" becoming,[152] and as such it is the "pure form of sensibility." [153] In this form, time is not the "pure" concept but rather the "simple" concept that is still in its complete externality and abstraction,[154] the "concept itself that is *there* and presents itself to consciousness as empty intuition." [155] That the time "grasped" or "intuited" by finite mind, by the pure self-consciousness—i.e., the becoming that posits itself in the time dimensions—is a "temporal," hence finite, occurrence is incontestable. Here, however, the matter lies in the realm of the "phenomenology of finite spirit." As finite, "spirit necessarily appears in time, and it appears in time so long as it does not *grasp* its *pure* concept, i.e., so long as it does not annul time." [156] Only Absolute Spirit, which grasps itself in absolute comprehending [*Begreifen*], as Hegel expressly declares,

---

pp. 168 ff.). The Idea is meant to have a "specific temporality," which Hegel wished to reserve by setting it off from natural temporality and hence addressed it in terms of "eternalness." Eternalness, however, is meant to be "itself time" (*ibid.*), since Hegel, in the passage cited by us, called it an "absolute present."

148. *Enz.* § 258.
149. *Enz.* § 259, add.
150. *Ibid.*
151. *Ibid.*
152. *Enz.* § 258.
153. *Enz.* § 258, add.
154. *Ibid.*
155. PG 558 (800). Alexandre Kojève, in *Hegel, Kommentar zur Phänomenologie des Geistes*, trans. and ed. by Iring Fetscher, with reference to this passage in the *Phenomenology*, declared that Hegel "identified the concept and time" (p. 96), and therefore there is no eternalness in Hegel. On the basis of this analysis, Kojève constructed his stimulating interpretations, which, however, are untenable, for the reason that Hegel in no way temporalized the concept but on the contrary expressly acknowledged its "eternalness." One need only read to the end the passage quoted by Kojève to see that Hegel distinguished between the "concept that is there" and the "pure concept," between the sphere of finite spirit, which "is not yet complete within itself," and spirit completed within itself which sublated the "time form" of the concept and thereby first comprehends it in its true nature as timeless and eternal concept.
156. PG 558 (800) (italicization of "pure" is by the author).

"sublates" the "time form" of "the concept apprehended only through intuition," "comprehends intuition, and is intuition comprehended and comprehending." For the concept, "in its free identity existing for itself and in itself as I = I, is in and for itself absolute negativity and freedom; thus time is not its power, nor is it in time and something temporal; rather it is much more the power of time, which is only this negativity as externality." [157] The pure concept, the Idea, is not a matter of the intuiting of finite spirit but the "eternal intuiting of itself in the other." [158] The "pure" concept of time is such an "eternal" comprehended and comprehending intuiting; it is the logical process which does *not* posit itself in the time dimensions precisely because its "time form" has been sublated.[159]

Being, however, in its highest fulfillment, is the "absolute self-knowing Idea," and this is the "concept of philosophy." In the Introduction to the *Phenomenology*, Hegel says of absolute knowledge which realizes this "concept of philosophy" that it has grasped its essence. It knows that it is the "ray itself" of the Absolute "by which the truth touches us" and that the Absolute "in its very nature" is and wishes to be "with us from the start." [160] This means that the Being which is known in speculative self-knowing "shows" itself in the form of absolute knowing. The self-knowing Idea, the "eternal process of selfsameness in otherness," *presents* itself. Perhaps one might see in this "self-presenting" a "kind" of temporalizing that once again surely lies outside the Aristotelian comprehension of time. The "eternalness" of *ousia* also defined itself for us as a self-presenting, but in this case the presenting consisted in an arriving, a lasting, and a

157. *Enz.* § 258.
158. *Enz.* § 214.
159. On the other hand, J. van der Meulen (*Heidegger und Hegel*, p. 91) offers the interpretation that even the notion of time contains "the three dimensions of time in pure form as the moments of its process." The concept of time as absolute present is the "pure conversion [*Umkehr*] and inversion [*Einkehr*], the negation of the negation, which the future (the moment of negation, of the distinction as contradiction) turns back into past (the moment of immediacy or identity), while it takes up both moments into itself as it posits them from itself." In our reading, the textual passage (*Enz.* § 259, add.) in which Hegel explained the process of the concept in time in relation to the dimensions of time refers to natural, beheld time and time "for the beholding of finite spirit" and does not involve the "pure" concept of time. Apart from this, van der Meulen's understanding of the notion of time as "primordial time" or "pure temporality" is interesting insofar as he sees in it the "root of time in its appearing" (*op. cit.*, p. 45). Cf. Heidegger, *KM* 171 ff. (193 ff.), and below, pp. 98 ff.
160. *PG* 64 (132).

returning-enduring of the same. Such a movement cannot be recognized in Being's "showing itself" as absolute knowing. Absolute knowledge already has "behind its back" the "pathway," [161] consciousness "externalized into time." [162] This is important to mention, since Heidegger, in his work *Hegel's Concept of Experience*,[163] determined the meaning of Being in Hegel as a permanent "presenting" [*Anwesen*] and understood the "kind" of presence prevailing here from the movement and structure of the "pathway of experience."

In *Being and Time* Heidegger had shown only that Hegel moved "wholly in the direction of the way time is ordinarily understood," [164] since he remained bound to the Aristotelian concept of time. Heidegger did not discuss there whether this "ordinary understanding of time" also lay at the basis of Hegel's notion of "eternalness," i.e., of the infinite movement of Being-with-self in otherness. Heidegger's attack on the concept of eternalness in the sense of the *nunc stans* [165] does not bear on Hegel's position, since the latter is concerned with a "creative" and "living" inner movement of a process.

The basic trait of the intelligibility of Being has already been defined for us on the basis of Hegel's conception of the essence of the "truth of Being." It is to be noted further that the fulfilled expression of intelligibility, the "concept for itself," is understood from selfsameness as that which is "mediated through itself and with itself" and that this self-mediation is called a "play" [*Spiel*].[166] This is of particular interest, since we shall encounter the word "play" as the decisive category of forethought Being in Heidegger. In Hegel, Being as concept "plays" in the sense that it mediates with itself in otherness. The universal mediates itself in that it "particularizes" [*besondert*] itself into the particular [*das Besondere*] and "individualizes" [*vereinzelt*] itself into the individual [*das Einzelne*].[167] This judging [*Ur-teilung*, "originary dividing"] is the movement in which the universal "with undimmed clarity remains with itself in its other." [168] Similarly, in the demonstration of the *Science of Logic* the various kinds of judgments and syllogisms are the expression of such self-mediations; the high

161. *PG* 564 (808).
162. *PG* 563 (807).
163. *HW* 105 ff. Cf. below, pp. 135 ff.
164. *SZ* 431, 432.
165. *SZ* 427.
166. *Enz.* § 161, add.
167. *Enz.* § § 163 ff.
168. *Enz.* § 163, add.

point of the *intelligibility* of Being is reached when the Idea
operates as the "process" [169] of "subjectivity," the process that, as
"eternal creation, eternal validity, and eternal spirit," [170] is the
expression of the ever renewed self-ordering movement-to-self, of
Being-with-self in otherness.[171]

169. *Enz.* § 215.
170. *Enz.* § 214, add.
171. Kant's transcendental consciousness is also in its way "creative,"
for the " 'I think' that must be able to accompany all my representations,"
the pure apperception, is "primordial." Prior to all empirical perceptions
it spontaneously effects a logical transformation in that it categorially organizes of itself, and thereby into one, the "given" manifoldness of the
material, i.e., "prescribes the laws to nature." The form-giving, to be sure,
is concerned only with the objectively valid construction of the world of
appearances through the function of an intellect that is finitely bound to
what is "given" to receptivity in its forms of intuition; it is not concerned
with the creating of a universe of "things in themselves" through an infinite, absolute intellect. The "practical reason" in Kant is "creative" in a
more far-reaching sense. The "moral consciousness," independent of all
natural causality, autonomously forms the unconditional moral law, the
Categorical Imperative, and submits to it in "freedom." Fichte, proceeding
from the conception of the "primacy of practical reason," developed the
essence of reason as such in this transcendental sense as productive or
"creative." The "I" as a "deed-act" [*Tathandlung*] shows itself to the "intellectual intuition"; it posits itself absolutely, so that it proves itself to be
what is given to the mind as a transcendentally produced representation.
The early Schelling similarly understood the unconscious and conscious
production of the absolute subject, which, according to him, had an aes-
thetic, artistically productive consciousness, in addition to a theoretical
and practical consciousness. The meaning which German Idealism in general assigned to the "power of imagination" within the powers of consciousness characterized the meaning of "the creative" that it developed.
To the "intellectual intuition," the "I" of the traditional starting points is
shown as fulfilled.

With a view to the meaning of the "creative" in Heidegger, it must be
emphasized that the producing of German Idealism always concerns a
producing by the *universal* transcendental subject and that this producing
always fulfills itself categorially.

3 / Being, Essence, and the Essence of Man

AS A FURTHER PRELIMINARY to our presentation of the thinking of Heidegger, it remains necessary to clarify the role that man, by virtue of his essence, plays in the relationship to Being and essence conceived in the traditional manner. For in Heidegger the question of the "relationship" of Being to the essence of man retained central significance. In *Being and Time* Heidegger had already indicated that only a complete determination of the "idea of Being as such" can lead to an adequate comprehension of the essence of man.[1] He thus saw that the starting point for the determination of the essence of man ought not to be man, *anthropos,* but the meaning of "Being and essence," and consequently the analyses of Dasein in *Being and Time* were not performed "anthropologically."

Even the tradition did not always define the essence of man anthropologically. Aristotle at the beginning of the tradition and Hegel at its end conceived the essence of man from the starting point of "Being and essence." In the present chapter we shall demonstrate the conceptions of Aristotle and Hegel to enable us better to think along with Heidegger in his attempt to arrive at a different understanding of the relationship of Being to the essence of man.

1. *SZ* 6, 13, 17, 48, 93, 94, 183, 206, 208, 231, 241, 286, 328, 333, 357, 366, 403, 436.

1. Being, Essence, and the Essence
of Man in Aristotle

We saw in what sense the Aristotelian *ousia* is "intelligible." [2] The basic trait of an intelligibility that is in principle unobstructed followed for Aristotle from the supposition of an unconditional sovereignty of the principle of complete transparence, the *nous*. Owing to the *nous*, *ousia* is illuminated, transparent, and, as a *noēton*, "thinkable." Since in antiquity "gnosiology" always follows "ontology," this basic trait of the intelligibility of *ousia* "founds" its thinkable character for human thinking. Because *ousia* ontologically is "thinkable," gnosiologically it is so organized for human thinking that man is able to think it intuitively in *noēsis*. And because this intelligibility ontologically is "unobstructedly" disclosed, human *noēsis* grasps *ousia* without possibility of error or semblance.

On the basis of this relationship, of this coordination with noetic, mindlike [*geistig*] Being and essence, Aristotle determined the essence of man as noetic and mindlike. In the *Nicomachean Ethics* [3] he stated that the *nous* constitutes what is highest, most powerful, and most worthy in the essence of man. The way of Being in which man develops this mindlike essence to the full is the *noēsis noēseōs*, the thinking that abides wholly with its own thought and in this sense is with itself or "free." In fulfilling this pure, mindlike way of Being, man, according to Aristotle, is akin to God, whose life is this pure actuality of mind. [4]

According to Aristotle, however, even in this high point of man's unfolding of his essence in his "similarity to God" man remains a "servant" and never becomes a "creator" or "cocreator" —any more than the Aristotelian God is a creator-God. Man's thinking illuminates the *ousia*, which is already "pregiven" as "thinkable" and which, by virtue of its total form as well as the basic characteristics of "eternalness," necessity, selfsameness, and intelligibility, is the expression of a "moving order." Thinking throws light on this order; it neither establishes it nor alters it. The philosopher serves the order and God, toward which everything is ordered. [5] Thus the philosopher's thinking is not to be understood as a "highest doing and achieving," as in Heidegger.

2. See above, pp. 37 ff.
3. *Nic. Eth.* 117a14–20 and 1178a5.
4. *Meta.* 1072b28.
5. *Meta.* 1075a12 ff. Cf. here the author's *The Meaning of Aristotle's "Ontology,"* p. 64.

The philosopher's task is in no sense a destroying or overcoming nor a "preparatory building" for the coming of another meaning of Being and essence and for the "saving of the essence of man."

Just as Aristotle determined the essence of man as "mindlike" from the noetic character of Being and essence, so too did he comprehend the essence of man as "logical," as the *zōion logon echon,* from the logical nature of the "attributes of an essentially coincident character." Only because everything stands in necessary, ordered relationships can man in various ways bring these order-structures to the light of day through his everyday and "scientific" (*epistēmē*) endeavors. Thus in speaking he articulates these structures in joining and setting them apart in meaningful sentences and judgments, thereby in his *legein* expressing the *logos* in the syllogism and apodictic demonstration, as well as in definition. Both in his everyday and his scientifically perfected knowing, man remains subject to the logical order and is its "servant."

Aristotle, however, also defined man as the essence that is able to practice *technē,* "art." Art, for Aristotle, includes not only architecture and literature but also the simple skill of the craftsman. The Aristotelian artist is not really a "creative" man in the modern sense. Such a "creativity" would contradict the basic trait of the selfsameness of essence, the meaning of which has already been demonstrated. As a consequence of this basic trait, the change in essence, as well as the sheer coming-to-be of essence, is a movement wherein something basic persists. This excludes the possibility that the Aristotelian artist is able to "create" something really new, something that has never been there before.

This does not mean that Aristotle did not regard *technē* as a way of *poiēsis.*[6] The structure of *poiēsis* is shown to consist in the fact that, as the generating power (*dynamis poiētikē*), it lets come forth, in a patient suffering this generating, an essence like that of the generating agent—this like essence having already been contained potentially in the patient. In the realm of *technē* the artist embodies this poietic force through which the generating occurs. The *ousia* of that which is generated is pregiven to the artist's soul in the form of an image—as *eidos* without *hylē.*[7] Thus the *ousia* of a complete house is in the soul of the architect,

---

6. *De. Gen. et Corr.* 324b14 and *Meta.* 1013b24; also compare, with what follows, K. Ulmer, *Wahrheit, Kunst und Natur bei Aristoteles,* pp. 101 ff. and 131 ff.

7. *Meta.* 1032b1.

where, as *telos*, it determines the planning and executing measures of the *poiēsis*, the production of the house. Thus it determines above all the *hylē*, the matter, in which the essence, the house, shall arise; it determines in a conditionally necessary way that only these and no other kinds of brick, wood, or other building materials are suitable for this house. In these appropriate materials the house is already present in potentiality. In this sense the *poiēsis* of the architect generates out of the building materials an essence that is not "new" but like the pregiven essence.

Seen in this fashion, the movement of *poiēsis* is completed in something basic that remains the same "according to genus" [8] and is only the conversion of potentiality to actuality in an actuality already present. What concerns us here is merely to see that Aristotle understood the course of *poiēsis* as ousiologically determined. The artist can actualize the human potentiality for *technē* only within the fundamental forms and figures of essences and their order, always pregiven to him. His doing is not a "creating" but, in the sense described, an "imitating" (*mimēsis*) of the already pregiven *ousiai* and the logical order.

It is not surprising that this conception of the artist and his work no longer suffices for a time that has learned to view the essence of the artist in terms of "genius" and expects to experience in his work something that has in principle never been present before. This problem of art is one that stirs Heidegger. He therefore seeks to free himself from this traditional problematic as such and thereby also to "overcome" the Aristotelian comprehension of art as *technē*.

The Aristotelian concept of *technē*, whereby man is only a "servant" of the ousiological order and does not emerge as the maker of "new" essences, let alone as their "creator" or "co-creator," can no longer satisfy times in which man has apparently shown that he can "master" nature and with the help of mechanical and atomic technology produce new beings of an essential character. This altered self-interpretation of "technological man" and his "labor" manifestly concerns Heidegger in a very particular way. And here too, through an overcoming of the problematic that reaches back to Aristotle, he seeks to gain another insight into the "essence" of technology and from it to determine anew the role in general of the essence of man in his relation to Being and essence.

8. *De Gen. et Corr.* 324a5 ff.

Aristotle also did not regard man as a "creator" in the sense that he can "project" his own moral order. No doubt Aristotle distinguished the human way of Being from the ways of Being of other living and animated beings. Man is shown to move in a realm (*ethos*) of his very own by virtue of determinately structured interconnecting movements of *praxis*, in which man is the *archē*, the author of his actions. But this "freedom" means only that man is "responsible" for his actions and has a certain leeway in deliberating about "means." As for "end purposes," or the "moral guidelines" of his particular actions, these are never his "products" but the pregiven *logoi* to which the "appetitive part of the soul" may or may not pay heed. Aristotelian man does not "project" the order that Aristotle defined on the basis of the ethical and dianoetic virtues. Man can attain only through practice to the right condition, *hexis*, of a good man, an *agathos*, and, in the manner suitable to the particular virtue (*kat' aretēn*), "hit" the mean (*meson*) between the extremes. Through this *eupraxia* he comes to share in *eudaimonia*.[9]

The same relation to Being and essence is also shown in the particular sphere of human praxis in which man, by reason of his essential constitution as *zōion politikon*, is always at home: the sphere of the *polis*, the "state." The citizen and even the statesman are always bound to a pregiven order. They act in accordance with their essence in obeying the prevailing order. Revolution, meaning the arising of what is new and unprecedented, is for Aristotle an evil to be avoided, as is shown by the discussions in Book V of the *Politics*.

2. Being, Essence, and the Essence of Man in Hegel

Hegel dealt with the essence of man in the *Phenomenology of Spirit* as well as in the third part of the *Encyclopaedia of the Philosophical Sciences*. The *Phenomenology*, to be sure, treats only of human consciousness, and for Hegel that means "knowing." The history of the "experience of consciousness" shows [10] the development of finite, and therefore untrue and unreal knowing, to infinite, absolute, true, and real knowing. Hegel derived the necessity of this "path" from the particular structure of human consciousness and demonstrated it as the

9. Cf. Eugen Kullmann, *Beiträge zum aristotelischen Begriff der "Prohairesis,"* pp. 13 ff., 21 ff., 93, 99.
10. With what follows, cf. *PG* 66 ff. (134 ff.).

movement from immediate consciousness to self-consciousness, beyond reason and finite mind to infinite spirit. To that extent he showed the essence of man as alterable within itself and in this sense, therefore, "historical."

In proceeding thus, however, did Hegel also present the essence of man as "historical" in the sense that man is able to change the meaning of Being and essence? What role did Hegel ascribe to the human essence in its relationship to Being and essence? If we take into account only Hegel's later writings, such as that on the philosophy of right [11] and the lectures on the philosophy of history,[12] then we are forced to conclude that he reserved for man a great power over the meaning of Being and essence. The insights of these works into the structures of those situations that can be altered by man have had great influence on the history of the problem. For example, Hegel's views [13] of world history as a "progress of the consciousness of freedom," of the lawlike succession of great national spirits, and of the deeds of the "great world-historical individuals" have formed the object of the great split between Right and Left Hegelians. But even the kind of presentation of the *Phenomenology of Spirit* of 1807 seemed to post-Hegelians, particularly Marx, to be the expression of a "historical" power of man that can bring about change.[14] Starting out from the "ontological" insight that "self-consciousness and Being are the *same* essence," [15] Hegel dealt in particular with the "acts" of this self-consciousness. Self-consciousness in rudimentary form is conceived by Hegel as "desire," since it strives to change the prevailing situation.[16] The struggle for "recognition," [17] the "fight for life and death" between master and slave,[18] are understood as forms of consciousness which at the same time move to change the structure of relationships. The slave consciousness conquers the master consciousness, overcomes its own "alienation" by being able to "work" and "give

11. *Hegel's Philosophy of Right*, trans. T. M. Knox.
12. *Die Vernunft in der Geschichte.*
13. *Ibid.*, pp. 63, 64, 97 ff.
14. Cf., for example, Karl Marx, *Economic and Philosophical Manuscripts of 1844*, ed. Dirk J. Struik, trans. Martin Milligan, p. 177.
15. PG 178 (276).
16. PG 135 (221); cf., here, A. Kojève (*Hegel*, pp. 11 ff. and 34 ff.), who, it seems to us, under the influence of specific motifs in Heidegger's *Being and Time*, interpreted the *Phenomenology* in a radically "historical" manner.
17. PG 141 (229).
18. PG 144 (232).

form," [19] whereby it brings forth itself as well as its world. And in the same way, the later chapters, which deal with the "actualization of the rational consciousness through itself," [20] show how man, through "activity" [21] and "work," [22] can alter not only himself but always at the same time the relationships or—as it is later expressly termed [23]—the "world."

The *Phenomenology* itself, however, reveals that Hegel also had quite a different conception of the role of man in his relation to *Being and essence*. The sections "Reason" and "Spirit" are evidence that the individual never can alter the relationships freely and unrestrictedly. Rather he is always determined beforehand by the "ethical realm," by the "ethical substance" [24] of the "free people," [25] by the absolute and common "objective subject matter" [*Sache*] [26] that is always given beforehand to all endeavors of the "law-giving" [27] or "law-testing reason," [28] by the universal "mores." [29] The individual, "in his actuality," is "confined within the limits of the activity of all," [30] and he must therefore identify himself with the universal substance as the "immovable irreducible basis and the starting point for the action of all and every one." [31] Nevertheless, all this is not yet the final "truth" of the essence of man. It concerns man only as "finite" or "existing" spirit insofar as it has "externalized" itself and has "fallen" within "time in its appearing." [32] The concluding chapter,[33] "Absolute Knowledge," shows that the "truth" of finite spirit is infinite or "Absolute Spirit." If the "truth" of the human essence lies in Absolute Spirit, then, as regards the determination of the essence of man in his relation to Being and essence, we ought to consider the ways of Being hitherto developed only as ways "to be sublated or having been sublated." For, writes Hegel, "spirit

19. *PG* 148 (238).
20. *PG* 255 ff. (374 ff.).
21. *PG* 257 ff. (377 ff.).
22. *Ibid.*; cf. also *PG* 287 ff. (421).
23. *PG* 313 (457), esp. 315 (460); cf. also *PG* 317 (462).
24. *PG* 256, 302 (375, 440).
25. *PG* 258 (378).
26. *PG* 294 ff. (430 ff.).
27. *PG* 301 (440).
28. *PG* 306 (446).
29. *PG* 257 (377).
30. *Ibid.*
31. *PG* 314 (588).
32. *PG* 562, 563, 558 (805, 806, 800).
33. *PG* 549 ff. (789 ff.).

as spirit *is* not finite, it has finitude within itself, but only as that which has to be and has been sublated." [34]

The highest way of Being of man in his "truth" as "infinite spirit" is for Hegel the knowing realized in the "self-thinking Idea," [35] the *noēsis noēseōs*,[36] the "concept of philosophy." [37] If the essence of man is defined only from this viewpoint of his highest fulfillment, then man certainly does not appear as a mighty "lord of Being" whose meaning and essence he is able to change, but rather as its "servant." Absolute knowledge, which brings forth "the organic self-constituting process" [38] of the concept and allows it to attain to demonstration, is "productive" only in the sense that it brings to light "what already in and for itself" is and wants to be with us.[39] Absolute and infinite knowing itself "is" the "self-showing" of the Being of the "Absolute" in its "infinity," it is the "ray" [40] through which the light of the "truth" touches us.[41] The philosopher demonstrates the "simple essentialities" that rule in him [42] and which he has known as the "powers" [43] that have him in possession.[44] Unlike the world-historical individuals, who have no intimation that and how they are only "instruments" of the "cunning of reason," [45] the philosopher knows that "his" comprehending is the "concept" itself [46] and that "his" knowing therefore cannot be mightier than "the concept."

In the *Science of Logic*, Hegel clearly circumscribed the "power and the weakness" of the concept. However, to draw conclusions without further ado from the logical determinations of the concept to the essence of man, would contradict Hegel's "system" as later expounded in the *Encyclopaedia*.[47] Even insofar as man in his "truth" is as "infinite spirit," he is "concrete" [48] and

34. *Enz.* § 386, add.
35. *Enz.* § 574.
36. *Enz.* § 577.
37. *Enz.* § 574.
38. PG 562 (805).
39. PG 64 (132); see above, p. 69.
40. PG 64 (132).
41. *Ibid.*
42. PG 101 (177).
43. *Ibid.* and *Logik I* 14 (35).
44. *Logik I* 14 (35).
45. *Die Vernunft in der Geshicte*, p. 105.
46. PG 558 (800).
47. Cf. here *Logik II* 231 ff. (592 ff.), according to which the concrete *sciences* have and retain the "logical" and the concept as the immanently formative.
48. *Enz.* § 380.

requires "nature as his presupposition." [49] But perhaps we might, with the necessary reservations, draw upon certain references to the logical determinations of the concept in its relation to the objective categories, since for Hegel "the concept is nothing other than the ego, or pure self-consciousness," [50] or "the concept has the nature of the ego" [51] and the "ego has the nature of the concept." [52] To be sure, the talk of the "ego" and "self-consciousness" must be understood here within the context of transcendental logic. Hegel expressly refers to one of "the profoundest and truest insights" [53] of Kant: the "original and synthetic unity of apperception, as unity of the 'I think.' " [54]

It is important to stress that the "concept for itself" "posits nothing new" but only brings out a change of form in what, as concept, was "already present in itself." [55] Seen in this way, the conceptual thinking of the concept of "divine and therefore creative thoughts" that are the "very heart of things" [56] and are that whereby "things in the world have their subsistence" and "are what they are" [57]—such a conceptual thinking is only a "becoming conscious to itself of its concept." [58]

Such an emphasis on the "weakness" of the "concept for itself," however, does not give proper due to the power of "subjectivity." Without the "concept for itself," the "concept in itself" can never attain to the "freedom" of the light of thinking and knowing. "Conceiving Being" [*begreifendes Sein*], subjectivity, especially in its developed form as self-knowing Absolute Idea, has the tremendous power of "idealizing" reality.[59] In this specific sense it is "creative." [60]

49. *Enz.* § 381.
50. *Logik II* 220 (583).
51. *Logik II* 222 (584).
52. *Ibid.*
53. *Ibid.*
54. *Ibid.*; but cf. below, n. 60.
55. *Enz.* § 161, add.
56. *Enz.* § 166, add.
57. *Enz.* § 213, add.
58. *Enz.* § 166, add.
59. Cf. *Logik II* 410 (757); *Enz.* § 377, add.
60. Cf. above, p. 71, n. 171. Subjectivity in Hegel is "creative" to a greater degree than Kant's theoretical consciousness. Although the "concept for itself" has the "nature of the original transcendental apperception," it is not restricted to what is given to sense and to what is intuited. Rather, the "concept for itself" has as its object thought-determinations, i.e., determinations of the "concept in itself," and therefore it can know "things in themselves." Regarding the use of the word "creative," see below, p. 139.

If we draw upon these logical relationships as indicating the essence of man in his highest development as philosopher, then perhaps we ought to say that Hegel, unlike Aristotle, did not view man simply as a "servant." Although man is not able to change "reality," he can and must, on the basis of the self-realizing subjectivity within him, "idealize" it. This is his role, and for that he is "needed." Even in Heidegger, man, and above all the thinker, is "needed." But the meaning and purpose of this being needed is different. The distinction can already be drawn in one respect: that Hegel constructs his doctrine of subjectivity on the basis of the traditional doctrine of substance. Substance, however, even in the power of thought and its character as process, as conceived by Hegel, excludes the coming of the new. So understood, the meaning of Being and the relationship of the human essence to Being remains in principle "uncreative." [61] Presumably Heidegger, for this reason also, regarded as his first task the "overcoming" of the traditional presumption of Being as substance and subject.

61. Viewed in this light, Kant's theoretical and practical consciousness would also be "uncreative." Objective knowledge of phenomenal reality is made possible and regulated by traditional categories deriving from the Aristotelian table of judgments. Even the "practical reason" was conceived by Kant in accordance with the guide of the traditional categories: for example, causality, in the determination of freedom ("causality from freedom"); reciprocity, in the community of rational beings; and presumably even substance, in the determination of the "person." Cf. here H. Heimsöth, "Die metaphysischen Motive in der Ausbildung des kritischen Idealismus," *Kantstudien*, XXLX (1924), 123 ff.

PART II

"Overcoming" the Tradition

1 / The Attempt to Overcome Substance and Subject in the Early Works†

HEIDEGGER IS NOT, LIKE ARISTOTLE, determined by the cosmic model of a mobile order nor, like Hegel, inspired by the confidence in a movement of thought ordering itself to itself. He is imbued with profound misgivings with all the traditional approaches, especially with those that approach Being as substance and as subject. Within the manifold and complex motivation of the early work *Being and Time,* we must acknowledge that the main motive is the attempt to "overcome" these approaches. He wishes to show that these traditional categories are inappropriate for the adequate apprehension of the *Being of man* as well as the *Being of the things* among which man lives in his day-to-day activities. The goal, which is frequently indicated in *Being and Time,* is to show that these models are also insufficient for the understanding of the *Being of being in general.*

Heidegger proceeded in two directions in this work. He sought the *sense of Being* underlying the traditional concept of substance in order to show that it cannot hold for the Being of man and his things when this Being is rightly understood. He developed broader and "more original" categories for the Being of man and of things; many of these are thought in opposition to the traditional categories, so as to overcome substance and subject.

† For the sake of a better contrast of the "tradition" with Heidegger's views, the determinations which were made in the preceding part will be briefly repeated in the pertinent sections of the following parts. This procedure will allow the reader to begin with the parts concerning Heidegger and to go back afterwards to the detailed expositions of these traditional determinations.

One thing which proved to be highly fraught with consequences is that Heidegger, in the line of questioning pursued in *Being and Time,* took particular and detailed issue with the *res extensa,* the Cartesian substance defining the essence of things. For it was in opposition to the *res extensa,* as Descartes allegedly understood it, that he determined the idea of Being which seems to guide all considerations in *Being and Time.* The interpretations of substance as *res extensa* indicated to him that it has the sense of something that *"constantly remains,"* [1] and that it is based on an *idea of Being* "not established in its own right," which he understood to be the state of "constantly being on hand." * [2] He stipulated the meaning of this state further by the appellations "permanently on hand," [3] "purely on hand," [4] and especially "pure thingness on hand" and "reality." [5] We stress this because in *Being and Time* he also speaks of a broader meaning of Being-on-hand, that of "presence," which constitutes the sense of Being in Parmenides and the sense of the Aristotelian *ousia.* [6] But a detailed discussion of the sense of Being of ancient ontology was withheld for later chapters, [7] and these chapters remain unpublished. The following investigations [8] will in fact show that for Heidegger this ancient and the modern sense are significantly related, that the Cartesian *res* is also a Being-on-hand in the sense of "presence." But in *Being and Time* the discussions attacking the traditional sense of Being were oriented toward the

---

* *Vorhandenheit, Vorhandensein, Vorhandenes:* Literally a state of being "before the hand," these will be translated by appropriate variants of the idiom "on hand," to convey the sense of reification, objectivation, and indifference of a substantial presence (e.g., extant stock). Something which is only on hand is a bit more conspicuous and static than the "handy" (*Zuhandenes*), inasmuch as it has been taken out of the immediate circulation of daily commerce in which things are in use, and is merely there. It is on hand as a burden and is thus something to be taken "off your hands." We have found this idiom to be more grammatically and stylistically adaptable than the awkward "presence-at-hand," while still preserving an orthographic kinship with the handy that suggested translations like "substantial reality" or "mere entity" do not. Even hyphenation will be avoided wherever possible, when no ambiguity of sense is thereby interjected.

1. *SZ* 92, 96.
2. *SZ* 96.
3. *SZ* 98.
4. *SZ* 99.
5. *SZ* 99, 201, 211.
6. *SZ* 25, 26.
7. *SZ* 26, 39, 100.
8. Cf. below, p. 135.

narrower meaning of "Being on hand" as "Being like a thing," "Being reified."

For Heidegger, this sense of Being lies at the basis of the modern understanding of not only the Being of things but the Being of man as well, generally dominating its ontologies and doctrines of substance. It led Descartes to his conception of substance as *res extensa* and "prevented him from bringing the modes of behavior of Dasein into view in an ontologically suitable manner." [9] It thus determines the Cartesian conception of *res cogitans* as well. And from "Descartes's *res cogitans* to Hegel's spirit," philosophy stands under the "seemingly self-evident jurisdiction of the ontology of the substantial." [10] And so for Heidegger, the selfness of the self or ego in Kant also has the sense of Being of the "permanence of something which has been on hand all along." [11] Likewise, when reference is made to the Aristotelian *hypokeimenon* in the characterization of the idea of Being which underlies the modern conceptions of man, this is done in order to clarify the meaning of Being-on-hand as "Being reified" and not generally as "presence." [12] What was decisive for Heidegger was that these determinations conceived of the essence of man as the subject "in the sense of the *Being-on-hand* of other created things." [13]

In opposition to this particular sense of Being, *Being and Time* projected a rich variety of modes of the Being of man and the Being of the things with which man meaningfully lives. Several of these determinations will be discussed in what follows.[14] Each testified to Heidegger's view of the unsubstantial character of the Being of man and of things and thus served the purpose of "overcoming" the traditional categories.

The Being of man is called *existence*. This term is given to

9. *SZ* 98.
10. *SZ* 320. On the other hand, it may be indicated that in Fichte the Being of the "deed-act" [*Tathandlung*] of the subject was expressly conceived "without substrate" (*Grundzüge der gesamten Wissenschaftslehre* [1794], § § 96, 97).
11. *SZ* 320; cf. also *SZ* 203, 204.
12. *SZ* 46, 319.
13. *SZ* 49.
14. An exposition which carefully develops and interprets these determinations of *Being and Time* can here be dispensed with, all the more so as they are sufficiently familiar through a discussion which has now lasted for over thirty years (cf. the bibliography of Heidegger literature by Herman Lübbe in *Zeitschrift für philosophische Forschung*, Vol. XI, no. 3). Cf. Peter Fürstenau, *Heidegger, das Gefüge seines Denkens*, pp. 17 ff.

the being which comports itself in a unique way to its Being, as that which is "in every case mine," for whom "Being is at issue" and "who has undertaken it in order to be." [15] It aims to counter the terms *essentia* and *existentia* pertaining to the conceptions of substance and subject and to show that the Being of man is simply not a "case and exemplar of a genus" which could be grasped "indifferently" as a "what of content" in terms of the traditional essence.[16] The term "existence" shall moreover attest that the human Being cannot be understood in terms of the traditional *existentia,* inasmuch as this category has its sense of Being from Being-on-hand. Man is not something "on hand," he is in his Being the movement of a self-relation.[17] When Heidegger explains in intentionally paradoxical turns of phrase that the "essence" [18] or the "substance" [19] of man is his "existence," it is in this consciously antisubstantial sense that the term "existence" is to be understood. The opposition to the substantial also leads to the distinction whereby all determinations which comprise the existentiality of existence are called "existentials," while the traditional designation of "category" is reserved for nonhuman beings.

The unsubstantial character of the human Being is further elucidated by calling this being which stands out from all other beings the *Dasein.* In *Being and Time* [20] this term signifies a being whose "here" [Da] is always already "disclosed," a being which *is* in the mode "of being its here." The decisive determination lies in the stand of this being in an "understanding relation" to its Being, so that it exists as an *understanding of Being.*[21] The categories of substance and subject are particularly inappropriate for the comprehension of a being which comports itself all along to its "ability to be," its "possibilities to be," in an understanding way, so that it is constitutionally disclosed or "cleared to itself." [22]

Dasein's "modes of comportment," the modes "of being its here," are given a decisive direction when they are characterized as modes of *Being-in-the-world.*[23] *Being and Time* actually deals with the world only as an "environment" within which man

15. *SZ* 12, 42.
16. *Ibid.*
17. *Ibid.*
18. *SZ* 318.
19. *SZ* 117, 212.
20. *SZ* 11 ff., 132, 133.
21. *SZ* 12, 85, 133.
22. *SZ* 133.
23. *SZ* 52 ff.

dwells with the things he uses in a circumspective manner.[24] The worldliness of this world is defined there as a meaningful totality of references.[25] This referential totality of the world confers a significance upon the Being of things as well as upon the Being of man which the traditional ontologies and anthropologies oriented to substance and subject had completely passed over. Considering the things as substances overlooks the fact that the human modes of comportment which work circumspectively have all along assumed references which are all "for the sake of" Dasein.[26] These "inner-worldly" things are ultimately geared in their significance to the being whose Being is defined as Being-in-the-world. Because of this, they are "close" [27] to Dasein, they are "near at hand" and "handy" to it, and have the ontological sense of *Being handy.** [28]

This determination of the Being of things seeks to overcome the traditional conception whereby the things as substances had the ontological sense of a Being-on-hand considered as reified. Of course, it is possible for things to change over into this sense of Being.[29] When the referential connections of an everyday circumspective activity are disturbed, when, e.g., the handle of the hammer breaks in the course of hammering and the "in order to" and "for" of the tool "for the sake of" the working mode of behavior are interrupted, then the possibility of such a change-over of the Being of things manifests itself, from the referentially meaningful "Being handy" to the mere persistence of "Being on hand." Heidegger has not indicated whether the category of substance would be applicable to these limit cases, in which the Being of things has changed over into the mode of Being on hand.

But it is not only the Being of things, but above all the Being of man, his "existence," which is determined by the "existential" of Being-in-the-world, since it makes manifest how man exists "in" [30] the world. Man is simply not an extended substance in

---

* *Zuhanden:* "Handy" conveys the sense of being (1) close at hand and conveniently near and (2) suited for use. The intimacy between man and his utensils, which "fit like hand in glove," gives the handy a much more familiar and therefore implicit presence in human existence than do the things on hand.

24. But cf. also *WG* 33.
25. *SZ* 87, 88, 364.
26. *SZ* 86; *WG* 35, 36.
27. *SZ* 102.
28. *SZ* 69.
29. *SZ* 71 ff.
30. *SZ* 53 ff.; cf. also *SZ* 202 ff.

space, nor is he in the mode of such a substance together with other substances. His essential insertion into the world totality prohibits approaching the essence of man in a Cartesian way, as an isolated substance or a subject which stands opposite another substance or a basically alien object. This holds for the relation of man to things as well as to "other" men. The Being of man is to be understood from the start as a *"Being-with,"* and the world into which man is essentially inserted as a "with-world." [31] In such a world, it is not isolated substances on hand which encounter one another, but rather beings who, because they are of the order of Dasein, essentially belong together with other Dasein simply on the basis of a common Being-in-the-world.

The "original" (transcendental) modes of behavior whereby Dasein "discloses" itself as "in" the world are disposition,* understanding, and articulation.** [32] The hermeneutical-existential analyses of these basic modes likewise attest in many respects to how unsuitable it would be to define the human modes of Being categorially as relations between beings on hand. Dasein discloses the world as a whole in an "attuned" way, "projects" it in an understanding way, and "communicates" its meaningful totality—on the basis of its Being-with—in an "articulate" way.

The modes of knowledge in the terms transmitted to us in the basic conceptions of the traditional ontologies and doctrines of substance, such as *noēsis* or *intuitio, legein, cogitatio,* repre-

---

* *Befindlichkeit* for Heidegger means to find oneself situated in a certain way in a disclosure that is basically affective. "How do you find yourself?," which in German is equivalent to "How do you feel?," is thus a question with regard to a person's disposition, whether good or ill and the like. The question also carries some suggestion of "How do you stand?," in the sense of a condition, state, or situation, i.e., a "position." To be dis-posed is therefore to have been placed or "thrown" into such a situation. Thrownness stresses the irrevocable "that," and mood the changeable "how" of the findings of disposition. The changes are "set off" by the modulations of an attunement which is beyond the control of the person disposed. Some justification for translating *Befindlichkeit* as "disposition" is given by Heidegger himself in WP 36 (77), where he relates the attunement of moods to disposition.

** *Rede* is normally "speech," "language," "discourse" but, since Heidegger here is trying to point to the precondition of speech and language, we prefer to translate it as "articulation," with the stress on the etymological sense of dividing into joints and then reuniting, i.e., the polemical and gathering process of *logos*. Heidegger's preparatory example here is the interpretation of "something *as* something" in the prepredicative world of work, an interpretation for which *Rede* is the prior condition. Heidegger himself describes *Rede* as "the articulation of the understandability of the there" (SZ 161).

31. SZ 118.
32. SZ 134 ff.

sentation, and conception, have not taken into account that all "understanding" is originally "attuned" and co-originally articulates the meaningful whole of the world. Nor have they taken into account that all the modes of theoretical behavior, in which beings are taken to be on hand, are likewise derived from these originary basic modes.[33]

Now these basic modes of Dasein are in no way to be construed as "free-floating." [34] Dasein "exists factically." [35] The fact "that this being is" and is "relegated to existence" points to its *thrownness*, which belongs intrinsically to the sense of the Being of man. This "facticity" has nothing to do with the "matter of fact which belongs to Being-on-hand." [36] For this "that it is" and "has to be" has been understood in an attuned way all along and has thus been assumed into existence. Moreover, thrownness is never a "finished" fact,[37] since Dasein must continually reassume this "that it is and has to be." [38] This structure provides further evidence of the unsubstantial character of the Being of Dasein.

Dasein is not a "self" in its everydayness but, under the dominion of the "crowd" [*Man*], it has persistently lost itself in "Being with others" among the things within the world.[39] But this essentially *immersed* * state in no way signifies that man has somehow "reified" [40] himself, hence become a substance in the sense of a "thing on hand." As an immersing, it rather has

---

* Since *Verfallenheit* is not intended, according to Heidegger, to have any basically negative connotations, we shall break with a custom for which Heidegger's own choice of terminology is responsible and translate it, not as "fallenness," but as "immersion," since its decisive sense is that of being absorbed in the things of the "world." It is only as a consequence of this absorption in beings that one becomes oblivious of Being. "Immersion" has the further advantage of stressing the "in" character of this existential category. More specifically, its Being-in is that of being "among" things and too much "with" the "world" (i.e., the totality of things). The German *bei*, which translates both of these prepositions, is equivalent to the intimacy of the French *chez*. Finally, "immersion" etymologically refers to a "plunge into," which from a slightly different vantage point could be taken as a fall. The term itself is suggested by Heidegger's reference to an *Aufgehen* ("absorption, merging") in his discussion of *Verfallenheit* (*SZ* 175) and the in-sistence in beings which is the erratic part of ex-sistence (*WW* 21 [344]).

33. *SZ* 67, 147.
34. *SZ* 276.
35. *SZ* 135, 179, 276.
36. *SZ* 135.
37. *SZ* 179.
38. *SZ* 276.
39. *SZ* 114 ff., 175 ff.
40. *SZ* 437.

the structure of a movement, which moreover admits of being taken back into an "authentic" mode at any time.

But it becomes particularly evident that Dasein in the mode of everydayness cannot be defined in terms of the traditional categories of reality and substance,[41] when daily Dasein as a "whole" is defined existentially and ontologically as *concern*.[42] Concern is the name given to the unity of existence, immersion, and facticity in the sense of its Being. In understanding Being, the existence which projects itself into its possibilities of Being is essentially "ahead of itself," which characterizes the Dasein that has always been in definite possibilities, in being "thrown into a world" and immersed among the beings within the world. This "Being already ahead of itself in the world" as "Being among beings encountered within the world" cannot be grasped by the traditional categories of substance and subject.

This structure also determines the particular way in which Dasein "discloses" beings within the world in an attitude of "discovery." For Heidegger, the original sense of "truth" lies in the worldly "disclosure" of Dasein itself. It is on the basis of this disclosure that beings within the world are "discovered." This second kind of truth is for the most part "disguised" by error and illusion within the immersed state of daily coexistence. Accordingly, Dasein must always first tear this truth away from beings within the world, to wrench it from "concealment." Inasmuch as factic truth is always a "robbery," the Greeks had conceptualized the essence of truth privatively as *a-lētheia*.

The meaning of concern is conceived even more profoundly in the second part of *Being and Time*, which determines in an initial respect that characteristic feature of the human Being which is decisive for all the determinations of Being that have already been cited. This trait is the *finitude* of human Being.[43]

The problem of the finitude of Dasein stands at the center of Heidegger's thought. The implication of the early works was that the evidence for the finitude of the understanding of Being at once demonstrated that "Being itself is finite in its essence."[44] For Heidegger, the understanding of Being signified the "self-showing" of Being, since "there is a giving of" [*es gibt*] a sense of the Being of being only insofar as there is understanding of Be-

ing.[45] Accordingly, in the evidence for the finitude of the understanding of Being, as the self-showing of Being, there is at once
a determination of Being itself. This should be stressed from the
start, in order to indicate in what sense the various demonstra-
tions of the finitude of Dasein are not meant to be anthropologi-
cal but are intended purely and simply to promote the "inquiry
into the sense of Being" which, in the introduction to *Being and
Time*,[46] was designated as the sole purpose of this work.

It might be worthwhile to refer on occasion to Hegel's "absolute knowledge" in the course of our presentation of this problematic of the finitude of the understanding of Being. For—in
sharpest contrast to the finite understanding of Being—it was
shown [47] that this "concretion of the infinite spirit" [48] proved to
be "infinite." Absolute knowledge has freed itself from all one-
sided objectivity and knows that, in its "knowledge of knowledge," the absolute is "at home with us." And so it "is" the idea
knowing itself in its movement of being at home with itself in
otherness, the "fulfilled Being" in its "infinitude." It was in this
sense that we said [49] that, in Hegel, Being "shows" itself as infinite to infinite knowledge.

Heidegger has specified the sense of the finitude of the understanding of Being in various respects. One of these lies in the
"dependence" of Dasein.[50] The "need" of Dasein lies in its dwelling "in the midst" of beings by which it "is sustained and on
which it is dependent" and over which it "can never basically be
master, for all its culture and technology." Dasein would not
comport itself at all to beings which it is not and to the being
which it itself is if it could not project beings in their sense of
Being, if it had no understanding of Being. It is in this sense that
the "privilege of existing" contains the "need of the understanding of Being" within itself. Understanding of Being is "the most
finite in the finite."

In contrast with this extreme dependence of the understanding of Being, absolute knowledge in Hegel is an expression of the
highest freedom. After all "foreignness," all "otherness," is sub-
limated, the infinite spirit as infinite is a "self" (though not like
finite spirit) and in this sense is "at home with itself." This inde-

45. *SZ* 212.
46. *SZ* 1.
47. Cf. above, p. 69.
48. Cf. *Enz.* § 386, add.
49. Cf. above, pp. 66 ff.
50. *KM* 205, 206 (235, 236).

pendence of absolute or philosophical knowledge ultimately rests on the traditional conviction that man as a sensory being is indeed dependent on the external world but that, at the same time, as a spiritual noetic being, he is the *nous* itself and can acquire this kind of independence in the philosophical life, in the *bios theōrētikos*. But along with the approaches to Being as substance and subject, the power of the *nous*, of the spirit, as well as the traditional hierarchy of the powers of the human soul, has become questionable for Heidegger.

Heidegger has specified the sense of the finitude of understanding further in terms of concern and its structural moments.[51] Facticity (thrownness) constitutes Dasein as finite insofar as it has not been brought of itself into its "here" and yet has to be its ability to be, which it did not give itself of its own accord. Dasein knows all along in an attuned way that it must continually project itself anew into the possibilities into which it is thrown. It must "be" the "thrown ground" of its Being, even though it "can never become master" of this ground, can never get behind it. It must "exist" the Being pervaded by this "nullity." Its existence, its existential "projecting" of possibilities of Being, is further finite because it must always bear "not having chosen" possibilities. And finally, its "Being immersed" is an expression of its finitude because this structure is in truth nothing other than a "flight" from itself. Evidence of this is found in "dread," [52] which in a phenomenal way also manifests the other two structures, facticity (thrownness) and existentiality, and thus the totality of the Being of Dasein, "concern," as well as its finitude. In dread, a mood over which man has no control, Dasein displays itself in its finitude in an "original" way, in a way which eludes the categories of substance and subject. Dread suddenly calls a halt to the everyday flight of Dasein from itself, to its immersion in beings. It tears Dasein out of its "domestic familiarity" with the handy things within the world and with its daily coexistence and plunges it into "unfamiliarity," the state of "not Being at home," into the "unearthliness," the uncanny state which characterizes its essence in an "original" way. When all beings within the world are "nothing and nowhere," when all referential contexts of the environing world have become inoperative, then all that remains is the experience of naked worldli-

51. *SZ* 284 ff.
52. *SZ* 184 ff.

ness into which Dasein is factically thrown and the experience that Dasein is "thrown back upon itself." Through dread, Dasein becomes the "individualized" being which must project itself upon its own possibilities without any help from "anyone" [*Man*]; it can no longer be relieved by "everyday coexistence" of its own ability to be. Dasein, which through dread has been transmuted into "Being-free for choosing itself and taking possession of itself," is still finite because it can choose only the possibilities into which it has already been thrown. It is through this finitizing "individuation" that it is an independent "self."

THE LECTURE *What Is Metaphysics?* [53] also defines the finitude of Dasein on the basis of "dread," but more broadly, for it seeks to overcome the "logical" categories of substance and subject even more fundamentally. Here, a phenomenological and speculative analysis of this "basic experience" shows how Dasein experiences "Nothing." Dread attunes Dasein not only on occasion but in its very constitution, even if mostly in a hidden way. Accordingly, the relation of "Dasein and Nothing" revealed by dread characterizes the "unsubstantial" essence of man in a fundamental way. Dasein, which always finds itself already "disposed" in the midst of "being as a whole" [*das Seiende im Ganzen*], experiences in dread that and how this "being as a whole" suddenly sinks into indifference and offers "no" further support to Dasein. Such an occurrence is not a logical negation of this being as a whole. Logic with its categories would come too late; it could only negate after the fact, but it could never conceptualize "the more original" prevailing of "Nothing," which makes this "no" possible and which dread experiences. This "Nothing" is neither a being nor an object, nor is it the *nihil negativum* of logic. Rather, it is a prevailing, an "essencing," and thus a "giving" Nothing. This Nothing "gives" Dasein, from which being as a whole slips away in dread, the original openness whereby this being is "as such." It manifests this being in its "full and hitherto hidden strangeness as the pure and simple other over against Nothing." So the "essence" of the original "nihilating" Nothing is determined on the basis of its "bringing Da-sein for the first time before being as such." This determina-

53. *WM* 28 ff. (360 ff.). Cf. also W. Schulz, "Über den philosophie-geschichtlichen Ort Martin Heideggers" in *Philosophische Rundschau*, I (1953–54), nos. 2 and 3, pp. 79 ff.

tion yields the "finitude" of Dasein. It is because of this that Dasein can comport itself to being as being only when it has gone beyond being as a whole in order to hold itself out into Nothing, which first enables this openness of being as such for Dasein. Dasein is the transgression, the "transcendence" which *meta ta physika* goes *beyond* beings. It is in this sense that "metaphysics" belongs to the "nature of man" and that he is a "place-holder of Nothing." The finitude of Dasein lies in its constitutional dependence on Nothing and, more particularly, in its incapacity to place itself directly in dread through its own decision and will and thus bring itself "originally" before Nothing. "So unfathomably"—writes Heidegger—"does finitization plumb in Dasein, that our ownmost and deepest finitude eludes our freedom." Thus, for Heidegger, it is an expression of "deepest finitude" when the understanding of Being, "ready for dread and called by the voice of Being," can experience "the wonder of all wonders: *that* being *is*" and when, in philosophizing, it can ask "the most original question": why is there being at all and not rather nothing?

The "permeation of Dasein" by the essencing ways of Nothing which ground its finitude is also manifest in the modes of behavior which precede logical negation: opposition, abhorrence, refusal, prohibition, and want. But it is not only the Being of man which is finite. In *What Is Metaphysics?* Being itself was also specified as finite, precisely because "it manifests itself only in the transcendence of Dasein holding itself out into Nothing." Since the understanding of Being needs Nothing, is therefore "finite," and since it displays the "self-showing" of Being, Being must also be "finite." But the finitude of Being for Heidegger also issues from the pertinence of Nothing to the Being of being. It is not the "indeterminate opposite for being," and in particular it "enables" the overtness for being as such. Insofar as it "gives" or "essences," it must belong "to the essence itself." On the basis of this brief elaboration, Heidegger holds that "the nihilating of Nothing occurs in the Being of being" and that "Nothing essences as Being." This Being pervaded by Nothing is not a logical-categorial Being whose "negativity" has always overcome every negation. It "shows itself" not as something known in self-knowledge but as something that can be experienced in a special attunement of a "self" which is simply not free from every "objective" determination but is instead dependent, finite.

The uttermost determination of the finitude of Dasein ensues for Heidegger from the ontological relation of "authentic" Dasein to its finish, to the possibility of its death.[54] The relation to death also plays a role in Hegel and determines the way in which Being shows itself to knowledge.[55] When man looks death, the negative, squarely in the face, sustains it, and holds himself in it, when he finds himself in absolute disruption and "tarries" in the negative, then, through the renewed negation thus realized, this negative turns "into Being." What manifests itself then is Being as the concept, the idea, the movement of being at home with itself in otherness, infinity.

"Being toward death" in Heidegger is not a "tarrying" but a "running forward in anticipation" [56] and a mode of behavior "acting in itself." [57] It does not have the form of categorially determined knowledge, as in Hegel. Instead, it occurs out of the attunement of dread, in which Dasein as "individualized," [58] as authentic self,[59] "faces death" [60] and overtakes its "thrownness unto death." [61] If in Hegel the finite spirit arrives at its "truth" when it knows itself as infinite spirit, then in Heidegger Dasein reaches the "truth of its existence" [62] when it experiences Being as circumscribed by the possibility of death as its total horizon and in this decisive sense experiences Being as "finite," as a finite whole. The sense of this experience defines itself originally for Heidegger from a temporality whose meaning is elaborated in the following chapter.

A Dasein which in "original individualization" runs forth into the resoluteness toward death, which is ready for dread, has acquired the "self-constancy" of a "self" which of course again and again lapses into "non-self-constancy." [63] In this insight into the possibility of an extreme "individualization," obtained from a consideration of the over-all articulated structure of concern and finitude, Heidegger has made an important contribution to the centuries-old problem of "individuation." But at the same time, this insight also manifests the larger attempt to overcome the categories of substance and subject. The "self" which is thought here is without any relation to something self-persisting

54. Cf. also *SZ* 235 ff., esp. 305 ff.
55. *PG* 29, 30 (93, 94).
56. *SZ* 302.
57. *SZ* 288.
58. *SZ* 250 ff., 263.
59. *SZ* 303 ff.
60. *Ibid.*
61. *SZ* 329.
62. *SZ* 297.
63. *SZ* 316 ff., 322, 323.

and to a self-consciousness. The "self-reliance" of man is still taken into account, and this precisely at the stage when he has extricated himself from the dominion of the "crowd," is wholly relegated to himself alone, and is prepared, on the basis of the insight into the "truth" of his Dasein, to shape anew the "possibilities" for an "authentic" ability to be. In *Being and Time* Heidegger sought to confirm this conception of "self" outside the jurisdiction of substantiality and subjectivity by a confrontation with Kant's "original transcendental apperception."[64] It is true that Kant no longer considered the "I" as a psychic substance, but he too "slipped into the ontology of the substantial." The "I think" is the formal subject of a "logical link." The "self" of self-consciousness was considered in the horizon of the Cartesian *res cogitans* as the "selfsameness and permanence of something which has all along been on hand," because Kant overlooked the worldliness of the world and the whole structure of Dasein's concern.

In the treatise *Kant and the Problem of Metaphysics*, Heidegger penetrates even further into the "metaphysics" which belongs to the nature of man, into the "transcendence," the "surmounting" which founds the essence of the "self." According to Kant,[65] the transcendence is constituted in the "pure synthesis" of pure thought with pure intuition (the form of time), in which the transcendental imagination unites these two stems of our power of knowing—as their root—[66] through the schematism, the forming of the "aspect of sequence." Kant's "unsaid" for Heidegger lies especially in Kant's "wish" to give time the decisive role within the primal occurrence of transcendence, not because it forms the movement of the "sequence of nows" but because as pure intuition it carries out the movement of a "self-affection."[67] The pure intuition affects itself, in that it "preforms the aspect of sequence and holds it as such *to itself* as the forming reception."[68] Accordingly, this "original" time constitutes the "self" as "related to reception," thus as "finite."[69] It makes possible both the "act of turning-toward which lets something take a position opposite,"[70] which underlies pure thought, and the "ho-

64. SZ 319.
65. On the "violence" of this interpretation cf. below, p. 108, as well as KM 182 (201–2).
66. KM 127 ff. (144 ff.).
67. KM 182 (205).
68. KM 171 (194).
69. KM 172 (195).
70. KM 172, 70, 110 (195, 94, 123).

rizon of objectivity" [71] founded by the transcendental imagination. The last section of the treatise attempts, in accordance with the structures developed in *Being and Time,* which are inimical to substance and subject, to lay a "foundation" for the metaphysics "belonging to the nature of man" [72] and to set forth the "finitude of Dasein in man." [73] It may be noted that the central role which Heidegger seeks to give to the transcendental imagination in Kant is symptomatic of the tendency of his thought toward the "creative," [74] which—in our interpretation—will be decisive for his later conceptions of the essence of man and of Being.

Heidegger made reference to the subjectivity in Hegel in his discussion in *Being and Time* of the "relation between spirit and time," where he dealt with the "spirit" that "falls into time." [75] To be sure, this "finite" spirit is for Hegel the object of anthropology and phenomenology. But the "truth" of the finite spirit in all of its forms lies—as we saw [76]—in the "infinite spirit," whose logical determinations are given by the *Science of Logic.* If Heidegger in *Being and Time* intended to overcome the subjectivity in Hegel, then he would have had to take issue with either the infinite "self-knowing idea" in the *Logic* or the last figure of the *Phenomenology,* which is not a "finite" self but the self-realizing, absolute, infinite, and in this sense "eternal" subjectivity. Since Heidegger has not gone into the problem of whether and how Hegel's "vulgar understanding of time" temporalizes this "eternity," we can leave it with the indications which have already been given in our remarks on the history of the problem. [77] But it is certain that Hegel's subjectivity as the "creative" and "living" inner mobility which produces the dialectical thought process and orders it to itself in no case has the sense of a reified "Being on hand" understood in a Cartesian way. Another question is whether there is at its basis a state of Being on hand in the sense of a temporally understood "permanent presence" that—in Heidegger's view, which only becomes explicit later—determines all the ontological conceptions of the tradition and is to be derived from the sense of Being of Aristotle's *ousia.* But more about this later.

71. *KM* 172, 75, 111 ff. (196, 100, 123–24).
72. *KM* 13 (4).
73. *KM* 204 (233).
74. See above, p. 71, and below, p. 139.
75. *SZ* 428 ff.
76. See above, p. 67.
77. See above, p. 70.

Since the aim of our treatise lies specifically in determining the "other sense of Being and essence" in Heidegger's late writings, we do not intend—beyond what has already been said—to go into the question of whether Heidegger's "attempt to overcome substance and subject in the early works" is to be regarded as successful. For that matter, a final decision on this question would be premature, since not all of Heidegger's confrontations with the tradition from this early period have been published.[78] It therefore remains an open question whether Heidegger's early works have dissolved the idea of the "categorial" and the "logical" in a "whirlpool of original inquiry" [79] and have shaken the "dominion of reason and understanding." [80]

One must certainly grant to Heidegger that he has in fact made the dominion of reason "problematic." One can of course point out that Schelling already disputed Hegel's philosophy of spirit and reconciliation, that the postidealists, that Feuerbach, Kierkegaard, and Marx, that Nietzsche and life philosophy already looked with contempt and scorn on the promise of reason which heals and reconciles all. It can readily be shown that their ideas already mightily shook the idealistic structures of reason and the concept, so much so that, influenced by them, the Western order in the "world of appearances" threatened to go out of joint through war and revolution. But it is doubtful whether any of these thinkers aimed his ax at the strategically decisive joints of the traditional structure as unerringly as Heidegger. The foundations upon which this structure rests are ultimately the traditional categories of substance and subject. Only an effective onslaught on or overcoming of these categories could bring the entire house down along with its foundations and make room for the construction of a new house.

It will be shown in what follows how the further grounding of the wholeness and finitude of Dasein out of its temporality and historicity points to a "construction method" by which Heidegger will attempt the new construction while still utilizing the stones of this old house.

78. In lectures given at the end of the 1920's and the beginning of the 1930's, Heidegger dealt with the subjectivity in Fichte, Schelling, and Hegel. Whether he also confronted the issue of substantiality in Spinoza and Leibniz at this time is something that is not known to the author. On Aristotle, cf. the seminar of 1940, now published in *Il Pensiero I* and *II*.
79. *WM* 33 (366–67).
80. *KM* 219 (252).

2 / Temporality, Historicity, and the Retrieve

ONE OF THE MOST CRUCIAL POINTS made in *Being and Time* [1] is that the Being of Dasein, concern, is "whole" in an authentic sense only when Dasein "holds and relates" to the possibility of death concluding its Being. Dasein "is" such a "relation to its finish," "is" in this pregnant sense "finite," if it *comes forward* to itself in this ownmost possibility of being toward the possibility of the impossibility to be and approaches it as a possibility, if it in this sense "runs forward" to it and *holds* it *out* as a possibility, i.e., withstands it. In such an anticipation Dasein has at the same time, in the "disclosing" attunement of dread, *gone back* to its "thrownness unto death." Through this anticipation and return it has "permitted itself to be summoned out of being lost in the crowd," it has withdrawn itself from the state of "being immersed" in the beings encountered within the world and is drawn forward into the "situation" in which it can encounter and deal with these beings in a "resolute and open" way. As such a "concern for death," the Being of Dasein is "whole."

But what *enables* the "wholeness" of this whole Being of Dasein, of this authentic concern in the unity of its different structures? [2] Wherein lies the "sense of the project" of this authentic understanding of Being which exists as thrown? For Heidegger, the "conditions of possibility" of this sense of Being are found in a *temporality*. It is temporality which enables the structures of concern, the "ahead of itself" which anticipates in running forward, the "back to" thrownness, and the resolute mode of "Being among." These three modes in which Dasein in

1. *SZ* 234 ff., 301 ff., 305 ff., 316 ff., 232 ff.
2. *SZ* 324 ff.

[101]

its Being is "outside itself" or "beside itself," these three ecstasies, are based on the three modes of temporality. The first mode is called the "coming" or the "forth-coming" [*Zu-kunft*] of the future, because it enables Dasein *on the whole* to come forward to itself in its possibility, to hold out this possibility so that it *can* exist "authentically." Insofar as the "coming" is the "condition of possibility" for the ability of Dasein on the whole to run forward to the possibility which finishes it, it is the "finite future." Since it thus enables the "truth of existence," it holds a "priority" over the other two modes of temporality.

Accordingly, this finite future must also be considered the "primary" sense of the project of the authentic understanding of Being, because only a Dasein which exists on the basis of this coming as a "coming-to-itself" can go back to its thrownness unto death, to this null ground of its potentiality of Being which it "always already was," and assume it as *its* having been which still *is*. The mode of time which enables this kind of coming back to itself is called "what is as having been," which is to be distinguished from the mere "past," which applies only to "facts on hand" and "substances on hand."

This coming and having-been enable Dasein to come toward and to come back to *itself*, so that it can be an authentic "self" which can "resolutely and openly" grasp the things that it encounters in its dealings, hence can "make them present" in their sense of Being without distortion. This mode of time of making present is the "condition of possibility" for Dasein's actually "Being-here" in the situation thus disclosed. Hence it is the "authentic present" or "momentousness." *

Further analyses [3] show how the modes of inauthentic concern, as well as the "vulgar concept of time" which is usually applicable to the beings "within time" that are on hand, are derived from this "original" temporality. There is no need to discuss this topic here. But in view of our concern with the history of the problem, we might note for the sake of contrast just where the conception of the finitude of the Being of Dasein—and accordingly of the Being of being in general—which is determined by this original temporality differs from the determinations of Aristotle and Hegel.

---

* *Augenblicklichkeit* refers to the momentous moment fraught with significance, an opportune moment (*kairos*) of resolution in which Dasein comes to terms with its total situation, especially the primordial limit situation of Being toward death (SZ 349).

3. SZ 334 ff., 411 ff., 420 ff.

It is evident that time and its modes as conceived by Aristotle,[4] in terms of the now, number, and movement in geometrical space, are not identical with this "unspatial" temporality and its ecstasies. Thus "momentousness" is not the "now," the "forthcoming" is not the "not yet now," and "what is as having been" is not the "no longer now." But it is extremely significant that Aristotle considered time as a "power" and from it determined the "transitory pastness" of the beings which are "in it." These beings, man included, are "passing," "transitory," in this sense "finite," because the time which encompasses them affects them in such a way that they must ebb away. But on the other hand, Aristotle considered Being as such to be completely free from subjugation to the power of time. On the contrary, he along with Plato founded the traditional conception, which holds that Being and essence are "not in time" and are thus more powerful than time. The sense of the "eternalness" of the *ousia* of the *synholon*, e.g., of the Being of man, gave us the clue to a "kind" of time which lies outside the Aristotelian conception. The Being of man occurs, endures, and recurs as ever the same from one generation to another on the basis of a "presence" completely different from that which is represented by the *nyn*. From the perspective of the early works, Heidegger would reject this sense of "eternalness" because Being "is" only insofar as there is understanding of Being. And understanding of Being is finite through and through. This finitude of Dasein lies primarily in the thrown "Being toward the finish" and not in the fact that the individual is affected by the "power of time."

In his *Logic* and *Encyclopaedia* Hegel[5] based the meaning of finitude on neither the creatureliness of beings nor their temporality but on the ontological structure of every something. To repeat, every something is transitory, finite, and thus temporal in its process, because it passes away and must go to its finish. But his decisive insight lay in the fact that every something, as it goes beyond its bounds, defines itself and returns to itself, so that accordingly the "truth" of the finite is the infinite. Likewise, the finite spirit, the essence of man, is in truth an infinite spirit. To be sure, the *Phenomenology* is concerned with the finite spirit which, because of its finitude, is "in torrential time" and for which time signifies "fate and necessity." Here time is conceived in Aristotelian fashion from the philosophy of nature. As "in-

4. Cf. above, p. 26.
5. Cf. above, p. 64.

tuited becoming," this time which determines the finite spirit is the "pure form of sensibility," "the concept which is *there* and represents itself to the consciousness as empty intuition." The relation to time as conventionally understood indeed plays a role in Hegel's determination of finite spirit. But the decisive factor lies in the fact that spirit "no longer appears in time when it has grasped itself in its pure concept." The idea which knows itself, the "concept of philosophy," which realizes itself as absolute knowledge, can "abolish time." In sharpest contrast to Heidegger, Hegel understood the Being of man as well as Being in general as "the power of time," i.e., more powerful than time. Absolute knowledge is "infinite," like "fulfilled Being," the absolute idea. It is really a matter here, not of an infinity or eternity in the sense of *nunc stans,* but of a movement of being at home with itself in otherness.

By contrast, *Being and Time* shows that time, i.e., the temporalizing of original temporality, is the "power of Being," inasmuch as temporality constitutes the horizon, the range of vision of the understanding of Being, and thus defines Being temporally. The temporal analyses of *Being and Time* [6] not only provide the deepest foundation for the finitude of human Being but also are the most important expression of the attempt to "overcome" the sense of Being in the traditional approaches of substance and subject.

Let us now show how *Being and Time,* against Descartes's reified idea of Being, characterizes the Being of Dasein as a "happening" or an "occurrence." In the process, the Being of Dasein will be further defined in its uniqueness. But even more important, out of this structure of occurrence or happening, the "historicity" of Dasein, there emerges a "method" for thought.

As "coming toward itself" and "coming back to itself," hence as "project and thrownness," Dasein is a "stretched self stretching." [7] Inasmuch as Dasein "holds together" its thrown Being-born with the Being-toward-death, it is, in the sense of this happening, "historical." But it is also "historical" in the strict sense that it is always a matter of an occurrence of Dasein which, as a Being-in-the-world, essentially occurs together with others. [8] Hence it is a "co-occurrence" which takes place in the "community of people." Dasein is historical because, in being rooted in

6. *SZ* 323 ff. Cf. also *KM* 157 ff., 160, 171, 172, 175 ff. (178 ff., 181, 194, 195, 198 ff.).
7. *SZ* 375.
8. *SZ* 384.

the collective destiny of the community, it is a "personalized collective destiny."

Regarded in this way, the movement of Dasein lies in the fact that its coming back to itself is always a coming back to the facticity of a definite community. It is taken over by "authentic" historical Dasein as the world of definite possibilities in which Dasein always already finds itself "thrown." The existence which comes back to itself on the basis of its finite future, having experienced itself in its limited wholeness out of its possibility of death, transmits to itself the possibilities of the community which "still perdure" [wesen] as a "heritage." [9] But this "retrieve" is not merely "suffered" by historical Dasein. On the contrary, it "counters" these inherited possibilities and "countermands" that "which in the today turns out to have 'passed away.'" [10] Dasein is thus personally destined in being open "for its time." It may be asked why the understanding of Being in its authentic existence, which has individualized itself in anticipation of its "ownmost potentiality of Being," its possibility of death, so that all "relations to another Dasein are dissolved," [11] seeks to overtake that dimension of its facticity in which it is thrown into its community. But in terms of our own interest it is simply necessary to stress here that, in the three ways in which historical Dasein temporalizes itself as "standing by itself," in the retrieve, the countermand, and the counter, a decision on the part of Heidegger with regard to the role of man becomes manifest. That the human being can retrieve what is as having been in countering the possibilities coming to it and at once countermanding the today indicates that it is constituted in such a way that it can generally transmute the sense of the possibilities of Being. Even if this is possible only in relation to the facticity of the community, hence not "freely creative" but happening only by referring to the possibilities which "have been there," we must still observe that in Being and Time Heidegger has relegated a transmuting power to the essence of man. Of course, even then he already saw that the role of the essence of man can be decisively determined only after the "idea of Being in general" has been clarified. Accordingly, the later writings have first of all expressly inquired into the essence of Being itself, in order to establish from this the role of the essence of man. But it seems to us that, in spite of this "turnabout," Heidegger in the later determinations

9. SZ 383.
10. SZ 386.
11. SZ 263 ff.

has fallen back on the structures which he developed in *Being and Time* on the basis of historicity and temporality. To that extent, the "method" of his expositions and of his thought in general remains oriented toward these structures.

Heidegger could arrive at this determination of Dasein as an essence capable of historical transmutation only because he conceived neither Dasein itself nor the possibilities projected by it in a traditional fashion [12] as substance and subject. The basic trait of the selfsameness of *ousia* prohibited the pure and simple emergence of the new because, just as in alteration, an underlying essence perdures as a relation which remains in itself. And so the *poiēsis* of the artist and the statesman could not itself "create" or cocreate anything new. Just like the philosopher and the scientist, they served a preordained order which in itself moved teleologically. Even the essence of man was for Aristotle an *ousia*. Man remains in the movement of "praxis" and can thus not be "historical" in Heidegger's sense. The other basic traits of *ousia* developed by us likewise contradict the assumption of such a historicity of man.

It is true that in the *Phenomenology of Spirit* Hegel showed how "finite" spirit, through work, education, and other kinds of activity, as well as through the works themselves, can produce itself and its world. And yet he saw the "truth" of the finite spirit in its infinity. But the infinite is the movement of being at home with itself in otherness, which has a completely different structure from the movement of historical Dasein. Both the self-knowing idea as such and all the steps in its dialectical process have a circular structure. In this circle as expression of the spirit with itself, an ousiological resistance to the advent of the new manifested itself to us. Hegel's infinite spirit, like the Aristotelian *telos*, is in all its alterations self-determining within itself. In this power over all "facticity" also lies the claim that there can be nothing new, because the infinite spirit has all along included the whole within its circle.

Hegel defined the role of man from this essence of infinite spirit. Man attains the highest development of his essence when he, as the self-conceiving of the concept, develops the science of logic as the "circle returning unto itself" and thus brings all history to a standstill. This absolute knowledge of the absolute as the "true" essence of man is Hegel's expression of an ability *to overcome history*. By contrast, the "authentic understanding of

12. See above, pp. 34 ff., 59 ff.

Being" as the "true" essence of man is Heidegger's expression of an ability *to found history.*

For Heidegger, an essential way in which man can exercise his power to found history is thinking, i.e., "ontological interpretation." In *Being and Time* the "thinking way of asking about Being," the way in which the question of Being is here developed as a hermeneutic of the existence which understands Being, was conceived as the "assignment" [13] which of necessity follows from the historicity of the essence of man. Dasein grasps the "possibility lying in it," [14] not only "to make its existence transparent to itself," but "more basically to inquire into the meaning of Being in general." "If in such an inquiry its eyes have been opened to its own essential historicity," then "the development of the question of Being out of the most proper sense of the questioning as a historical one must itself head the assignment of inquiring into its own history." [15] This "historical questioning" of historical Dasein, in the form of the "destruction," or, as it is later called, the "overcoming," has a "positive aim." In *Being and Time* the aim of this inquiry is to work out "the original experiences in which the first and thereafter guiding determinations of Being were won" and to authenticate the origin of their "ontological birth certificate." [16] As a thinking which interprets history, it wants to reveal the possibilities of history which "are in having been," so that "the power of the possible penetrates into factic existence, into whose futurity thinking then comes." [17] When "retrieve" is understood in this way, this "countering" of the retrieve of an interpretation at once "countermands" "the prevalent manner of dealing with the history of ontology." [18] In this sense, it "criticizes" the "concealments" of traditional concepts.

Historical Dasein can interpret "originally" in this way because, on the basis of its thrownness, it has always moved itself "factically," as a being which "is as having been," in definite historical possibilities which have been in the tradition of its community, inasmuch as all of its projecting is tied to them. These possibilities do not represent a "past on hand." Insofar as they belong to a precedented Dasein, and therefore belong to a historical "Being-in-the-world" as "world-historical" possibilities,

13. *SZ* 21.
14. *SZ* 20.
15. *SZ* 20–21.
16. *SZ* 22; cf. *SZ* 220.
17. *SZ* 395; *KM* 185 (211).
18. *SZ* 23.

they themselves have the "mode of Being of *precedented* Dasein." [19] Their significance has already brought projecting Dasein out of the totality of the world project in such a way that it anticipates itself in a preunderstanding. But the explicit interpretation must itself adopt that which is already implicitly understood in this anticipation. [20] It must explicate the "upon which" of its project, its sense or meaning in the form of "something as something." In this way, every interpretation comes to that which it presupposes. In this sense, it comes back to itself and necessarily has the structure of a circle.

The countering, countermanding retrieve, which historical Dasein carries out as a "questioning of Being," is just such a circular interpretation of precedented historical possibilities. It strives to disclose them and develop them as possibilities in their impending powers. [21] In circular fashion, a textual interpretation makes the "prejudice" of an interpreter explicit. The interpreter has always already "taken the first cut" of "what stands there" out of the totality of his preunderstood project. He thus makes this provisional interpretation on the basis of his *predisposition*, [*Vorhabe*] and with a definite view, the *preview* [*Vorsicht*]. He is thereby guided by the definite conceptualization, the *preconception* [*Vorgriff*], which he has decided upon from the beginning.

But such a "disclosure" of the meaning of a text is "original"; it can "retrieve" a fundamental problem as a precedented possibility which is now forthcoming only if it consummates itself as a "discovery." As essentially disclosed and "discovering," Dasein is "in truth." But as "immersed," Dasein finds itself "in untruth." Consequently, the factic discovery concomitant with every interpretation, the truth, must be wrested from the historical object. [22] This holds particularly for the analysis of Dasein itself, which "conquers" the original meaning of the Being of this being "against its own tendency to cover up." [23] Every interpretation has the character of "violence," [24] because every interpretation is a discovery of something which until now had been distorted and concealed.

The "violence" of every "retrieving" interpretation thus lies not only in the countermanding of the current conceptualization but also in its countering rejoinder. In a textual interpretation,

19. *SZ* 393.
20. *SZ* 150 ff.
21. *SZ* 231 ff., 310 ff.
22. *SZ* 311.
23. *Ibid.*
24. *Ibid.*; also H. G. Gadamer, *Wahrheit und Methode*, p. 473.

the countering occurs in such a way that, in the light of its "predisposition" and its "preview," it reads "what is said" so that through it the "unsaid" emerges.[25] The text, this historically precedented possibility, is thereby so "transmuted"[26] that the problematic treated by the author comes to us, not as he intended it, but in a new way which until now had been concealed. Through this transmuting exposition, the problem is to be kept "free and alive" in those powers which "make the problem possible in its essence."[27]

The analysis of Dasein carried out in *Being and Time*, but even more so in the early work *Kant and the Problem of Metaphysics*, are examples of "retrieving" interpretations which, because of the violent nature of every historical inquiry, are necessarily carried out violently.[28] What Heidegger wanted to do in the Kant book was to violently transmute, in the light of the predisposition, preview, and preconceptions that he had acquired in *Being and Time*, the problematic of the finitude of Dasein and its wholeness, now regarded as Kant's "unsaid" possibility, into one that was said by Kant, so that, as a new possibility now determining us, it would preserve and maintain the power of an original problem.

In view of this intention of any "retrieving" interpretation, it in fact appears doubtful whether it is to be refuted in detail by arguments from traditional research. If a position is taken in the course of our own references to Heidegger's interpretations in the context of the history of the problem, this is done in full knowledge of the fact that Heidegger undoubtedly pursues another goal. But contemporary philosophy must expose Heidegger's particular "prejudice" in the specific texts interpreted by him, first in order to elucidate the many extremely brilliant insights in their own right, but also to safeguard the traditional interpretations or to arrive at interpretations which are independent of Heidegger.[29] But first of all, the critique must confront the method of interpretation in a way which permits the examination of the structures which found it. Of course, this task raises the difficulty that the thought now recognized as authentic by

25. *KM* 182 (206).
26. *KM* 185 (211).
27. *Ibid.*
28. Cf. Heidegger himself in the Foreword to the second edition of *KM*; also *EM* 134 (176) and above, p. 98.
29. An excellent example of this is offered by Dieter Henrich, "Über die Einheit der Subjectivität," *Philosophische Rundschau III* (1955–56), 28 ff.

Heidegger no longer seems to "legitimate" itself on the basis of the structures developed in *Being and Time*.

With regard to the violent interpretation of the Dasein analytic, Heidegger in *Being and Time* explicitly posed the question as to whether there was a "guideline" or "regulation" for it.[30] He found it in the "idea of existence" always presupposed by the interpretation. There is also a place in *Being and Time* [31] where he says that an interpretation cannot permit the predisposition, preview, and preconception "to be guided by fancies and popular conceptions" but must secure the scientific theme "out of the things themselves." But it would be remiss to assume that there is for Heidegger a thing "in itself" which could "from the outside" yield a "criterion" which would determine whether the "unsaid" in what is said in a definite text has been disclosed "correctly" or "falsely." The discussion on the essence of truth in *Being and Time* makes a brief reference to the difficult problem of "verification." [32] An assertion is verified to be true insofar as what is asserted shows itself as "the same." Verification means: beings showing themselves in sameness. It is accomplished "on the basis of a self-showing of beings." Heidegger has unfortunately not discussed whether and how the hitherto hidden possibility, "discovered" in each instance through interpretation, is *verified* in the "how of its discoveredness." Precisely because such a possibility, in accordance with the "preconception of phenomenology," [33] is a phenomenon, and in this sense a "thing" which "in an outstanding sense" remains *hidden* or even falls back under *cover* (and only to that extent is something which "shows itself"), a treatment of the problem of verification would have been desirable. Since Heidegger gave only a few indications on this matter, the question soon arose whether his interpretations could be considered as "binding," without attempting to apply "scientifically rigorous" standards to his thought.

Heidegger's reference to the "power" of the precedented historical possibility which is now forthcoming already points to the foundation for the "method" of his later thought. Already here, "possibility" has a meaning similar to "essence," without of course corresponding to the traditional conception of "essence."

Aristotle's "possibility," the *dynamis*, since it is a fundamental mode of *ousia*, also has a power characteristic of essence. As

30. *SZ* 234, 312.
31. *SZ* 153.
32. *SZ* 218.
33. *SZ* 35.

a disposition, it is the prestructured range of possibilities. These "possibilities" press toward their "actualization," the *energeia*. This occurs as the movement in which what is prefigured comes forth and out into the open in a circular form as the remaining-with-itself of the *telos,* as the teleological self-actualization in which the *ousia* returns to its beginning, the *archē.* The "modal category" of "possibility" at the end of the tradition, with Hegel, is likewise a kind of "essence which appears." As a "real possibility," it is the modal category of "immediate actuality" which the category of "new actuality" bears within itself. This possibility "actualizes" the modal category of "actuality." The essentializing power of possibility and actuality lies in the circular movement of being at home with itself in otherness, the movement of "self-sameness."

Inasmuch as Heidegger's efforts in *Being and Time* were directed toward "overcoming" substance, he at the same time dismissed the modes and categories belonging to every ousiology. Only by fixing this in our minds can we truly acknowledge that the notion of possibility in *Being and Time* can no longer have anything to do with the traditional concept of possibility.

It is true that, in a paradoxical way, this work establishes a relationship with the traditional concept of actuality. It is expressed in an introductory chapter in the following way: "Higher than actuality stands possibility." [34] But against the tradition, "possibility" is here understood as a mode which simply cannot come to an actualization. Thus the distinctive mode of man's Being, existence as a "Being toward possibilities," [35] as a relationship to them, as the "ahead of itself" within them, is thought in such a way that its "actualization" would completely contradict the ontological definition of man. The projective disclosure of the "can be" of possibilities, the undertaking of the possibilities into which Dasein is thrown, especially of the Being toward the finish, the anticipation of death, is to be out toward possibilities which must be held out as possibilities in their forthcoming character without becoming "actualized" in the traditional sense. And so history is a possibility of "precedented existence" because historical Dasein can hold out the facticity of its community as a possibility in its emerging power and let it come to itself. This possibility is simply not an already prestructured *telos* which can be actualized only in a specific way. And it is not an order permeated by the process of being at home with itself in otherness, in which

34. *SZ* 38.
35. *SZ* 43 ff., 143 ff.

there can be no "new actuality." This kind of possibility, which is not thought from the actualizing actuality, is an "existential" which is fundamentally "open" and can be transmuted into a new "power of possibility." The altering and history-founding power which the early works ascribe to Dasein is ultimately based on the fact that the possibilities in which Dasein is thrown and which it projects are not closed and so are capable of new developments. From this concept of an open possibility, the essence of man is shown to be "creative" in a completely new and radical sense.

But Heidegger has not gone any further into the essence of this "power" of possibility described in *Being and Time*. Instead, without any transition, the *Letter on Humanism* twenty years later states: "Being as that which empowers in wanting is the possible. Being as the element is the still power of the empowering that wants, i.e., of the possible." [36] Possibility so understood "empowers" the relation of the human essence to itself as a possibility, i.e., "appropriates" [*ereignet*] it. Accordingly, "thought" is understood to be "enabled" by the empowering of Being. This empowering "sends" or "com-missions" * its "ground pulls" (basic traits) ** "to" thought and is, in a sense to be explained more precisely later, a "com-mission" to which thought sub-missively responds. This "sub-missive" thinking, which now no longer "legitimates" itself out of temporality and historicity but out of the "wanting power" of possibility, Heidegger calls *rethinking* [*Andenken*] and *forethinking* [*Vordenken*].

With this change in direction, Heidegger's endeavor to overcome the traditional conceptions of substance and subject is intensified. The early works still admitted that Dasein was in a cer-

---

* *Zuschicken:* "Commission" seems particularly apt in describing the "sending" of the mission (*Geschick*) of Being, since it sends itself in such a way that it empowers and authorizes those receiving its word. At times, *Geschick* itself will be translated as "commission," which is synonymous with "mission." Though its orthographic kinship to *Geschichte* (history) cannot be maintained in English, this is no real handicap inasmuch as the English "mission" is fraught with historical overtones.

** *Zug* is first a "tug," "pull," "draw," and then a "feature." It is best rendered here by its etymological equivalent, "trait." The tractability of traits is linked by Heidegger to the attraction of mystery. The traits of Being attract experience and provide traction for thinking, inasmuch as Being draws thought in a withdrawal (*Entzug*) that draws the creative man with it. Being pulls by wanting thought, in a wanting (*mögen*) that empowers (*vermögen*) its possibility (*Möglichkeit*) to be thought. In wanting thought, Being calls out to be thought in an appeal which Heidegger will eventually describe as a silent "saying." The traits of Being are therefore its "gift" of "language."

36. HB 57 (273).

tain sense a "self." But now, man thought "from Being," with an essence which is presumed to lie in its "standing out into Being," is no longer considered as "standing on his own." This change of direction even "neglects" the "self-standing" character of things, as will be shown. Generally speaking, the thought emanating from Being no longer seems to reach back far enough in order to apprehend the concrete ways of human behavior and the concrete structures of serviceability which pertains to things. Now, in addition to the basic determinations of Being, only the basic relationship of Being and man is still treated as such.

In following Heidegger's change of direction, our investigation will have to expose these basic determinations and this basic relationship in order to find out exactly what Heidegger seeks to put in the place of the "overturned" categories of substance and subject. But let us keep in mind that the "overturned" concept of substance safeguarded for the understanding of beings that order of basic traits already cited, and that the concept of subject, when thought to the end, was capable of instituting the specific order of Being considered as thought. Moreover, the change in direction has made "productive retrieves," like the one in the Kant book, impossible for Heidegger himself. Instead, there has been an increase in the attacks against all traditional thinking which starts from self-consciousness. Regardless of whether it proceeds in a transcendental-logical or a speculative-logical fashion, it is traced back to the Cartesian representation of self-consciousness dogmatically knowing itself and certain of its knowledge and is thus reduced in its richness and its multiplicity. The deep insights of critical and speculative philosophy into the "self" as well as into the structures of the reality thought by this "self" no longer get their full due, just because they are concerned with the "self" of "self-consciousness." To be sure, rethinking and forethinking are still understood in relation to this "metaphysics," but at the same time they are carried out as a "leap away" from it. This will be shown in more detail in the following chapter.

3 / The Structure of Rethinking and Forethinking and the Range of Tasks

HEIDEGGER HAS CHARACTERIZED the rethinking and forethinking which are enabled by "empowering" Being as a "leap." It is first carried out as a "leap away that sets off." It sets itself off from the Platonic-Aristotelian *noēsis* and *eidenai* as well as from the *idea, eidos,* and *ousia.* It leaps away from the Cartesian *cogitare* of *res cogitans,* the "representational" thinking of the "subject," as well as from the *cogitatum,* the "object" thought in the representation, from the transcendental knowledge of the "objectivity of the object" as well as from the "objects of experience," from "conceptualizing" and "absolute" knowledge as well as from the concept and the idea. And it leaps away from the current interpretations and representations of the essence of man, e.g., *animal rationale* or *ens creatum.* This "leap away that sets off" is like the "countermand" of *Being and Time.* What in *Being and Time* was the "past" in the "today" is now the metaphysical "jump-off" zone." Similarly, just as in *Being and Time* this countermand temporalized itself out of momentousness, so too the leap away that sets off in rethinking happens in the "abruptness of the opportune moment." [1]

The "leap away that sets off" leaves the metaphysical jump-off zone in order to "appropriate" itself anew and originally in the "leap that rethinks." [2] The rethinking does not think back to "what has passed" but to "what is as having been," which still approaches thought and, indeed, so that the hitherto unthought and unsaid is forthcoming to the thinker in such a way that he

1. *ID* 65 (67).
2. Cf. *SG* 158.

[115]

must think "what-is-as-having-been as something not-yet-un-folded," [3] as "what is to be thought." This structure of rethinking does not seem to be essentially distinguished from the structure of retrieve in *Being and Time*.[4] The retrieve in *Being and Time* in fact went back—aside from several references to Heraclitus and Parmenides—only to Plato and Aristotle as the still "essenc-ing mission," while the rethinking first of all goes back to the "experiences" of the pre-Socratics. It is in these experiences that Heidegger now sees the "inception" [*Anfang*] * of the Western conceptions of the sense of Being and essence. In them lies "the source," [5] the "root," [6] the "ground" [7] of the "metaphysics" which begins [*beginnt*] * with Plato and Aristotle. The rethinking must therefore be a "backtracking into the ground of metaphysics." [8] Through such a backtracking, the "sense of Being in the first be-ginning," the basic traits of Being in the first beginning, as well as the "essence" of the "metaphysics" resting on this "ground," are appropriated anew. Thinking experiences itself as "ad-dressed" by the *experiences* which the early Greeks had with Be-ing and essence in the first beginning, which were deposited in *works,* especially in *linguistic works,* in *ground words.* On the basis of this "address," he seeks to unfold *thoughtfully*—in this sense "rethink"—the hitherto "unthought" *basic traits* or the *sense* of the experiences of Being in the first beginning out of the basic words of the early Greeks. The rethinking develops *"an-other sense of Being,"* in opposition to the tradition, as that which

---

* Heidegger distinguishes between the explicit beginning (*Begin*) of metaphysics in the reflections of Plato and Aristotle and its much more implicit and basic inception (*Anfang*) in the experiences of the early Greeks. Although we shall generally not make this distinction in trans-lation, since it is usually clear from the context which of these Greek beginnings is under discussion, it will be grammatically and stylistically convenient at times to translate *Anfang* by its closer etymological approxi-mation, "inception" and its close cousins, "incipience" and "incipient." Accordingly, a phrase like *erstanfänglicher Seinssinn* will usually be translated as the "sense of Being in the first beginning," but, at times, translating it as the "initially incipient sense of Being" results in a more graceful English sentence. At times, also, it may be desirable to emphasize the nascent process of "catching on" (*An-fang:* cf. *Nietzsche II* 29) and "taking hold" (in-ception) which occurs in the "initial incipience" and the "other incipience." Accordingly, as opposed to "inception," "incipience" is intended to stress the *process* or *quality* of beginning.

3. HD 95.
4. See above, pp. 107 ff.
5. HD 137 ff.
6. WM 8 (208).
7. WM 7 (207).
8. *Ibid.* This is the subtitle of the "introduction" of *WM.*

is *to be thought* for a *forethinking*, which in turn seeks to determine still *another* sense, the sense of Being and essence for another beginning.

Heidegger has not always distinguished very sharply between these two "ranges of tasks" of rethinking and forethinking. It can be said that every rethinking is always already a forethinking,[9] even if it elaborates the sense of Being in the first beginning only to the point where it becomes that which is to be thought. For even what is hitherto unthought in the early Greek experiences deposited in the basic words becomes something to be thought only through an "adoption and transmutation of the tradition." [10] But several of Heidegger's later writings present examples of a forethinking in the narrow sense, insofar as the "to-be-thought of the rethinking" is transmuted anew into a sense of Being for another beginning.[11]

Despite all the similarities, "essential" thinking distinguishes itself from the historical questioning and interpretation of retrieving thinking, in that it no longer legitimates itself out of the historicity and temporality of Dasein but out of "empowering" Being itself. This thinking is, according to Heidegger, "appropriated" by Being itself; Being shows itself or hides itself in it; it "commissions itself to it" or "withdraws itself" from it and is thus a "commissioning" or "historical" Being. All of this will be more carefully explained in the later expositions. For now, it is only a matter of seeing that the relation between historical Dasein and the historical possibilities that "are forthcoming in having been" —which have the mode of Being of Dasein and belong to it—has been *reversed*.[12] If previously Dasein projected possibilities into which it was thrown and expressly interpreted and transmuted this project, its sense, so now the historical "possibility" determines historical Dasein and "appropriates" its asking and thinking. If historical Dasein thus now belongs in this reversed mode to the historical wanting-empowering "possibility," then the determinations which were valid for the projective interpretation can no longer apply. In fact, Heidegger has even recently declared that the "hermeneutic circle structure" of interpretation is not valid for essential thinking.[13] Oddly enough, several of Heidegger's later interpretations are still constructed as though they

9. Cf. *SG* 159.
10. *WP* 33 (71).
11. Esp. "Das Ding," *VA* 163 ff.
12. See below, pp. 173 ff.
13. *US* 150.

were retrieves.[14] Their "violence," to be sure, may also be explained by the fact that essential thinking is a "leap that sets off and rethinks."

More specifically, it is the sense of Being which the early Greeks "experienced" in the first beginning that "commissions" itself to thinking as the empowering possibility and in this sense is the "granting." The rethinking as well as the forethinking are legitimated in that the sense of the first beginning is manifested to them in the words in which the early Greek experiences of Being are conserved. The rethinking that seeks to explicate the sense which lies at the basis of these words is understood as a "dialogue." We shall have to inquire later [15] as to the laws or rules to which Heidegger's dialogues are subject and whether they establish their "binding character." But inasmuch as rethinking and forethinking are not a matter of a hermeneutic interpretation and a "discovery" of Dasein, the problem evidently no longer lies in whether "that which shows itself" verifies itself in its "discoveredness."

Heidegger has defined both ways of thinking on the basis of their relation to metaphysics. Rethinking remains related to metaphysics when it endeavors to loosen itself from it in the "leap away that sets off" and when it strives to appropriate itself anew in the "leap that rethinks." Forethinking is a relation to metaphysics to the extent that it wants to overcome it in the leap.

This definition of rethinking and forethinking in relation to metaphysics indicates that Heidegger's confidence in the transmuting and history-founding power of thought, in its ability to determine concrete events, has in no way diminished. But this becomes completely clear only when one realizes that for him "metaphysics" is not simply a "discipline" of academic philosophy. It is true that the term "metaphysics" designates the direction of the Aristotelian question which remained decisive for traditional "philosophy," insofar as it surmounted beings and then from the point of view of beings represented "Being" merely as the "surmounting," the transcendence, the "Meta-physical." But this "Being" metaphysically represented by thinking has in its various "stampings" [Prägungen] determined the West in its concrete historical appearances and institutions. "Metaphysics" prevails in all areas which constitute the whole of being. It puts its stamp on the "world" and the "earth" of Western man, on what

14. E.g., "Hegels Begriff der Erfahrung," *HW* 105 ff. Recently translated in book form as *Hegel's Concept of Experience.*
15. See below, p. 229.

is at any given time conceived as nature, culture, politics, ideas and ideologies, and on what the "real" is. In particular, it determines the nature of man and his planning, representations, and calculations. Metaphysics permeates all of these appearances, though at different stages of its dominion. Today we live, according to Heidegger, in the time of "metaphysics consummating itself," also characterized as the metaphysics of "nihilism" consummating itself and as the "metaphysics of the atomic age."

The currently prevailing "essence" of technology is in particular a stamping of metaphysics. Not only is "machine production and implementation" "metaphysical," but also these are the ways in which man deals with his things as he comports himself to other men or to the state and social institutions.

We must always keep in mind this very broad meaning of "metaphysics" when Heidegger speaks of the "dominion of metaphysics" and the "overcoming of metaphysics." It is to this broad sense of "metaphysics" that rethinking and forethinking relate themselves.

Though "metaphysics" thus by no means constitutes the essence of philosophy, it nevertheless plays a decisive role for Heidegger. For a dominion of metaphysics came about only because the "true sense of Being" was "withdrawn" from Platonic and Aristotelian philosophy and remained withdrawn from philosophy for the next two thousand years. Traditional thought, determined by this "withdrawal," has left its stamp on the over-all sense of each of the eras of Western history. Heidegger thus calls the different historical periods the "epochs" of metaphysics.[16]

Hence, for Heidegger, traditional thought plays a role in determining history, even though the true sense of Being remains withdrawn from it. Consider how much stronger must then be the history-founding power of a thought in which the true sense of Being no longer "withdraws" itself but "commissions" itself.

In fact, this thought must accomplish nothing less than the overcoming of a metaphysics which has been dominant for two thousand years. It has to overcome its "oblivion of Being" and exhibit Being in all of its fullness, in order to thus prepare "another beginning" for mankind.

Hegel also spoke of the history-founding operation of thought. He thus writes: "Day by day, I am more and more convinced that theoretical work brings about more in the world than does the practical. If the realm of representation is revolutionized, reality does not hold out." [17] But for him, the highest power of thought still lay in the sublimation of every temporal reality as a moment of a timeless process. Accordingly, the most important aim of his endeavors was to describe the infinity of thought as the movement in which all alterities are reconciled and made whole. He wanted above all else to develop categorially, through an absolute thinking removed from "torrential time," the "unhistorical" course of Being, i.e., the *Science of Logic*. Hegel did not seek to prepare the advent of another sense of Being and thereby alter the concrete historical world. Rethinking and forethinking do not move in the "free aether of pure thought" in which history is brought to a halt, but instead they think out of the "historical situation," out of the "need of the oblivion of Being." And they do not attempt to develop the categories of an absolute Being absolved from history but only "categories" which rest on "experiences" as they were once actually undergone within a definite historical space of the West during a definite era. The experiences which at one time lay at the basis of the actually spoken basic words, the history-determining "categories" of "Being in the first beginning," are determined by rethinking in order to be then thought-forth to the "categories" of a "Being of another beginning."

Our particular concern in this work is to elaborate the "other sense of Being and essence" which this history-founding rethinking and forethinking have developed in relation to metaphysics, in setting themselves off from it. Our reflection on the structure of these modes of thought and their range of tasks showed that the *other* of the sense of Being and essence is to be sought in a threefold direction and in a definite sequence. First of all, the *other* sense of Being in the first beginning exposed by rethinking is to be described. In other words, the *basic traits* of the Being of the first beginning, which rethinking thought out of the experiences underlying the basic words of the early Greeks, are to be developed. Insofar as these ground words constitute the "ground" of metaphysics, this description already implements the second task, namely, to make the *essence* of metaphysics manifest by referring to this history of experience and thought, the "history of Being," and to show to what extent the "stampings" of metaphysically represented "Being," thought by Heidegger in the light of the Being of the first beginning, are *other* than the conceptions of Being of traditional philosophy. In the course of this second

17. *Hegels Briefe*, I, p. 194.

task, the "structure" of the history of Being in particular is worked out, and the "terminal configuration" of "metaphysics," the "essence" of technology, is described.

From this terminal configuration, thinking is naturally led on to the third task, the task of forethinking (in the narrow sense), which determines the sense of Being and essence of another beginning. It is this sense which is the genuinely *other*. Even if what matters most to us is its determination, if we were to restrict our discussion to it alone, this would only militate against Heidegger's "historical" way of thought. It is, moreover, important to clarify the "relationship" of the other beginning to the first beginning, in order to be able to determine to what extent forethinking and its forethought really still go back to the experiences which, according to Heidegger, lay at the basis of the basic words of the first beginning. For here we have a reference point for the problem of the legitimation of his thinking, which will concern us later.

This threefold otherness of the sense of Being in Heidegger will be clarified by referring back to our discussion of the history of the problem. The following expositions will not give a full account of the "interpretations" by which Heidegger sought to make the basic traits of Being manifest, nor will they follow in detail the steps which at various stages have led Heidegger to the determinations of these basic traits. Here, instead, we shall—in conscious violation of the special historical mode of his thought—present these basic traits as they appear today in Heidegger's works as an "over-all result," as if they were "categories."

PART III

The Basic Traits of Being

in the First Beginning

1 / The "Distinction" of Being and beings

LET US FIRST SHOW how Heidegger "rethought" the basic trait of Being in the first beginning, the trait which he has called the "difference," the "distinction," and the "twofold."

The early writings were already pervaded by the insight that "there is a giving" [*es gibt*] of the distinction of Being and being. This distinction, which there was called the "ontological difference," was treated only in its relation to Dasein and to the essential ways in which it "gives truth" to Dasein. In the essay on *The Essence of Reasons*,[1] Heidegger started from the distinction which prevails between the prepredicative overtness of being, the "ontic truth," and the unveiling of Being which makes this overtness possible, the "ontological truth." The unveiling of Being is always the truth of the Being *of* being, and in turn such a truth of Being already lies in the overtness of being. This means that ontic and ontological truth belong together on the basis of their relation to the *distinction of Being and being* (ontological difference). These ontic-ontological modes of truth are "one with the breaking-open of this distinction." In the early works, Heidegger dealt with this question only with regard to Dasein. The decisive factor was that "the ability to distinguish," in which this ontological difference "becomes factic," "has struck the root of its proper possibility in the ground of the essence" of that being which is capable "of comporting itself to being by understanding Being." Later, on the contrary, it is a question of how the "distinction of Being and being prevails." [2] The "unique state of affairs"—that, and how, "Being" makes "being" possible out of the

1. WG 14, 15 (21, 23).
2. WW (3d ed.), 26 (351).

[125]

occurrence of the difference—is now the "topic" of his thought.[3]

This "topic" is approached by Heidegger in a threefold way. First, the words of the early Greeks were rethought in order to determine from them the experiences which were undergone in the beginning with the "occurrence of the difference." Second, it was shown that decisive aspects of the subsequent "history of Being" and the "essence" of metaphysics are "grounded" in these incipient experiences of the distinction of Being and being and that the essence of metaphysics is determined out of this "prevailing of the difference." And third, this "to-be-thought" distinction was thought-forth to the "distinction of world and thing."

The "grammatical form" of the word *eon* indicates that the early Greeks expressed Being "participially." The experience which necessitated this grammatical form holds for Heidegger "the riddle of Being." [4] Every participle is the expression of a twofold.[5] Thus the participle "blooming" nominally or substantively names a specific blooming thing, e.g., a rose, and at the same time verbally names the "in bloom," in contrast to being "in wither." But in *eon* we have an "outstanding" participle, since all other participles are grounded in it. It names the fundamental difference between nominal, substantive "being" and verbal "Being." Without this twofold character of Being, no particular participial modes could in general "be."

"Anaximander's Aphorism" [6] is of value as "testimony" to the fact that the early Greeks not only experienced a "twofold" of "Being" and "being" but also experienced this twofold as the occurrence of a "referential relation" or "bearing" [*Beziehung*]. This bearing, which brings it to pass that Being enables being to "be," "expressed" itself in the basic word *to chreōn*. This word is translated into the German *Brauch*.* For *to chreōn* has the same

3. *ID* 43 ff. (47 ff.).
4. *HW* 343.
5. *WD* 133 ff. (220 ff.). [Here Heidegger treats the Epic (Ionic) participle *eon*, the Attic *on*, the Latin *ens*, and the German *Seiendes* (being) as the "same."—Trans.]
6. *HW* 296 ff. On the relation of *eon* to the essence of man cf. Heidegger's interpretation of Parmenides' Fragment B6(1) (*WD* 110 ff. and 136 ff. [182 ff., 223 ff.]; cf. below, pp. 217 ff.).
* *Brauch* and *brauchen* normally mean "need," "want," "use," which also enter into the Greek *chreon*. But all of these ring too anthropomorphically as translations for the impersonal *chrē* ("it is fated, necessary, befitting, proper") that Heidegger stresses (*WD* 115 [188]). The quasi-impersonal verb "behoove" evokes a constellation of connotations and etymological intersections remarkably similar to both *brauchen* and *chrē*. It is gradationally related to "have" and the English *heave*, "to seize, hold, take up, make use of," and therefore finds somewhat similar distant

meaning that originally pertained to this German word, namely, "to hand out something to its own essence and to keep it as so present in the protecting hand." [7] *Brauch* says "to let the behooved into its essence" and "to preserve it there." [8] In the manner of such a "behooving," the distinction of Being and being holds sway, Being approaches being, makes it possible for it "to be" as a being. Only on the basis of this occurrence of the difference carrying itself out as a "behooving" are Being and being "given" at all, i.e., "Being *of* being" or "being *of* Being." The experience of this occurrence is "deposited" in the participial form of *eon* and has been "preserved" in this word as a basic word.

But the early Greeks did not *think* the experience which they had with the occurrence of the twofold of Being and being. The difference "as difference" did not "commission" itself to their thought and even less to the thought of the subsequent tradition of philosophy. In the succeeding ages, this basic trait of Being was instead "forgotten," in the sense of a "withdrawal" from thought. Thus, for Heidegger, the "essence" of metaphysics is

---

resonances to the metaphors of actions of the hand that Heidegger finds in his two words (*HW* 337 ff.; *WD* 114 [186–87]). But more importantly, "behoove" suggests a need, want, or use which does not imply a lack but which accrues to one's behalf. This positive connotation is particularly manifest in its noun form: "Importers for their behoof of provisions and corn" (Carlyle); "In youth . . . methought it was very sweet to contract the time for my behove" (the Clown's song in *Hamlet* V.i.71). It is this direction that Heidegger wishes to emphasize: Being "behooves" man in a way that fulfills man in his essence, brings him to fruition (*frui: HW* 338–39). In other words, Being suits man and it behooves him to respond in a befitting manner (see below, pp. 217, 226). "Behoove" is most often used in the following impersonal formulation: "And thus it behooved Christ to suffer" (Luke 24:46); "It behooves the rock to have shafts, and the earth furrows" (Hölderlin, "The Ister River"; cf. *WD* 117 [190]). But other patterns are possible, e.g., "If you know aught which does behove my knowledge thereof to be inform'd, imprison't not in ignorant concealment" (*The Winter's Tale* I.ii.395). Besides the impersonal sense of "it is necessary, useful, befitting, proper for," "behoove" has had a history of usage in the more active sense of "to have use for, need, require" (object originally genitive!), as in: "He had all those endowments . . . which are behoved in a scholar" (Hacket, *Abp. Williams* I, 39 [1670]). As Heidegger uses it, *Es brauchet* (where "It is necessary" becomes "It requires") tends toward the same active character that *Es gibt* (where "There is" becomes "It gives") assumes in his texts. In conclusion, it is believed that such a word, with all of its archaic reverberations, rather than the "use," "want," and "need" of common parlance, with all their anthropomorphic overtones, is preferable in expressing a relation that Heidegger considers to be unique and incomparable to any other relation (*HW* 337), as well as deeply rooted in the beginnings of our tradition. See the Translator's Introduction for a further discussion of *Brauch*.

7. *HW* 339.
8. *WD* 114 (187).

especially determined from this "forgottenness" of the difference.[9] But the "experiences" of the early Greeks have nevertheless determined, through their basic words, the entire history of
thought in this "unthought and unquestioned" way, inasmuch as
philosophy from Plato on into modern times has in fact distinguished between Being and being. Plato must have experienced
the distinction between Being and being, or he would not have
been able to think the *chōrismos* between Being, the *ontōs on*,
and transitory being.[10] And Aristotle must have experienced it,
for both the *on* and the *ousia* mean on the one hand the enabling
and on the other the enabled.[11] And out of this experience, Kant
—to take an example from modern thought—distinguished between "objectivity" and "object" in a transcendental way.[12]

These Heideggerian interpretations of traditional philosophy
are certainly not at issue, since many of its thinkers have distinguished between "Being" and "being," either explicitly or implicitly. Our own reflections on Aristotle and Hegel served to confirm this.[13] But it is disputable whether this distinction between
Being and being really has to do with the "experiences" that the
early Greeks had with the "distinction." This question is connected with the problem that lies in the particular "historical
structure" of "rethinking and forethinking," a problem that will
concern us later as the problem of "legitimation." [14]

Since all of Heidegger's interpretations serve his specific purposes,[15] it does not appear to be necessary here to investigate
whether they are tenable and convincing according to the standards of the philosophical and philological tradition. For our purposes of a "reconstructive investigation" of the *total context* of
the basic traits of Being developed thus far by Heidegger, it is
first of all important to know only the meaning that this basic
trait of *eon*, as the "governing distinction" of Being and being,
has for Heidegger.

Hegel viewed "difference" as a category of Being.[16] But Being
itself was posited by him as a thought and was demonstrated in
its healing and reconciling power. Hence the category of difference must at once be drawn back into the category of identity.

9. *ID* 47 (51); *HW* 336; *VA* 264.
10. *WD* 135 ff. (222 ff.).
11. *Ibid.* Cf. *SZ* 89 and *HW* 161 (105–6).
12. *WD* 148 (243); on Hegel, cf. *HW* 161 ff. (105 ff.).
13. See above, pp. 17 ff., 45 ff.
14. See below, p. 177.
15. See above, p. 110.
16. See above, p. 61.

"Nonidentical identity" is the categorial model for the occurrence of Being *qua* thought; it determines the "substance" and the "subject," the "concept," the "idea," the movement of "being at home with itself in otherness," "affirmative infinity." Because Hegel persisted in the traditional presuppositions, he did not first question what this state of affairs implies, so that he also conceived Being without further ado as the Being *of being* and understood being as the being *of Being*. Hegel thought "categorially," in the traditional sense, and saw the purpose of absolute thinking in the demonstration of the total "organization" of the "logic" of Being. In contrast, Heidegger asks the "simple" question of how to think the occurrence in which Being makes it possible for "being" to "be." In the essay "The Onto-Theo-Logical Constitution of Metaphysics," [17] he characterizes this enabling movement as a "transition" to being, whereby this transition is certainly not to be represented spatially, as if Being, "leaving its place, goes over to being, as if being, previously without Being, could simply be approached by it."

In this essay, Heidegger has himself distinguished his thought from Hegel's in the following way:

> For Hegel the topic of thinking is Being with regard to being as it is thought in absolute thinking and as this thinking. For us too the topic of thinking is the same, therefore Being, but Being with regard to its difference to being. To put it more precisely: For Hegel the topic of thinking is the thought as the absolute concept. For us the topic of thinking, provisionally named, is the difference *as* difference.[18]

This distinction strikes us as wholly apt and to the point. For us, of course, Hegel's topic of thinking is Being not only with regard to being as it is thought but also with regard to Being itself as It is thought.[19]

17. *ID* 62 (64).
18. *ID* 42 (47).
19. See above, p. 45.

2 / The Temporal Sense of Being: The Presenting Process

HEIDEGGER HAS TRANSLATED the Greek words *eon* and *on* as well as the Greek *ousia* with one and the same word. And he has also used the same word to designate the different "stampings" of Being and essence, as these "have manifested themselves up to the most recent times of our own century." [1] This word is *Anwesen* (presenting, the presenting process). Accordingly, the *eonta, onta*, the "beings" are called the *Anwesenden* (those present).

In our introduction, we emphasized that Aristotle and philosophy after him distinguished between *on*, Being, and *ousia*, essence, even though it was Aristotle himself who asked the question of Being as a question of essence. By translating *on* and *ousia* as one and the same word, is Heidegger simply trying to sublate the distinction of Being and essence or is he really trying to overcome the metaphysical meanings of Being and essence? According to Heidegger, Being was for metaphysics "the indefinable, self-evident, most general concept," [2] an "empty word," [3] or, in Nietzsche's words, "vapor and smoke." [4] It has no naming power either as an infinitive or as a substantive [5] and has been depleted by the four "limitations" and "restrictions" or "separations," by "becoming," "appearance," "thinking," and the "ought." [6] Likewise empty is the hitherto and current concept of

1. *SF* 21 (62).
2. *SZ* 3; *EM* 52 (68).
3. *EM* 38, 53 (50, 69).
4. *EM* 27 (36).
5. *EM* 42 ff. (56 ff.).
6. *EM* 71 ff. (93 ff.). Cf. esp. *EM* 155 (203).

[131]

essence, "the whatness," the "quiddity, the general genus and the universal." [7] But we might recall from our discussion of the basic traits of Being and essence in Aristotle and Hegel that their conceptions of Being and essence did not prove to be so completely "empty." [8] It can even be shown that Hegel thought these four "separations" together with Being, in which it was of course a matter of "Being" in the "element of thinking," of determinations of thought. [9]

One must in any case reject the view that Heidegger proposes nothing but replacing the traditional and presumably "empty" words "Being" and "essence" with other words. On the contrary, the word *Anwesen* is intended to designate the *sense* which lay at the basis of these traditional words as well. Not only the early Greek *eon* but also the *idea* of Plato, the *ousia* of Aristotle, the *res* of Descartes, objectivity in Kant, all conceptions of objectivity as well as all forms of self-knowledge within the subject-object relationship, like Hegel's "experience" and Nietzsche's "will to will," are modes of presenting, in which, to be sure, the kind and mode of such "presenting" has been changed in many ways.

But "what is thereby gained," asks Heidegger, [10] when the customary words Being and being are replaced by the less customary "presenting" and "what is present"? Nothing in fact would have been gained if Heidegger had not elaborated the sense of "presenting" and "what is present" in a variety of aspects.

In *Being and Time,* the temporal sense of both the Being of Parmenides and the Aristotelian *ousia* was designated as "presence" [*Anwesenheit*], and presence there was also identified as "Being on hand." [11] This early work at the same time associated the term "Being on hand" with the narrower meaning which had been obtained from the interpretation of the Cartesian *res extensa,* the meaning of pure reified stability, [12] which simply does not pertain to the sense of Being in Parmenides and the sense of the Aristotelian *ousia,* [13] as Heidegger's later writings also con-

7. Cf. VA 37, HW 39 (676); cf. also above, p. 19.
8. Cf. above, pp. 18 ff., 48.
9. Within the limits of the traditional approaches, Hegel considered "Being and becoming" together (cf. above, p. 46 ff.). He explicitly thought of "Being and appearance" together (*Logik II* 11 ff. [394 ff.]); likewise "Being and thinking" (*Logik II* 212 ff. [600 ff.]) and "Being and ought" (*Logik II* 383 ff. and 477 ff. [735 ff., 818 ff.]).
10. WD 141 (233).
11. SZ 25.
12. See above, p. 86.
13. With regard to *ousia,* cf. above, p. 21.

firm.[14] The word "presenting" contains the sense of "presence" [*Präsenz*], of "the present" [*Gegenwart*], and thus of "time." "Time" was also the decisive aspect from which Heidegger sought to determine the sense of Being in *Being and Time*, entitled with this in mind. There he pursued this "project of Being toward time"[15] by investigating the temporality of the understanding of Being.[16] It was thus that the "guiding field of vision,"[17] the "horizon of every understanding of Being,"[18] was to be secured. But the last sentence of *Being and Time* asks whether "time itself manifests itself as a horizon of Being."[19] This is the question that Heidegger pursued. For now he wants to think the temporal sense lying at the basis of the early Greek *eon, einai, ousia*, the metaphysical "stampings" of "Being"; he wants to think "the present" prevailing "unthought and hidden" in the presenting process. It is thus a matter not of time in the sense of Aristotelian time constitution, which measures changeable being according to movement taking place in space, but of another "kind" of time residing in Being itself.

It is because of the enormous difficulty of this problem that thus far such a "time sense" has been explicitly determined only for the early Greek *eon* and simply intimated for all subsequent determinations of Being. The time sense of *eon* for Heidegger comes from the presenting process occurring here as a verbally conceived movement of *pareinai* and *apeinai*, as the "struggling of a strife" between "emergence and coming forth," *genesis*, and the "ever possible absence," *phthora*.[20] In the especially "violent" interpretation performed in "Anaximander's Aphorism,"[21] it is shown how presenting occurs between "coming," *genesis*, and "going," *phthora*, so as to constitute, in the sense of such a "between," the "joint" of a "transition." It is from this transitionality that the temporal sense of such a presenting is determined. Transitionality proclaims that it is not a matter of a "mere continuing" and "persisting." In *Being and Time*, the authentic present was called momentousness. A similar momentousness describes the kind of "the present" that pertains to this transitional occurrence, this upsurge and shining-forth out of the

14. *KM* 217 (250); *EM* 147 (194).
15. *KM* 216, 217 (249, 250).
16. See above, pp. 101 ff.
17. *EM* 157 (205).
18. *SZ* 1.
19. *SZ* 438.
20. *WD* 144 (236–37).
21. *HW* 296 ff., 315, 327 ff.

darkness. As the present, it is indeed a "while," but it "whiles" only in an "abrupt" manner.[22] The temporal sense of *eon* is a presenting and, as such, a kind of "the present" which has the character of an "abrupt while." Accordingly, the time sense of the early Greek being is of "something present for a while" [*je Weiliges*] which appears "abruptly."

Eon becomes a ground word because, according to Heidegger, all subsequent determinations of Being "ground" in the experience of the first beginning, through which Being in general had the sense of presenting. This sense of Being as presenting, and thus as the present, persisted "until the early part of the twentieth century." To be sure, this transitional presenting, this abrupt way of the while, was already transformed in the Platonic *idea* and the Aristotelian *ousia*. Underlying these is the sense of a "constant" presence.[23] This "Being constant" is here temporally a "Being always" and a "Being permanent." The *idea* is the "always existing" model, and the *ousia* is that which "always already" lies before, a *hypokeimenon*, and as something which "always already has been," a *to ti ēn einai*.[24] Both the *idea* and the *ousia* were, according to Heidegger, thought in "contrast to becoming" and hence already temporally represent a "remaining."[25] The temporal sense of the *idea* and the *ousia* resides in a "while" which is no longer abrupt but which remains.

Our own representation of *ousia* started from the assumption that Aristotle did not determine it by contrasting it with becoming but that, guided by the cosmic symbol of a unity of order and movement, he considered Being and becoming to be together in it. Hence the inner mobility of *ousia* that results should directly contradict the time determination of "remaining." However, our own determination of the temporal sense of the "eternalness" of *ousia*[26] agrees with Heidegger in its result, insofar as we also described this eternity as a "mode" of the present, as a "presence." This present is a "remaining" to the extent that the same "endures in recurring." But since here the same "arrives" and "continues" again and again, it is not a question of a "remaining" which can be thought in "contrast to becoming."

On the other hand, it seems to us that Heidegger's determination of the temporal sense of *res extensa* in *Being and Time* as an

22. WD 144 (236–37).
23. EM 147, 157 (194, 205).
24. EM 147 (194); KM 217 (250).
25. EM 154 (202).
26. See above, pp. 30 ff.

"everlasting remaining" and "constant remainder" is completely correct, corresponding to the thingness, to this kind of Being on hand. To the extent that we are dealing with a mode of the present in the time sense of both the *res* and the *ousia,* there is an interconnection in the "history of Being" that rules between these two "stampings of Being." If Heidegger had in *Being and Time* oriented the sense of all modern conceptions to his determination of *res extensa,* he now determines the entire modern conception of Being on the basis of an interpretation of *res cogitans.*[27] Since Descartes, the only true and certain "forelying" dimension is the self-certainty of the subject knowing itself unconditionally. This cognitive representation possesses the basic trait of "presentation." It "presents" the object in that it represents it to the subject, in which representation the subject presents itself as such. This presentation is an essential mode of presence (*parousia*); as such a modality of essence it is a presenting. From this time on, the sense of Being for Heidegger lies in a presenting which occurs within the subject-object relationship. As he sees it, this kind of presence is also found in Kant's "objectivity" of the objects of experience for knowing and cognition [28] and in Hegel's concept of experience. In the essay *Hegel's Concept of Experience,*[29] he explains to what extent in the *Phenomenology of Spirit*

27. *HW* 121 ff. (33 ff.).
28. *VA* 75.
29. *HW* 105 ff. (5 ff.). This interpretation has the structure of a "retrieve." To be sure, the sentence on page 143 (70) shows that it was written after the "turn" (see below, p. 173); the "language of thinking developed from its mission" (i.e., Hegel's) evokes the "thought of another thinking [i.e., Heidegger's] into the light of its own thinking, in order to deliver the other over to its own essence." It is thus a matter—as in a retrieve (see above, p. 108)—of bringing to light out of its previous "concealment" the "other" of what is thought by Heidegger, i.e., what is "unsaid" by Hegel himself in what the text actually says. The necessary "violence" of this interpretation is a result either of the discovery character of retrieve or of the basic trait of rethinking as a leap away from metaphysics in order to reappropriate it.
In the terminology of the "retrieve," Heidegger here has proceeded from the over-all project of the history of Being (mission) (*HW* 161 ff. [105 ff.], esp. 164 [110], 174 [128], and below, p. 163 ff.) as his "predisposition." He had already determined its eschatological sequence, indicating that it terminates with the stamping of Being in Nietzsche as "will to will" (see below, p. 170). To this over-all project also belongs the already established determination of the essence of metaphysics (*HW* 179 [135–36], 184 [143], 186 ff. [147 ff.]; see above, pp. 118, 127). The "preview" guiding this interpretation is the already established determination of the sense of Being as presenting, prevalent since the first beginning. On the basis of this view, the text is "cut out" to let "experience" in Hegel be seen as a mode of presenting. The interpretation (*HW* 125 [40], 166 ff. [112 ff.], 175 ff. [129 ff.], 187 [148]) brings to light the sense of the occurrence un-

the "presenting of the absolute" occurs as "experience." Being shows itself here, "appears" in the sense that it is knowledge which appears or that it is consciousness which is at once Being [*Bewusst-"sein"*], where Being "presents" itself as the "way" of "experience." The particular movement in which experience advances on this way as an "outreaching reach that attains its goal" characterizes for Heidegger the specific mode in which presenting occurs here.[30] Experience goes ahead of itself and in doing so comes back to itself; and in this coming-back it unfolds itself as a presenting. It is thus in each instance a matter of an "exteriorization" which nevertheless remains as "interiorization" [*Er-innerung*]. As such a pervasive interiorization, "the power of will of the *parousia*" holds the fullness of appearing to itself. It is in this definite sense that the presenting is "constant" here.[31] This constancy of presenting is of an entirely different kind from that of the presenting of the Aristotelian *ousia*. But it is also

---

thought by Hegel himself, according to which the absolute on the "way of the experience" of consciousness "wants to be at home with us." It shows that the manner in which this consciousness as a subject-object relation "represents" the absolute "to itself," as presence, is thus the presenting of the absolute itself, whose "will" is a first step to Nietzsche's "will to will."

This determination came about with the help of the "preconceptions" which Heidegger had worked out in the early works, e.g., the ontological difference (*HW* 161 ff. [105 ff.]), the essence of truth (164 [110]), the sense of presenting (122 [34], 170 [120]). The "violence" of the interpretation can be shown from traditional Hegel research in many respects, e.g., Heidegger's conception of the essence of truth in Hegel (see above, p. 53), his determination of the "goal" of the way of experience as a goal already reached at the beginning of the way (146 [78]; see above, p. 70), the overinterpretation of the expression that the absolute "wants" to be with us, which for Heidegger becomes the "will of the *parousia* of the absolute." But the one which is especially "violent" is the reading of *PG* 74 (159), line 2, whereby it is not the self-conceiving concept that holds sway in the consciousness which brings about its "reversal" but the "ontic-ontological dialogue" which is "our addition"—even though the deed for Hegel is only our scientific "contemplation of the topic." In his exhaustive analysis (*Heidegger und Hegel*, pp. 27 ff.), van der Meulen has already pointed to several of these "violences" and a series of others. Generally speaking, his book may be said to secure the traditional interpretation of Hegel, but—with the exception of the footnote on page 35— perhaps has not sufficiently taken into account the intentions of Heidegger that we have stressed above. For us, within the limits of our specific purpose of a presentation of the basic determinations of Being in Heidegger, only these intentions are important. Accordingly, and for the reasons already indicated (see above, p. 109), we shall forego a more exhaustive treatment of this Heideggerian interpretation here.

30. *HW* 170 (120).
31. *HW* 176 ff. (131 ff.); van der Meulen (*Heidegger und Hegel*, p. 39) is of the opinion that Heidegger drew the "standing permanence" of presenting from his view that Being means "objectivity," with its character of "standing over against" [*Gegen-ständlichkeit*].

different from that of the Cartesian *res*. Heidegger has not defined the temporal sense of this kind of constancy any more closely. He in fact suggests that the presence prevailing here "essences from a yet unthought essence of a hidden time." [32]

It is still possible to ask whether the *Science of Logic* and "absolute knowledge" would not provide a more suitable horizon for the determination of the sense of Being, as well as for the attempt to characterize the "kind" of "time" in which the absolute "presents" itself in absolute knowledge. Heidegger's discussions relate themselves to the "way of experience." But the absolute does not show itself "in its truth" on this way. This occurs only when consciousness has pressed on to its "true existence" and has become absolute knowledge. Only then does it become manifest just where to locate the "truth" of that movement which accomplishes itself—in the medium of "torrential time"—as the experiential way of "exteriorization" and "interiorization." When one sees, as Heidegger does, a mode of presenting in the mode in which the absolute presents itself in knowledge, and wishes to infer the more precise character of this presenting of the movement of the absolute, then it seems necessary to pay particular attention to this movement when it shows itself in its "truth."

As absolute knowledge, the absolute no longer "presents" itself as the "way of experience"; the movement has arrived at its "goal." [33] Here it "presents" itself as the "pure" movement of the self-knowing idea, of being at home with itself in otherness. It is questionable whether such a presence or presenting of a pure movement can be characterized as "constant."

For Heidegger, there is a presenting not only in the presentation of the absolute, in knowledge, but also in the manner in which the absolute idea conceives itself in the *Logic*.[34] This movement, which for Hegel himself—in the light of his guiding concept of time [35]—was extratemporal, "eternal," is for Heidegger—in the sense of another kind of time—a presenting. However, Heidegger has not developed this interpretation any further.

32. *HW* 142 (69).
33. *PG* 564 (808); also *HW* 146 (78).
34. *HW* 181 (139).
35. See above, p. 68.

3 / *Physis*

HEIDEGGER USED THE GERMAN WORD *Anwesen* (presenting) to "translate" not only the early Greek *eon* but also the early Greek *physis* in several interpretations, particularly of fragments of Heraclitus and Parmenides and of a chorus from Sophocles' *Antigone*, in order thus to exhibit further *basic traits* of Being from the *experiences* "preserved" in this basic word. His justification for translating two different Greek words into the same German word is based on the assumption that *eon* and thus Being "revealed itself as *physis*" [1] to the early Greeks. For "being as such as a whole" [2] was apprehended as *physis* in a "poetizing-thinking ground experience," and all the later and regionally understood views of the essence of nature are derived from this apprehension.

This "trans-lation" of *physis* into "presenting" is intended above all to express the "creative," the *poiēsis* of *physis*. Everything comes down to recognizing and keeping in mind that, for Heidegger, "presenting" has the original sense of a *creative occurrence.* [3] The pregnant meaning which the Greek *poiēsis* has

1. *EM* 11 (14).
2. *Ibid.*
3. In this treatise, the word "creative" has already been employed to characterize the *poiēsis* in Aristotle, the absolute idea in Hegel, and the consciousness in Kant, and in each case its sense has been specified. Furthermore, it was pointed out that there is a new sense of the "creative" in the determination of the essence of man in Heidegger's early works. The use of such an overworked word is justified by the fact that it "combines the meanings 'to create' [*schöpfen*] and 'to produce or do' [*schaffen*]" (Johannes Hoffmeister, *Wörterbuch der philosophischen Begriffe* [Hamburg, 1955], p. 544). This coherence of meanings will prove to be very

in the pre-Socratics must therefore be associated with the word "creative," unfortunately so overworked. This definition of the sense of "presenting" does not contradict Heidegger's use of the same word to designate even the metaphysical "stampings of Being," which become increasingly "uncreative" in the course of the history of Being. For this indicates that for him these uncreative modes of presenting are "grounded" in a creative occurrence, the original sense from the first beginning.

The mobility of Being in the first beginning has already been characterized in the "prevailing" of the distinction and in the "momentous while." But the character of the "poietic," of the creative, first comes to light in the basic traits which Heidegger has developed from the word *physis*. For the early Greeks, the occurrence of Being was not the prevailing of "thought" but the way in which the "overpowering powers" of "Nature" prevail, like the waves of the sea, "tearing open their own depths and flinging themselves into them," or like the domination of the overpowering powers of the "burgeoning, nurturing, and towering" earth.[4]

Physis is the basic word for the "how" of this "activity" of Being, which does not mean the "absolute activity," the "method" of Hegel's Being posited as thought. It is true that Hegel also thought of the occurrence of the idea as "creative," and he saw the "root of the movement and vitality" of thought in "contradiction." But this movement always resulted in a synthesis. But the prevailing of the overpowering powers of *physis* knows no "reconciliation"; they prevail, not as a "contradiction" which can be healed by synthesis, but as a "conflict" which remains essentially "antagonistic." [5]

Physis does not have the structure of a circle turning back upon itself. It is indeed "play," but not the "play of the concept." Its decisive basic trait is that it—like the *eon* considered as *parousia*—is a prevailing "emerging out of itself." [6] The early Greeks experienced the way in which a being comes into Being and "is" in it as such an "emergence out of itself." Herein lies the sense of "presenting" in the first beginning of the history of Western thought. Even now we still speak of an "emergence out of itself" of a rose, of an "evolving out of itself" and "opening out of itself," in order to express how a rose comes into Being.

---

indicative for the following conception of the sense of Being and particularly for the relationship of Being to the essence of man.

4. *EM* 118 (153).

5. *EM* 47, 120 ff. (62, 157 ff.); HW 37, 49 (674, 684); cf. here also van der Meulen, *Heidegger und Hegel*, pp. 78 ff.

6. *EM* 11 (14).

And in the same sense, we speak of the rising of the sun and of the burgeoning emergence of animal and man from their parent stock or of the fruits out of the earth. They all "present" in the sense of a "prevalence emerging out of itself."

Physis, moreover, had for the early Greeks the basic trait of "originating." It prevails in the mode of a "bringing-out," "exposing," and "producing." The "prevalence" of *physis,* the basic trait of presenting in the first beginning, therefore has the meaning of an occurrence that pro-duces, that brings products to light. Of course, this production must not be confused with human "making," so that the Greeks later on even distinguished between the "producing" of *technēi onta* and of *physei onta.* The producing of *physis* is an origination emerging "out of itself." Likewise, even today we still characterize "Nature" as "creative."

In the first beginning it required, according to Heidegger, the interplay of the *physis* in its "overpowering power" [7] with the "actively violent, the wielder of power," the man capable of *technē,* for a "creative" occurrence of presence in a narrower sense to take place. Being was meaningfully "opened up and revealed" in a reciprocal relationship of *physis* and *technē,* in which the overpowering powers of *physis* were harnessed into "works." This interplay formed a "world." In this world-opening event, something "hitherto unthought, unsaid, unheard" [8] is brought forth, produced by the "creators," something "new" [9] originates. Since we shall deal with the essence of man apart from the essence of Being in this book, it is important to note here that the essence of man thus plays a role in the occurrence of presence which is "creative" in this narrower sense.

As a presenting process that "emerges" and "comes forth," *physis* furthermore has the basic trait of *appearing,* of "showing itself," of bringing "itself forward" and "to light." But presenting as appearing and coming to light points to the darkness, the "obscurity" from which appearing comes and into which it must recede. *Physis* as an "appearing" presence is thus related to an absence without light. Likewise *physis* as "originating" or "coming to be" at the same time always prevails in a relation to "passing away." For every "rising" there is a "setting." [10] *Physis* as appearing, arising, emerging presence is at the same time the relation to that which has not appeared, arisen, emerged, to

7. *EM* 114 ff. (149 ff.).
8. *EM* 47 (62).
9. *EM* 110 (144).
10. *EM* 88 (116).

"concealment." [11] Heraclitus' aphorism *physis kryptesthai philei*,[12] "Nature loves to conceal itself," means for Heidegger that every luminous presenting is related to and pervaded by darkness. This sense will become clearer in the exposition of the basic word *alētheia*.

Heidegger sees an extremely decisive consequence for the essence of the subsequent "metaphysics" in the early Greek experience of *physis* as appearance. *Physis* with its basic trait of appearance led to "aspect," "view," and "look" becoming the "unique and standard interpretation of Being." [13] Hence with Plato the *idea* became authentic Being, the *ontōs on*,[14] which was no longer the occurrence of a "creative opening of Being," but the "apparent" or "visible," [15] the "foreground," there only for human vision. Through this "restriction of Being" [16] to the idea, Being becomes the "paradigm" for man.[17] There is in this at the same time a fundamental alteration of the role which man has to play in the occurrence of Being.[18] Likewise, for Aristotle and subsequent interpretations, Being remains a "foreground" affair, having meaning only in relation to man. Being loses the sense of a creative occurrence of presence.

Against this over-all view of the subsequent development of the history of thought, let us briefly recall the results of our reflections on Aristotle and Hegel. Aristotle thought of the *ousia* as "a certain *physis*." [19] It is true that this *physis* also appears, to the extent that, as *ousia*, it is *eidos*, and as such was conceived in relation to human vision, the *eidenai*. But other determinations of *ousia*, first of all as *energeia* and as *telos*, do not have the sense of "appearing" for "a knowing." It is not true that Aristotle's *ousia* is limited to merely being the "visible" in the foreground, since the occurrence of *energeia* and of *telos* are "inner" movements. Even Hegel's [20] "idea" is in no way simply an appearance as an "apparent and visible" foreground. For in the *Logic*, "appearance" is the way in which Being comes forth as "essence," where Being itself comes to full light. Being as the self-knowing idea is like-

11. *EM* 87 (114).
12. Cf. esp. *VA* 270.
13. *EM* 139 (182).
14. *EM* 140 (183).
15. *PW* 35 (262).
16. *EM* 71 ff. (93 ff.).
17. *EM* 154 (202); *PW* 39 ff. (264 ff.).
18. See below, p. 220.
19. See above, p. 25.
20. See above, pp. 54 ff.

wise not "in the foreground" but is the inner process which for Hegel signifies "eternal creation" and "eternal vitality." [21]

These "rethought" basic traits of *physis* in the first beginning, these determinations of the sense of the presenting process, are the "to be thought" which forethinking must transmute into another sense of Being and essence. Heidegger's attempts at forethinking have presumably been determined by the "creative" character of the presenting process of *physis*. In order to bring out its sense of the "creative" somewhat more clearly, let us recall that in Aristotle the *poiēsis* of *ousia* was bound in a twofold way. The *ousia* always bears the basic trait of a "conditioned necessity" as well as that of selfsameness, which forbids the emergence of any really "new" essence. The "creative" in the Aristotelian *poiēsis* is above all so restricted that it can only occur as an "approximation" of "what is to be produced" to the "producing," as well as the awakening of already existing predispositions. And even in Hegel the "creative" character of the idea and the concept does not mean that it is capable of producing "new" realities. The "process of necessity" always produces only that which has already been prepared as a "possibility" in the "old reality." This requirement is an essential consequence of the basic trait of self-sameness, which Hegel also attributes to Being.

If the early Greek *physis* does not hold to these requirements, this does not mean that its "creative" movement is a "self-dissipating" process. For every "coming-forth" emerges from a "self," returns "to itself," [22] is thus "gathered into itself." It would nonetheless be a mistake to interpret this double direction of the movement of *physis* according to the model of the ousiological *telos* or by Hegel's "good infinity," as a "return to itself" that circles out of itself into itself.

21. Cf. *Enz.* § 214.
22. Cf. *Il Pensiero I* 143.

4 / Alētheia

HEIDEGGER HAS "TRANSLATED" the early Greek word *alētheia* into various German words, in order to *think* further experiences that the early Greeks had with the essence of Being and essence. The sense of *alētheia* is primarily obtained from interpretations of Parmenides' fragments.[1] In what follows, the "results" of these interpretations are presented as further basic traits, as "categories" of the sense of Being in the first beginning, as further determinations of the presenting process, while the way in which the essence of man belongs to it is for the time being left out of consideration.

The basic word *alētheia* "preserves" experiences that the early Greeks had with the occurrence of Being. Hence it must stand in a "peculiar essential connection"[2] with the words *eon* and *physis*. The basic traits of the presenting process thought as *physis* were manifested in its "self-emerging prevalence" which as a coming to be, an appearing, a coming to the fore, is a stepping-forth into the *light*. Thus to the occurrence of *physis*, to the presenting process, belongs the light. The experiences pertaining to this relation to light were laid down by the pre-Socratics particularly in the basic word *alētheia*, which is traditionally translated as "truth." Heidegger adheres to this translation, and since it is a matter here of the role of light in the occurrence of Being itself, he speaks of the "truth of Being."

If, on the one hand, Heidegger now thinks of "truth" as

---

1. With regard to linguistic usage in the nonphilosophical works, cf. the important investigation of H. Böder, "Der frühgriechische Wortgebrauch von Logos und Aletheia," *Archiv für Begriffsgeschichte*, IV, 82 ff.
2. EM 78 (102–3).

"belonging to the essence of Being,"[3] he had, on the other hand, conceived of it on the basis of his "existential-ontological" aim in *Being and Time* as belonging to the "basic constitution of Dasein," as its mode of Being of "disclosure," which is there called "truth in the original sense."[4] Since it is "cleared in itself," "is" its own "here," Dasein in *Being and Time* is called "the clearing" [*Lichtung*].[5]

It is only with the essay *On the Essence of Truth*, which inquires "into the truth of essence,"[6] that Heidegger found it necessary to ask in what sense "Western thought in its beginning"[7] experienced being—and this means "that which is present"[8]—as *ta alēthea*. "In thinking this experience," Heidegger has translated *ta alēthea* as "the overt"[9] and "the open."[10] Here he goes further and asks just where the "openness" really lies, "in which each being stands and which it, as it were, brings with itself."[11] All human behavior is something which "stands open,"[12] insofar as it stands out into an openness which "is not initially created by human representation but is only entered into and taken over each time as a relational field."[13]

This openness of the Being of a being, of what is manifest and overt, is called a "clearing" in the "Letter on Humanism."[14] Here, "clearing" is now identified with the ever prevailing openness of the Being of being. And even the *alētheia* of the first beginning is translated as "clearing."[15] This translation is designed to express the openness characteristic of the occurrence of presence experienced by the early Greeks. But the sense of the word "clearing" that will truly be relevant to this experience becomes evident only when this word is thought "verbally." The early Greeks experienced every present*ing* as a clear*ing* or light*ing*. "Presenting" (verbal) was "clearing" (verbal). This implies, first, that the openness prevailing in the occurrence of presence is not without further ado "given," that it is not even

3. *Ibid.*
4. *Ibid.;* cf. above, p. 92.
5. *SZ* 133.
6. *WW* (1st ed.) 27 (351).
7. *WW* 15 (333).
8. *WW* 12 (328).
9. *Ibid.*
10. *WW* 15 (334).
11. *Ibid.*
12. *WW* 12 (328).
13. *WW* 11 (328).
14. *HB* 71; cf. also *HW* 41 ff. and 49 ff.
15. Cf. here esp. the essay "Aletheia" in *VA* 257 ff.

equivalent to a "state," and, second, that it is a coming-forth that comes out of the darkness.

That every being is "luminous" was Aristotle's basic conviction,[16] which then later formed the basis of the Scholastic view that *omne ens verum est*. Our reflection on the basic traits of *ousia* yielded the result that the Aristotelian essence as *noēton* is "totally intelligible." Since the *nous* holds sway and has already made everything transparent and overt, there cannot in Aristotle be talk of a "clearing" by which the openness would initially come forth, so that accordingly every experience of a being as it really is would be a "robbery," an *a-lētheuein* initially overcoming the fundamental *lēthē*, the concealment. Heidegger has—we think unjustly—taken the position in *Being and Time* that such a conception of the experience of truth was predominant in Aristotle.

Hegel[17] in fact conceived of the occurrence of Being as an occurrence of truth that realizes itself as a "coming to light," as a coming-forth in relation to "darkness." Because he experienced truth in the image of light, the following problem presented itself to him: What is the relation of untruth, error, evil, vice, death, and pain, these "realms of darkness," to the light of truth? He of course approached Being as thought and did not consider these "realms of darkness" in their own right but as "reconciled" and "healed" and "idealized" in the dialectical movement of thought. But it is of great importance in the history of the problem that Hegel at the end of the tradition experienced the occurrence of Being as an occurrence of truth and this as a coming to light in relation to that which is not luminous. It was here that we saw some "kinship," which perhaps had to come first in the history of the problem, before Heidegger's thought could think the *alētheia* of the first beginning as well as the truth of Being generally as "clearing," in a sense which goes beyond Hegel.

The decisively new factor in Heidegger's conception of *alētheia* as well as of the truth of Being generally is that he thinks of the "realms of darkness" and the "realm of light" as *equal partners* in the occurrence of Being and that he conceives of their relationship to each other as a "strife" which keeps the character of the occurrence of presence radically "creative." Hegel could not come to this "new" dimension because his thinking remained within the traditional approaches to Being as

16. See above, p. 38.
17. See above, pp. 52 ff., 57.

substance and as subject and because he understood Being as a movement of thought ordering itself to itself.

Already in *Being and Time* [18] truth was determined from its relationship to "untruth." "Untruth" belongs to "original truth," to the disclosure of Dasein, because Dasein—as a result of its essential immersion in beings—must again and again overcome "disguise" and "concealment" in order to come to the "discovery" of beings.

In *On the Essence of Truth* Heidegger distinguishes two modes of untruth belonging to truth. Untruth in the narrower sense pervades Dasein in the form of "erring," [19] so that it errs by "making a mistake," "committing an oversight," etc. Determined by "erring," Dasein turns only to the fleeting and transitory aspect of its concerns, and turns away from "authentic untruth," from "concealment," from which all "unconcealment" comes forth and which pervades Dasein as "mystery." [20] It is here that Heidegger deals for the first time with truth as unconcealment, as a relation to concealment. Later [21] he even identifies erring as "sham," the inauthentic untruth, with authentic untruth, mystery, insofar as he also views it in terms of its modes of concealment. And in like manner he considered the "absence" in *physis* as a mode of concealment.[22]

Heidegger translated the basic word *alētheia* as unconcealment in order to indicate that the early Greeks had experienced presenting as an occurrence of truth in the form of a relationship to concealment. As a "self-clearing" to be thought verbally, presenting for them always came about only in relation to concealment. *Alētheia* occurred as a self-concealing clearing or a self-clearing concealment.[23]

The realm of concealment should not be represented as a realm of "nothing" in the sense of *nihil negativum*.[24] The various modes of concealment which have been named are not "null" in this sense. The relation of the "essencing" Nothing to the various modes of concealment need not be discussed here. It is sufficient to point out that none of these modes is null in the sense of *nihil negativum* but that they all "essence" insofar as they continually

18. See above, p. 92.
19. WW 23 (346).
20. WW 20 ff. (344 ff.).
21. HW 42 (678).
22. Cf., above all, VA 270 ff.
23. Cf., e.g., SG 130.
24. WM 31 ff. (365 ff.).

"pervade" [25] the openness, the clearing. They are all indeed modes of "denial" [26] of the full light, but they also belong, "in the double form of refusal and disguise," [27] to the essence of the truth of Being. That which still or always "withdraws" itself, which remains hidden as "mystery" and so "refuses" itself to human knowledge, provides "the permanent origin for any clearing." That which "distorts" itself as errancy and sham gives every clearing the unmitigated harshness of error.[28] It is in this "countervailing" [29] mode of light and concealment that Being occurs. It is in this way that the sense of presenting in the first beginning is determined and that the "essencing" modes of concealment are to be considered in their own right. With this thought, Heidegger in fact goes far beyond Hegel. Hegel, to be sure, also wanted to show the power of Nothing in the occurrence of Being. His fundamental conception of Being as negativity led him to think Being and Nothing together.[30] The way in which the thesis negates itself in the movement of thought, becomes the antithesis, the contradiction, in order to be negated again into the synthesis, is an expression of the essencing power of "negativity." And the movement of affirmative infinity, which repels itself from itself but at the same time returns to itself, likewise testifies to this power. Heidegger in fact acknowledged in a later text [31] that the "nihilating in Being" comes to the fore in Hegel's dialectic, but he at the same time explains that this nihilating nonetheless veils itself in its actual essence. For anything logical is— according to a previously held position of his [32]—a negation which is merely derived from the original nihilating.

In fact, the "logical" prevented Hegel from giving proper due to the modes of Nothing, untruth, error, death, that in Heidegger are modes of concealment. It is true that they were acknowledged as important realms, but at the same time they were still placed in the service of the thought process. They became the medium which moves this process and were finally "healed and reconciled" by it. Hegel does not let the dark remain dark but wishes to illuminate it by thought, reason. The approaches to Being as

25. *HW* 43 (679).
26. *Ibid.*
27. *Ibid.*
28. *Ibid.*
29. *Ibid.*
30. *Logik I* 67 (73).
31. *HW* 114.
32. *WM* 36 (372).

substance and subject and their corresponding goal, to conceive of Being as a movement of thought ordering itself to itself, demanded that the idea always "overcome" its opposite. It is only because Heidegger no longer considered himself to be determined by these traditional approaches and goals that he can think of the modes of concealment in a relationship of equal rank with the realm of light. And only because of this was it possible to apprehend this relationship as a creative occurrence in a radical sense. The revelatory opening of Being in the first beginning is the decisive example of "the presenting process" as a creative relationship of concealment and clearing. The battle between the overpowering powers of *physis* and man, the violent wielder of power, was in this sense an occurrence of truth. In this "strife" of self-penetrating light with error, sham, mystery, the sense of Being in the first beginning is opened and revealed.[33] Unconcealment occurs when those who do battle, the "creative men," [34] nominate things to their meanings, when they wrest "works" away from concealment, works of language, of art, and of "founding states," [35] when the openness of a world is formed.[36] But then the unconcealment that prevails as a result of such strife is not the stationary "state" of a "total intelligibility." This unconcealment, and with it, as well, the works that have come forth to it and the world that has come to light in it, remains permeated by the powers of concealment, by error, sham, but above all by mystery. The strife between the equal partners of concealment and clearing remains "contentious." Wherever this battle ceases, "Being retreats from being" and the "world turns away." [37]

Heidegger has articulated the creative character of the occurrence of presence as an occurrence of truth in an especially striking way in the essay "The Origin of the Artwork." [38] Though this essay does not belong to the range of tasks that pertain to the rethinking of the basic traits of Being in the first beginning, we bring it in here because Heidegger's conception of the sense of *alētheia* in the first beginning is treated with the greatest penetration in his discussion of the essence of the artwork. The

33. *EM* 115 (151).
34. *EM* 47 ff., 120 ff. (62, 157).
35. *Ibid.*
36. *Ibid.*
37. *Ibid.*
38. For the following, cf. *HW* 38, 41, 42, 43, 48, 59 (675, 678, 679, 680, 683, 691). Cf. here the introduction to the *Sonderausgabe* (Reklam) by H. G. Gadamer, pp. 102 ff.

workings of the artwork is a setting-into-work of truth, a process of opening in which a clearing is wrested out, an "open position" is "struck" among the beings that are ordinarily on hand, "an openness in which everything is extraordinary." This clearing or unconcealment transmutes being as a whole in a new and unprecedented way. It has indeed been torn from concealment, but the two modes of "denial" continue to permeate it in "countervailing" fashion. The clearing that was wrested out continues to be "permeated by refusal and disguise, i.e., by mystery and by sham and error." It remains a "concealment at once in itself," the "playing field of openness," a "field of strife." In order for the artwork to "be" an artwork and experienced as such, the original strife must "remain a strife." In this contentious way, the artwork as an occurrence of truth "is" a *poiēsis* in a radical sense. It is bound by neither the basic trait of "conditioned necessity" nor the selfsameness of *ousia* but by the "institution" of the new and the unprecedented. We might note here that Heidegger views not only the setting-itself-into-work of art as an occurrence of truth but also the "act of the statesman" and the "thinking of the thinker," [39] as well as other modes of behavior that we traditionally relegate to the realm of the "ethical." [40] The unconcealment achieved from time to time as well as what appears in these modes of behavior is also pervaded by mystery, error, appearance, and evil. The grave consequences of this conception will be considered in our concluding chapter.

The experience of *alētheia* in the first beginning as a relationship of unconcealment to concealment was, according to Heidegger, already "forgotten" in Plato. The essay *Plato's Doctrine of Truth* [41] shows how this conception of the first beginning is transformed into the sense of truth as "correspondence," *homoiōsis*. When Being is thought only as "appearance," as the "apparent foreground," as *idea*, then the correctness, the *orthotēs*, of the view of the idea and the self-correction and self-approximation of knowledge to the idea are alone decisive, and the correspondence of knowledge and thing becomes the sole criterion of truth. There is no need to go into this "violent interpretation" of Platonic philosophy here, but it may be recalled that Aristotle [42] acknowledged an *alētheia* of *ousia* along with *alētheia* in the sense of

39. HW 62 (696).
40. HB 114 (300).
41. PW 32, 34, 41, 42 (260, 261, 265, 266). Cf. P. Friedländer, *Platon*, pp. 223 ff. (221 ff.).
42. See above, p. 38.

homoiōsis. It strikes us as noteworthy that Aristotle conceived the *alētheia* of *ousia* explicitly without any relation to a "concealment." The *noēsis* experiences the *ousia* through simple "contact," *thigein*, free from any possibility of error and dissimulation. Aristotle's conception is thus governed by a "total intelligibility," a fundamental luminosity and disclosure. In any case, this concept of *alētheia* no longer retains a trace of those experiences which, according to Heidegger, dominated pre-Socratic thought in such a decisive way. It remains to be seen whether this throws Heidegger's conception into question. On the other hand, Hegel's *Logic* [43] is governed by a conception of the essence of truth as a relation to untruth, as a relation of "light" and "darkness." We recall this once again only because for Heidegger "the final vestige of the concealment of Being disappears" [44] in Hegel's thought.

43. See above, p. 57.
44. *SG* 114.

5 / *Logos*

THE RETHINKING OF THE WORD *logos* exhibits further basic traits that define the sense of presenting in the first beginning even more closely.

In *Being and Time* Heidegger [1] dealt, not with the early Greek, but with the Aristotelian meaning of *logos* and *legein*. There it was a matter of demonstrating "that the logic of *logos*" is rooted in the existential analytic of Dasein. He wanted to show that the Aristotelian definition of the essence of man as a *zōion logon echon* rests on an "original experience" which even Aristotle did not see. It is true that Aristotle [2] conceived of the *legein* of *logos* not as an extrinsic theory of judgment but phenomenologically, as a manifesting letting-be-seen. But he did not see that the *logos apophantikos*, because of its apophantic character as an *alētheuein*, a taking out of covertness, had its existential origin in the interpretation that understands circumspectively, in the *hermēneia*. This process of interpretation is further founded in the "articulation" which, co-originally with "disposition" and a prepredicative "understanding," constitutes the disclosure of the Being-in-the-world that discovers and projects. It might, however, be remarked that Heidegger's conception of *legein* as an unconcealing *alētheuein* at any rate seems to us to be irreconcilable with Aristotle's basic conception.

Heidegger obtained the basic traits of the *logos* of the first beginning primarily from interpretations of the fragments of

1. See above, p. 41.
2. See above, pp. 37 ff.

Heraclitus and Parmenides.[3] The *Introduction to Metaphysics* sought to make clear that the *legein* of *logos* already in Homer had, "in terms of what it means, no immediate relation to language." [4] *Legō, legein* originally meant "to lay one thing with another, to bring together into one, in short, to gather." [5] Many years later, the essay "Logos" [6] developed the sense of *logos* more precisely as a basic trait which together with the basic traits of *eon, physis,* and *alētheia* constitutes the whole of the occurrence of Being, the entire sense of the presenting process. We shall briefly present the "results" of the interpretations of Heraclitus' Fragment 50 as further "categories" of Being in the first beginning, and again the way in which the essence of man belongs to them will for the time being be left out of consideration.[7]

Presenting occurs as *logos* in the form of a "laying." The laying lays "down" in unconcealment, and at the same time it is a laying "out" and a laying "forth" in it. Laying is a "bringing to lie," a "letting lie forth of the forelying (*hypokeimenon*)." It is in this way that a being as something present is "laid down" or deposited in the presenting process, "enveloped" [*geborgen*] in unconcealment and "developed" [*entborgen*] out of concealment. The occurrence of presence as *logos* has thus brought the seas, mountains, plants, animals, men to lie, has made them into the forelying, has laid them forth out of concealment into unconcealment and laid them down in it, developed out of concealment. The "developing-enveloping" occurrence of *logos* is not a human occurrence. Man has brought only a tiny part of the forelying into this "lay of the land," and even this minute contribution is present only with the help of what already lies before him.

The occurrence of presence as *logos* also rules by gathering all that strives apart and asunder out of dispersion and into the "One" (*hen*), into the "joint" of presence.[8] The *eon* as *hen* is essentially a *xynon*, "that which in itself assembles all things and holds them together." [9] In this sense, the occurrence of *logos* as laying is always also a "collecting" that brings together by selec-

3. Namely, Heraclitus' Fragments B1, 2, 7, 16, 30, 43, 50, 52, 53, 64, 67, 72, 73, 77, 123, 124, and Parmenides' Fragments 6(1), B5, 8(34–41). On the nonphilosophical sources cf. H. Böder, "Der frühgriechische Wortgebrauch von Logos und Aletheia," *Archiv für Begriffsgeschichte* (Bonn), Vol. IV.
4. *EM* 95 (124).
5. *Ibid.*
6. *VA* 207 ff.
7. *VA* 209 ff.
8. *VA* 221.
9. *EM* 100 (131).

tion and election. It is the ruling of an "assembly," it is a "gathering" or "collectivity." [10] Because of the gathering, assembling, and cohesive power of *logos*, things that pull apart and asunder, like life and death, are gathered in such a way that the "Being of life is always at the same time death." [11] Because of this basic trait of "logi-cal" unification in the occurrence of presence, whatever "absents itself from another and so against another, like day and night, winter and summer, peace and war, waking and sleeping, Dionysus and Hades," [12] is laid forth in a *single* "issue."

Does Heidegger with this conception of the sense of the early Greek *logos* return to the traditional sense whereby *logos* first of all meant "order"? Aristotle viewed the order of the necessary connections from *legein*, and, at the end of the tradition, Hegel described the *"Logic"* as the order of the "system" of the thought movement of subjectivity "ordering itself to itself." But, according to Heidegger, the early Greek *logos* of Being is neither the order of necessary connections nor a movement of thought determinations leading in a dialectical way from "contradiction" to synthesis through a circular movement. On the contrary, presence must be kept in contention as a "conflict," a "primeval strife," if it is not to lose its creative power, if it is to remain an occurrence in the original sense. It is in this sense that Heidegger interprets Heraclitus' Fragment 53, declaring that *logos* and *polemos* are the same.[13] *Logos* itself assembles only to the extent that this happens as a "setting-apart," [14] a strife, in which what is in conflict is never dialectically reconciled, in which, instead, "the one always drives the other to the self-assertion of its essence" [15] through strife. The assemblage is therefore a strife that knows no "rest" of the kind commonly associated with the sense of order. The "rest" of this assemblage is rather, strictly speaking, an "intense mobility." [16] It is in this way that the presence remains "creative"; it is not permitted to come to a "gathering" in which an "orderly" rest holds sway. The strife must be kept "in contention." In such a presenting process, there is a genuine *polis* only as long as the strife "over rank, standing, and position" prevails.[17] Wherever this battle comes to a standstill, "world turns

10. VA 209; EM 95 ff. (124).
11. EM 100 (131).
12. VA 221.
13. EM 47 (62).
14. Ibid.
15. HW 38 (666).
16. Ibid.; SG 143–44; WD 144 (237).
17. EM 100 (131).

away, Being retreats from being."[18] And an artwork has "unity" only by virtue of a gathering that keeps the polemically emerging world and the self-enclosed earth in contention.[19]

It is only because *logos* is such a gathering, which does not relate the occurrence back to a predetermined order, that the advent of the new and unprecedented is consistent with this basic trait. "New" in this sense are the political institutions and the "world" and its "works" in the first beginning. Is Heidegger now of the opinion that in the first beginning not only the works that originated in this "world," the works of language, art, and political institutions, but also "being" pure and simple has come forth "creatively" and was "creatively" "preserved"?[20] He writes that "being" becomes the merely finished, available to anyone, on hand, as soon as the sense of Being in the first beginning has retreated from it and its world has turned away. It may be asked whether for Heidegger the things in daily use at the time of the first beginning were determined just like the artworks from the creative basic traits of Being and from the wholeness of the world considered creatively. This extremely important question will later be dealt with in more depth. It concerns the limits of the prevalence of the "creative" sense of Being.[21]

Our interpretation, that Heidegger views the sense of Being primarily in its creative character, has been corroborated by his recent view of the sense of *logos* in a "groundless grounding." The nonhuman occurrence of presence lays "ground and foundation,"[22] gives measures, but has no ground of its own. It is the silent ruling that grounds of its own accord and not for the sake of the man who seeks grounds and principles. It is in this sense that Heidegger understands *logos* as a "play."[23] This character in the first beginning of presence as a play above all constitutes for Heidegger the "to be thought" that is to guide and determine the forethinking of the sense of Being of the other beginning.

This basic trait of *logos* as a groundless play was already forgotten by Plato and Aristotle. Because of this forgetting of Being, the "ground" was no longer conceived as a "groundless" grounding but as a "groundable" and "grounding" ground. The groundable ground is on the one hand considered as "the first from

18. *EM* 47, 48 (62, 63).
19. *HW* 38 (675).
20. *EM* 48 (63).
21. See below, p. 202.
22. *SG* 179.
23. *SG* 188.

whence," *to prōton hothen,* as *archē,*[24] as primal thing (*Ur-sache*) and *causa prima,*[25] and on the other as a way of being responsible for, being the cause of, contained in the meaning of *aition.*[26] These two modes of the groundable ground designate "the most general" of what is "everywhere and indifferently equi-valent" and common to every being as such.[27] The science studying this most general matter was "ontology," which according to Aristotle investigated the "principles and first grounds." [28] The grounding ground was also thought to be the highest being or God, who grounds the whole, the unity of the totality, whose essence was explored by "theology." Ontology and theology have their common source in the basic trait of *logos* in the first beginning, which as ground assembles and unifies in this twofold way of most general ground and highest ground. The "onto-theo-logical constitution of metaphysics" [29] is also rooted in this source. A more adequate demonstration that the "essence" of metaphysics goes back to this source can be made from the "ruling of the difference of Being from being." [30] "Being" in its metaphysical stamping of general ground goes "over" to that which—enabled by such a going-over—emerges as a grounded being. And yet, this grounded being in its part as highest being, as *causa sui* (God), grounds that general Being. This "ruling of the difference" is also ultimately grounded in the groundless play of *logos* in the first beginning.

The book *The Principle of Ground* [31] shows in another way how ground for a being with reason becomes *ratio,* where reason is likewise called *ratio.* Today our action and will in the form of *ratio* are determined by a grounding and founding that yields *rationes* to a knowing, willing, calculating, rational ego. With this double meaning of *ratio,* a "total rationalization" prevails throughout the history of Being.

In opposition to this version of the "history of Being" of ground, it might be recalled [32] that the Aristotelian *ousia* is also a ground in the sense of a ground of Being, an *aition tou einai.* Then, however, it does not take effect simply as something "most

24. *SG* 182.
25. *ID* 57 (60).
26. *SG* 182.
27. *ID* 55 (58).
28. *ID* 56 (59).
29. *ID* 35 (42).
30. *ID* 64, 65, 67 ff. (66, 67, 69).
31. *SG* 175 ff.
32. See above, p. 19.

general" but as a *physis* which causes a house to *be* a house and not a pile of bricks. Aristotle here also explicitly emphasized that this ground cannot be grounded by the usual questions and teachings. True, this *physis* is not "contacted" [33] by the *noēsis* as a "groundless" ground but as an "absolute" ground. One cannot therefore restrict oneself to the determinations of "ontology" that Aristotle gave in the first section of the third book of the *Metaphysics*. Of course, the *epistēmē* of the *syllogismos* conceives of a ground in the sense of the "everywhere and indifferently univocal" and the most general, a ground that refers to the "attributes of an essentially coincident character." "Science" grounds the "middle" in a general (*katholou*) and necessary (*anankēi*) way.

The "ground" in Hegel [34] as well, which as "resolved contradiction" is a stage of the process upon which the essence is constituted, would hardly pass as an actually groundable ground or as a *ratio* "re-presenting" itself to the rational ego, according to Heidegger's interpretation of the history of Being. Hegel expressly did away with the inquiry into the "grounds of things" as a standpoint of "reflection" [35] and showed why ground is to be viewed only as a "stage of self-determining thought."

Even though Heidegger holds the view that *logos* in the first beginning had nothing to do with speech and language but meant the nonhuman presence of a laying collection, he nevertheless declares that there was also an "essential intertwining" [36] between Being and language already in the first beginning. On the basis of the experiences that lay at the basis of the *Antigone* chorus of Sophocles, Heraclitus' fragments, and Parmenides' didactic poem, *Introduction to Metaphysics* tries to rethink the sense of *logos* in the first beginning insofar as it meant language. The basic traits elaborated here become for him what is "to be thought," which was then forethought in the *Commentaries on Hölderlin's Poetry* and lately in the lectures of *On the Way to Language*.

It was self-evident for Heidegger that the early Greeks "dwelt" in language. But it was the rethinking that first elaborated the "essence" of language by determining this essence out of the basic traits in the first beginning. Language as *logos* is an assemblage that lays forth and lays down. As *physis*, it is an

33. See above, p. 39.
34. See above, p. 62.
35. *Enz.* § 121 and addendum to § 121.
36. *EM* 41 (53).

"overpowering power" that "pervades" the essence of man. Man "administers" the *"physis*-like" language but does not have it at his disposal.[37] Language is above all *alētheia*, rethought out of the first beginning. It is the occurrence of truth through which Being is "opened." It is through language that that "irruption into Being" [38] occurs through which it is harnessed into works, which in creative fashion impart sense and meaning to being as a whole and to beings individually. Language is the "primeval poetry," [39] in which "Being becomes word." [40] In the original saying of language, the Being of being is opened "in the articulation of its gatheredness" and becomes "world." [41] The "powers" of language,[42] which hold sway as "understanding, forming, and building," make meaningful disclosures and bring everything into meaningful relations.

Forethinking will further "transmute" this "to-be-thought" essence of language into a significant moment of the sense of Being of the other beginning. But before we actually turn to the description of this sense of Being of the other beginning, we must examine Heidegger's conception of the development of metaphysics as a history of Being. The most important stages of this development have already been pointed out in the course of the preceding presentation of the basic traits. We can therefore restrict ourselves to the elaboration of the peculiar structure of the history of Being. However, the last form of the history of Being will be examined in some detail. This is the currently prevailing "essence of technology," the "terminal configuration" of metaphysics which at the same time seems at least to announce the new form aimed at by Heidegger, since it has occasioned his forethinking of a sense of Being of the other beginning.

37. *EM* 119 ff. (154 ff.).
38. *EM* 131 (172).
39. *Ibid.*
40. *Ibid.*
41. *Ibid.*
42. *EM* 120 (157).

PART IV

The History of Being
and the "Turn"

1 / The Structure of the History of Being

THOUGH ARISTOTLE HAD RECOGNIZED change *in* the essence, the basic traits of selfsameness and eternalness ruled out, even in the case of the so-called "coming into Being of the essence," an actual change *of* the essence. Being and essence in Aristotle are not "historical" but "absolute." And likewise in Hegel, because of the basic trait of the selfsameness of Being *qua* thought, there is no "new" reality but only a development of the "old" reality. Even though there is a "process" of Being in Hegel's *Logic*, this process proceeds circularly within itself. It is absolute insofar as it is "absolved" from the historical development underlying the "power" of "torrential time." The present "need of philosophy" lies, we repeat, in thinking a change of Being and essence in such a way that the advent of the "new" becomes possible, but without thereby relativizing or historicizing Being and essence. Being and essence must surely be thought "historically," but in such a way that any given change would not depend upon the power of man, even though a certain role in the occurrence seems to be due to man.

If we now ask to what extent Heidegger has responded to the current need of philosophy, then we must first of all recall [1] that already in *Being and Time* he understood the "Being and essence" of man, the Being of Dasein, "historically." The modes of the Being of man which were developed there in opposition to the substance and subject models permitted him to think of a change of the essence of man. For underlying the "how" of the execution of Dasein is not something that remains exactly the

1. See above, p. 104.

same with itself and that presents itself again and again as exactly the same and, in this sense, an Aristotelian ousiological "eternal" self. Instead, the Dasein is an occurrence that
"stretches" itself. Later this "substancelessness" of Dasein and
its historicity are further radicalized by conceiving Dasein as *ek-
sistence*, as a standing-outside-itself into the meaning of Being
as it presents itself and changes itself.

Being and Time [2] also considered the "Being and essence" of
the handy beings within the world as "changeable in themselves." The world in which beings are encountered has the
"mode of Being of historicity." But since the worldliness of the
world there represented an "ontological determination of Dasein," [3] this problem was decided, not by reference to the historicity of the world, but in terms of the historicity and insubstan-
tiality of Dasein.

The later writings did not expressly ask whether the sense of
Being in the first beginning and the world that came forth in it
were changeable in themselves and in this sense "historical."
Presumably this did not appear necessary, since "presence" in
the first beginning and its world were defined as a "creative" occurrence in such a way that they are actually *only* "change." One
might even say that here change itself has been posited "absolutely." For presenting "whiles" only in an "abrupt" way and
gathers itself only in a restless and contentious way, so that
there is no ousiological "selfsameness."

The question of whether Being thought in the first beginning
is "historical," i.e., changes itself in itself, is, however, expressly
asked with regard to the two millennia of the history of thought
that followed the first beginning. For Heidegger, the determining
factor in the history of Being is that the sense of Being of the
first beginning, its basic traits, did not "commission" themselves
to experience and to thought but instead "withdrew" or completely "concealed" themselves. The sense of Being in the first
beginning was a "mission" [4] insofar as it was "commissioned" to
the "experiences" of the early Greeks, although not to their
thought. It was also a mission insofar as it "withdrew" itself
from the thought of metaphysics, i.e., held to itself with its
"truth," its "draws" (traits). [5] This withdrawal, the *epochē* of the
creative basic traits of the Being of the first beginning, came

2. See above, p. 104.
3. SZ 52 ff.
4. On the meaning of "mission" cf. esp. SG 108 ff.
5. HW 311; WD 144 (236).

about in such a complete way that the "epochs" of metaphysics became "epochs of erring," [6] whereby its basic traits were completely concealed and thus "forgotten" by thought. This concealment became a "mission" as early as Aristotle, since his thought saw Being only in terms of its constitution of being and, in line with the "Meta-physical" drift of his inquiry, viewed Being merely as "transcendence," as surmounting. This "Being" in its various stampings is also a "mission" or a "history" because every epoch represents a change in relation to the preceding epoch and because any mission dominant at any particular time must again be transmuted into another oncoming mission.

Heidegger also calls the sense of Being in the first beginning "the granting." For it grants the individual "epochs of erring," and it grants his own thinking the possibility of explicating the creative sense of the first beginning through rethinking and, what is more, of forethinking what is to be thought of the sense of Being in the first beginning by transmuting it into a sense of Being of another beginning.

It is important for our earlier question, whether Heidegger has thought out a "change" of Being and essence, to work out the structure of this "history" of Being. Again and again, Heidegger has asked to what extent "something pervasive . . . goes through the mission of Being from its inception to its consummation." [7] The history of Being has an inception and a consummation. The full continuity from inception to consummation is called the "eschatology of Being." He thus writes: "Being itself as commissioning is in itself eschatological." [8]

We find the following remarks on this conception of an eschatology of Being in the essay "Anaximander's Aphorism": [9]

> The early age that determines Anaximander's aphorism belongs to the morning, the early hour of the early epoch of the Evening-land. But how, when the early overtook everything late, when the earliest would overtake the latest the farthest? The "once" of the early hour of the mission would then have come as the "once" to the very last (*eschaton*), i.e., to the parting of the hitherto hidden mission of Being. The Being of being gathers itself (*legesthai, logos*) in the last of its mission. The former essence of Being descends into its still hidden truth. The history of Being gathers itself in this parting. The gathering in this parting as the

6. *HW* 311.
7. *ID* 66 (67).
8. *HW* 302.
9. *HW* 301 ff.

gathering (*logos*) of the uttermost (*eschaton*) of its former essence is the eschatology of Being.[10]

This "eschatology" cannot be understood in the traditional sense of this word. For the traditional *eschaton* is an expression of the movement of *ousia* considered as *telos*.[11] Here, the end is already situated in the beginning and must yet be explicated to itself, so that this self-explication has a circular structure. Hegel's process of thought is eschatological in this traditional sense, for it is a return to itself in which the beginning is already prestructured by the end but must still develop itself toward it and in this sense "perfect" or "consummate" itself. The movement of returning to itself, dialectically forming a circle, comes to an end that winds back to its beginning.

It is therefore inconceivable for Heidegger to understand the eschatology of Being in this traditional sense, since he now considers the model for this eschatology, substance, to be "overcome." But the decisive difference from the traditional conception lies in his assumption that the "incipience" of the beginning, the institution of Being, the opening of Being, was the high point in time, the "great time"—and by no means "primitive times" [12] —which determined all subsequent development. This development, however, is not a teleological development that leads to a "fulfillment," to an adequate explication, in this sense to a "full-ending" (*Voll-endung*) or consummation of the pregiven end, but instead it is an "emptying-ending" (*Ver-endung*), a de-mise. The great beginning of the Western experience of Being comes to its "last" as a parting, which means downfall. The "very last" of the great essence of the early days is the downfall, in which not only the basic traits of Being of the first beginning are "veiled" in *their* truth but even the overtness of being is disguised.

Just as this eschatology of Being is not a movement that circles within itself and completes itself, so it does not manifest a selfsameness in the traditional ousiological sense. But Heidegger could not have spoken of an eschatology if he saw nothing in this general development which is "pervasive" [13] and "selfsame." [14] This "selfsame" that pervades the mission of Being, so

10. HW 301.
11. See above, pp. 22, 32.
12. EM 12 (14–15).
13. Cf. ID 66 (67).
14. SG 110; WP 28 (61).

that there is a continuity between an inception and a consummation, is, however, not Hegel's timeless and thus history-free thought movement of the "good infinity" but the onto-theo-logical way [15] in which "Being" in its various stampings has "commissioned" itself throughout the epochs of metaphysics to experience and to thought. But since this onto-theo-logical way of metaphysics for its part rests on the basic traits of Being in the first beginning, one must go further and affirm that it is this Being of the first beginning which in a definite "kind" of selfsameness founds the "continuity" of beginning with end.

Accordingly, a "kind" of selfsameness of Being in the first beginning would have to lie at the basis of the structure of the history of Being. Heidegger himself has thus far not dealt with this basic trait of Being in the first beginning. But he has observed that "the beginning contains the end in a still hidden way" [16] and that "with the parting, the former essence of 'Being' descends into *its* still hidden truth." [17] And in the essay *The Principle of Identity* he has even expressly declared that only metaphysics considered selfsameness as a "basic trait in Being." [18] The "kind" of selfsameness we have pointed to here is of course not a matter of an ousiological selfsameness. Manifestly, the Being of the first beginning is not a referential ousiological "underlying" that persists as "exactly the same." On the contrary, the creative sense of the first beginning conceals itself more and more and finally descends into the terminal configuration of the history of Being. And it is not a matter of Hegel's selfsameness of a movement of pure thought, for the "selfsame" of the first beginning leads in its terminal stage to the "collapse of the world and the devastation of the earth."

Even though Heidegger has not discussed it, it is only by presupposing this "kind" of selfsameness of the Being of the first beginning that it is possible to acknowledge that Heidegger succeeded in thinking a "change in Being" which is not historicistic or relativistic. The sense of Being in the first beginning as well as the subsequent metaphysical stampings of "Being" governs irrevocably, and that which as a result of them appears as "being" or as "real" is in no way subject to human influences. And since any particular governing sense of what is to be considered "real" determines all the other sense formations of an epoch, we

15. *ID* 56 ff. (59 ff.).
16. *HW* 63 (697).
17. *HW* 301.
18. Cf. *ID* 19 and 31 ff. (28, 39 ff.).

can speak of a permeating, universal, and in this sense "absolute" efficacy of this sense of Being. Heidegger's conception of a "change in Being," of a change of the Being of the first beginning in its "history," makes it possible to take into account the advent of any "new" sense of Being or mission of Being that may arise.[19] Allowance is made for the fact that at times another sense of Being governed, e.g., in the Middle Ages or the eighteenth century. Our "historical consciousness" has been given its due, and we need no longer accept the view that accords with the sense of the basic trait of the eternity of the Aristotelian *ousia,* which seems so unreasonable to us today, namely, that exactly the same occurs, endures, and continues to recur again and again throughout the ages.[20]

In the "kind" of selfsameness underlying this "change in Being" there also seems to be a "kind" of necessity. Heidegger has stressed that the history of Being does not have the necessity of Hegel's dialectical process.[21] It is not the "process of reality" that as "process of necessity" simply explicates the "new reality" already contained in the "old reality." What governs here is not the "constraint," determined by this necessity or ousiologically from the *telos,* of the series of steps that bring consummation.[22] But Heidegger has nonetheless conceived of the history of Being as bringing itself about in a definite series of steps. It begins with the "falling-away" of the early Greek sense of Being in Plato and Aristotle and goes across the Scholastics to Descartes, Kant, Hegel, and finally to Nietzsche. The different stampings of Being still follow one another in a certain line of "constraint," a "kind" of necessity that Heidegger has not dealt with thus far. This necessity it not only a structural element of the history of Being, but it must also be viewed as a basic trait of the Being of the first beginning, inasmuch as the series of sense determinations of this history are ultimately founded in it, even if in the mode of withdrawal.

But if such a necessity governs this over-all continuity, then it must also be clearly shown that and how each of these historical stages belongs in this continuity. If, for example, Heidegger's determination of Hegel's philosophy as "the beginning of the

19. Cf. here Max Müller in *Existenzphilosophie im geistigen Leben der Gegenwart,* pp. 38 ff. and 53 ff.
20. See above, pp. 30 ff.
21. Cf. *ID* 66 (67); *WP* 29 (63).
22. See above, pp. 32 ff.

consummation of metaphysics" should turn out to be unconvincing,[23] the over-all continuity would then have become questionable, inasmuch as its governing necessity would thereby have been interrupted.

With regard to the structure of the history of Being, it may also be asked what "kind" of necessity actually guided Heidegger in his particular selection of the philosophers that he discusses. Would another conception of the development of the history of Being have resulted if Heidegger had also acknowledged Plotinus, Spinoza, and the later Schelling among its "stages"? And since it is still a question of the "dominion of metaphysics," especially with regard to the effect that a "stamping of Being" has on the concrete historical manifestations and institutions of a people, why has he not discussed Locke, for example, who has had such an immediate impact on the culture, politics, and self-understanding of the American people? And since Heidegger's historical interpretations are largely directed toward a definite and preselected portion of the total work of a "metaphysical" thinker,[24] one may also ask about the "kind" of necessity that governs this selection of texts at any particular time.

Let us say in conclusion that all the determinations of sense of the history of Being have ensued either under the guidance of the antisubstantial "idea of Being in general" or in the light of the "creative" basic traits of the Being of the first beginning or of the already forethought Being of the other beginning.[25] They all therefore manifest the degree to which they in various ways are based upon the withdrawal of this "idea of Being" or of the "creative" basic traits and thus upon the "dominion of the oblivion of Being." Herein lies what is common to all of them, what constitutes the "essence" of metaphysics. This essence of metaphysics as well as the essence of each of its "stampings" is therefore of an entirely *other* sort in comparison with the "Being" and "essence" that concerned the tradition, insofar as it was mainly "ontological." The difference lies especially in Heidegger's concern for the determination of the "sense" of this metaphysically conceived "Being" and "essence." A further decisive distinction,

23. See above, p. 44.
24. An example of this is Heidegger's selection of the "introduction" to the *Phenomenology of Spirit* instead of the *Science of Logic;* see above, p. 137.
25. An example of the first case is *KM* 185 ff. (211 ff.), for the second and third case is the determination of the "essence" of technology; see below, pp. 173 ff.

as we saw, is that this "sense" or this "essence" of "Being" and "essence" is not determined on the basis of the constitution of being and from it as a vantage point.

We have referred throughout this book to Heidegger's determinations of the sense of Being in Plato, Aristotle, Descartes, and Hegel. We have very briefly touched upon his detailed interpretation of Kant in the treatise *Kant and the Problem of Metaphysics*.[26] Heidegger has now promised an extensive publication on Nietzsche.[27] What he has already published [28] indicates that he views Nietzsche as the "last thinker of the West," [29] who brings to fulfillment the consummation of metaphysics—a stage that began with Hegel.[30] Here, where the only issue is the structure of the history of Being, it might be mentioned wherein Heidegger exactly situates the fulfillment of the consummation of metaphysics. What is consummated is the Cartesian self-knowing representation and the "rational will" of Kant, Schelling, and Hegel. From the principle of knowledge, the rational will now knowingly posits "values" and thereby determines itself to the "will to power." [31] The essence of the will to power lies in its being directed not toward possession but only toward itself, so that it is accordingly a "will to will." [32] The will to will is the determination of "Being," unthought by Nietzsche himself, that consummates the eschatology of the history of Being. It is its "last step." [33] The creative basic traits of the Being of the first beginning become more and more withdrawn from the historical development of metaphysics. Hence the consummation of metaphysics fulfills itself with Nietzsche, because in his thought these creative basic traits of the Being of the first beginning are completely "buried." Now, fully and completely, "there is nothing doing with Being." [34] The "nihilism" that lies in this accelerating withdrawal of the creative sense of Being comes to consumma-

26. See above, pp. 98 ff.
27. Cf. here K. Löwith, *Heidegger*, pp. 72 ff., and *Nietzsches Philosophie der ewigen Wiederkehr*, pp. 222 ff.; cf. the Appendix, below, p. 257, on Heidegger's *Nietzsche I* and *II*, which appeared since this was written.
28. "Nietzsches Wort 'Gott ist tot,' " *HW* 193 ff.; *WD* 1 ff., 62 ff. (1 ff., 55 ff.); "Wer ist Nietzsches Zarathustra?" in *VA* 101 ff. and *VA* 81 ff. This particular essay has been translated by Bernd Magnus in *Review of Metaphysics*, XX (1967), 411–31.
29. *WD* 61 (46).
30. *HW* 344.
31. *HW* 214.
32. *HW* 217.
33. *HW* 229.
34. *HW* 243, 244; *SF* 34 (87).

tion when "Being" shows itself as "will to will" in this withdrawal. This historical "extremity of the consummation" henceforth leaves its stamp on the "world" and the "earth." The "long-lasting" time of the "de-mise" of metaphysics has begun, in which the "world is brought to collapse, and the earth becomes a waste-land, and man is forced into sheer labor." [35] Nature is now ob-jectified under the domination of the will to will, "culture" is cultivated, politics is "made to order," [36] and man becomes "home-less." The way in which terminating metaphysics rules today has been specified more precisely by Heidegger as the "essence" of technology. This essence of technology is characterized in more detail in the following chapter, not only because it is for Heideg-ger the most extreme form of the Being of the first beginning, but also because it at the same time represents for him the beginning of the dominion of a Being of another beginning.

35. *VA* 73 ff., 84 ff.
36. *VA* 73.

2 / The Essence of Technology and the "Turn"

IN ACCORDANCE WITH THE ESCHATOLOGICAL structure of the history of Being which has just been set forth, the initial inception of Being is consummating itself in a final configuration. It terminates in the essence of technology that prevails today. The *essence* of this essence may now be examined in its own right, because Heidegger has declared that it is technology "which demands from us that we think of what we normally understand by essence in another sense," [1] and because it is this essence of technology that leads over into another inception of the sense of Being. For Heidegger, it at once represents the "greatest peril" and the promise of a "deliverance." This deliverance lies specifically in the fact that what he has called the "turn" occurs within the dominion of the essence of technology.

Two directions must be distinguished with respect to this turn.[2] Heidegger has spoken of a turn which leads to an "overcoming of the oblivion of Being" and of the metaphysics and nihilism that this includes.[3] This turn from the oblivion of Being for him is due to his own thought—to use his terms—being "granted" the possibility of explicating the initially incipient sense of Being in its basic traits as well as the history of Being based upon this sense. Moreover, there seems to be another turn for Heidegger which goes in the direction of another inception

1. *VA* 38.
2. On the question of the meaning of the "turn" cf. esp. Walter Schulz, "Über den philosophiegeschichtlichen Ort Martin Heideggers," *Philosophische Rundschau*, I (1953–54), 85 ff., and K. Löwith, *Heidegger*, pp. 18 ff.
3. *VA* 71 ff.

of the mission of Being.[4] It is because Heidegger views the history of Being as a "commissioning" or "mission" that it can actually be transmuted into another mission. The turn into another *inception* of mission begins when thinking is capable of experiencing the "withdrawal" of the creative basic "draws" (traits). But this is possible only when the essence of that which today "is" *can be thought* as a "terminal configuration" of the initially incipient creative sense of Being. For then this terminal configuration of the first beginning at the same time emerges as a "withdrawal configuration" of another beginning of the creative sense of Being. Once this withdrawal configuration has been experienced and thought, then the basic traits of the other beginning of Being are "commissioned" to thinking and "the deliverance" takes place. It is in this way that we interpret Heidegger's cryptic suggestions. Since they are particularly important for our specific purposes, we shall support our interpretation further by considerations which will show how Heidegger, in the essay "The Question of Technology," conceived the essence of technology as both the terminal configuration of the first beginning and the withdrawal configuration of the other beginning.

The "essence" of technology is a mission "granted incipiently out of the dawn [of the West]."[5] Although Heidegger does not expressly say so, this determination suggests that this essence is to be explicated from the creative basic traits of the first beginning, i.e., from *physis, alētheia,* and *logos.* This must come about in such a way that the creative experiences of the first beginning that lay at the basis of these basic words come to the fore as terminating. The project of the essence of technology must therefore show to what extent this essence is no longer presence as *physis* (in the broad sense), no longer a *poiēsis,* the creative occurrence of a self-emergent prevailing, an opening, appearing, bringing-forth, and setting-up in interplay with the creatively violent ways of man. The "essence" of technology must furthermore show that it is not presence as concealing-clearing, the occurrence of *alētheia* in which something new and unprecedented comes forth in a way that is pervaded by mystery. And finally it must make explicit that the currently prevailing "essence" does not sustain the initially incipient basic trait of *logos* and accordingly does not rule in the mode of a "strife-torn"

4. VA 99. The designations "terminal configuration" and "withdrawal configuration" are mine.
5. VA 39.

gathering, of a creative laying-forth and laying-down of works and as the forming of a world.

The glance back to the *poiēsis* of *physis* brings to the fore in what way the essence of technology "stems" from this *poiēsis*.[6] While the Being and *technē* of the first beginning occurred as a creative pro-duction and in this sense, like the "setting-up" of a statue on the temple grounds,[7] display a creative interplay of Being and the human being, this reciprocating production of the currently prevailing essence of technology is a noncreative "positing."[8] The positing takes place because the human being is for his part "posited" by the prevailing "Being" to expose the "real" as something which "has been disposed of." And items which have been disposed of have the mode of Being of uncreative "stock."[9] The creative presenting of the first beginning, the *physis* in its *poiēsis* in its interplay with the creative man, prevails by terminating in this reciprocally provocative positing. The uncreative "Being" summons man "out," i.e., challenges or "provokes" him, to "labor" in uncreative ways, whereby the real comes forth merely as something "posited for disposition." If the current governing essence is regarded as a demise of the creative presentation, in this sense as a "terminal configuration," it has then made its appearance as uttermost "peril,"[10] which now in turn is to be experienced and thought. The peril can be experienced as the denial, the withdrawal of creative presentation. And it is precisely in this that the thinking which follows the "draw of this withdrawal" can begin to forethink the basic "draws" of another and "saving" sense of Being.

If the "essencing"[11] element of technology is considered in retrospect to the initially incipient *alētheia*, then the "unconcealment"[12] that now prevails shows itself as an openness which unveils the current prevailing sense of the Being of being as disposable stock. Corresponding to it are the "things" that come forth without any "true" Being. They are in this pregnant sense "without truth" and "annihilated" long before the "atom bomb" can do it. The currently prevailing openness and whatever appears in it as real are not permeated by the "mystery." Thus the real for modern science is "detectable and surveyable in its sequences,"

6. *VA* 28.
7. *Ibid.*
8. *VA* 22.
9. *VA* 24 ff.
10. *VA* 34.
11. *VA* 39.
12. *VA* 26.

"securely posited in its objectivity," by adapting it to the relevant objective context of the particular theory.[13] If the unconcealment now prevailing is experienced and thought as the terminating mode of the clearing and concealing *alētheia* of the first beginning, then the withdrawal of this mystery is acutely felt, a mystery which Heidegger has described as the "unapparent state of affairs." [14] But here is where we find the indications of the "saving" factor, of a new and coming mission of the "truth of Being."

If the "essencing" of technology is thought in retrospect to the creative *logos* of the first beginning, then it manifests itself as an uncreative "setting-forth and setting-down," as an uncreative gathering [15] which no longer "gives" a world and its works. Heidegger has named this currently governing gathering the "com-posite" [*Ge-stell*],* in order to express the existence and mode in which the essence of technology reigns as a reciprocally provocative positing which organizes itself in various ways. The insight into the reciprocity of this positing in the terminating configuration of the Being of the first beginning elucidates the "peril" and the "saving" character of the essencing of technology. The danger lies in the exhaustion of man's essence in obeying the provocation of the com-positing in a restless and never ending fashion and in becoming "fixated" as a "laborer," [16] so that his creative modes of life completely atrophy. But the saving factor is that man through this reciprocity experiences himself playing a significant role within the occurrence of presence, so that he has a "share in unconcealing," [17] and it is incumbent upon him "to guard the unconcealment and with it the prior concealment of every essence on this earth." [18] But the main reason why Heidegger views the essencing element of technology as the promise of a "deliverance" is precisely because it has, with this insight into this special "relationship" of Being and man,[19] "commissioned" the basic traits of another origination of the creative sense of Being to his thinking, because it has in this sense already turned out to be the "mission" of a "turn" into another

* *Gestell* ordinarily means "frame" (e.g., of furniture), but here, as hyphenated, it is made to serve as the name for the style, the way, the *logos*, the essence of technology, particularly the provocative positing that occurs between man and Being. Hence "com-posite."

13. VA 56 ff.
14. VA 59 ff.
15. VA 27 ff.
16. VA 28 ff.
17. VA 40.
18. *Ibid.*
19. Cf. *ID* 29, 31 (36, 38).

origination of Being. Thinking has by the "empowering possibility" already been enabled to forethink the basic traits of the "essencing world," of the "relation of world and thing," which will be discussed in the following chapters. This enabling possibility is now, according to Heidegger's explicit declaration, "that which incipiently continues out of the dawn," [20] hence the initially incipient Being. Although it prevails as the essencing element of technology, as com-posite in the stage of termination and acutest withdrawal, this Being with reference to Heidegger's thinking no longer holds its basic traits "to itself" but rather unveils itself "in its truth."

After the early works, Heidegger [21] no longer defined thinking and its thought on the basis of the particular structures of Dasein's temporality and historicity but as "appropriated" by "the wanting and empowering possibility," by Being. It is from this that his rethinking and forethinking now legitimate themselves. The historically enabling possibility which enables his historical thinking is the initially originative sense of Being that the early Greeks experienced and "preserved" as *physis, alētheia,* and *logos.* But how could this sense of Being enable the turn of thinking and what it thinks in the direction of specific basic traits that are clearly *of another beginning?* Since the essence of technology was projected in the light of the basic traits of the first beginning as their terminal and withdrawal configuration, we should expect that the experience of the withdrawal of these creative basic traits of the first beginning which was thus made possible would draw thinking back to *these* traits. But according to Heidegger, the experience of the withdrawal of the *initially incipient* basic traits draws thinking in the direction of basic traits that definitely *belong to another inception.* Or, to put it another way, the initially incipient sense of Being "grants"—by way of the terminating configuration of this sense of Being—the basic traits of the other beginning as well.

This account would be immediately evident without further consideration if the initially incipient sense of Being had persisted in somewhat Aristotelian fashion "beyond all coming to be and passing away" through the entire two thousand years, or if it stood, as in Hegel, in the relationship of the "one and *its* other" to the other incipient sense of Being. But, for Heidegger, incipient Being simply has no ousiological basic traits at all, and sameness of Being is to be found only in the metaphysically rep-

20. VA 39.
21. See above, p. 111.

resented formulations of Being.[22] Besides, neither rethinking nor forethinking go back to the "past" of two thousand years. Rethinking [23] goes to the "having been" that still goes on, and in such a way that what is hitherto unthought of this "having been" is forthcoming as the "not yet explicated." The "kind" of self-sameness that prevails between the unthought "having been" (the experiences of Being of the early Greeks) and what is to be explicated (the initially incipient basic traits) has not been clarified by Heidegger. In fact, he explicitly views the movement of rethinking as a "mystery." [24] And evidently forethinking would retain this character of "mystery." For he also has not clarified the "kind" of selfsameness which would here have to unite the initially incipient and the other incipient sense of Being if forethinking is to be drawn into the "turn" of specific basic traits that definitely belong to another inception. Now forethinking also goes back to the initially incipient sense of Being insofar as rethinking has provided "what is to be thought," but this expressly occurs only in order to *transmute* it.[25] And rethinking for Heidegger is not only an adoption but also a "transmutation of tradition." [26] But this transmutation still remains bound, inasmuch as it is an explication of the "not yet explicated." Forethinking is not bound in this way, so that it is much more of a "transmuting" than rethinking. The "kind" of selfsameness that prevails here unites in a much more tenuous way.

We feel that it is very important that these connections someday be exposed. Heidegger's intention to consider the movement and the power of rethinking and forethinking ultimately as a mystery can nevertheless be completely respected. And yet it is necessary to see that thereby the foundation of his "historically" operative thinking is held in the mysterious in a decisive way. And it is necessary to point to the difficulties that ensue from the indeterminate status of the "kinds" of sameness that prevail here, as well as from considering thinking as, on the one hand, "granted" by the experiences of Being of the first beginning and, on the other hand, as a "transmuting" power. This difficulty is particularly grave for forethinking, for here the talk of the "granting" which continues "out of the dawn" gives the impression that Heidegger still wishes to legitimate even that which

22. See above, p. 167.
23. See above, p. 116.
24. HD 94.
25. See above, p. 117, and WP 33 (71).
26. See above, pp. 117 ff.

is forethought exclusively from the experiences that the early Greeks had with Being. But it seems to us, on the basis of our previous considerations, that the basic traits of the Being of the other beginning which Heidegger has already forethought—insofar as they represent "transmutations" of the initially incipient basic traits—are to a large extent justified from the experiences *which Heidegger himself has had with Being.* It is only when we present the problem of the legitimation of forethinking and its forethought in this way that a second problem assumes its true gravity. This is the problem of the "binding" character of Heidegger's thought, which we can consider only later.

The import of these problems of legitimation and binding character can, however, be assessed only after we have investigated to what extent the forethought basic traits still actually refer back to the basic traits of the first beginning and to what extent they are transmuted. In what follows we shall describe the basic traits of the Being of the other beginning with explicit reference to this question, in order to determine more precisely the "kind" of sameness that holds sway here.

PART V

The Basic Traits of Being

in the Other Beginning

1 / The World

THE SENSE AND SIGNIFICANCE of the concept of "world" have altered repeatedly in the course of the development of Heidegger's thought. In *Being and Time* and *The Essence of Reasons* the world or worldliness was specified as a "constitutive character of Dasein," [1] as an "existential." [2] In the basic movement of the existence that understands Being, in the occurrence of "transcendence," the "world" is the "toward-which of the surmounting," [3] and this "toward-which" belongs to the unitary structure of Dasein. It is in this "transcendental" sense that the basic constitution of Dasein is a "Being-in-the-world."

As Heidegger sees it, the early Greek sense of *kosmos* refers to the "how of the Being" of "being as a whole," which in an "antecedent" way and "relative to Dasein" determines and makes possible every particular "how." [4] The "world" in *Being and Time* is also such a "how," but it is related to Dasein [5] even more decisively, for it now has the character of being "for the sake of Dasein." [6] The worldliness of the world—as environing world—is the unity of a referential context that bestows significance upon the relations of "in order to," "whereto," "for," and "for the sake of." Dasein moves itself with circumspective and preoccupational

1. *SZ* 52 ff. Cf. also, for the following discussion, G. Brand, *Welt, Ich und Zeit*, pp. 13 ff. and 20 ff.
2. *SZ* 64.
3. *WG* 18, 19 ff. (39, 41 ff.).
4. *WG* 22 (49).
5. *SZ* 86 ff., 144 ff., 364 ff.
6. *WG* 35 ff. (85 ff.).

familiarity in a totality of involvements because, as Being-in-the-world, it "is" always already "in" this totality of relations.[7]

We need not go any further into how Heidegger in *Being and Time* and *The Essence of Reasons* described the constitution of Dasein as a "relation" to this "world." It suffices to point out that the meaningful whole of the world does not stand "opposite" Dasein like a region of "ever existing ideas." Rather, Dasein in a "primal action"[8] "lets" the world stand before it as its "for the sake of," lets it "reign and world."[9] In letting the world "world," Dasein gives meaning to "itself" out of "its" world[10] and lets handiness be as the Being of "beings encountered within the world,"[11] as well as the co-Being of "others."[12]

There are tendencies in these determinations that first find articulation only in Heidegger's later writings, where the world is no longer regarded as related to Dasein in the way described. These tendencies already announce that the "worlding" of the world is a giving, in that it bestows meanings. This suggests that it functions as an "open*ing* of meaning," and here is where the relation of the *world and truth* lies. This relation is already indicated in *Being and Time*, where Dasein as Being-in-the-*world* is "disclosed," i.e., is Being-in-the-*truth*.[13]

Being and Time, moreover, already points to the relation of the *world to language*, inasmuch as articulation and language belong to the disclosure of Dasein, along with understanding and disposition. Here, of course, articulation and language were determined on the basis of the constitution of the Being of Dasein.[14]

It is possible to see the prefiguration of a connection of "*World and history*," in that Dasein as Being-in-the-world is "historical." For the historicity of Dasein, on the basis of its ek-static horizonal temporality, temporalizes the historicity of the world, which includes the beings on hand as well as the handy.[15]

The relation of *world and thing* is to be found in the indication in *Being and Time* that the totality of involvements which constitutes the handiness of beings within the world is based on

7. *SZ* 87, 88, 364.
8. *WG* 36 (89).
9. *WG* 40 (103).
10. *WG* 34 (85).
11. *SZ* 118.
12. *Ibid.*
13. *SZ* 221.
14. *SZ* 160 ff.
15. *SZ* 381.

the referential relations of the world. This relation to the world is proof to Heidegger that the things are not reified "substances" in the Cartesian sense, since man has understood them all along in an unthematic way as the "gear" of his "environing world." [16]

Notwithstanding all of these tendencies, however, it must be emphasized that, in these early writings, the "content" which the world has and gives is limited to the relations cited above. By contrast, "world" in the later writings is specified precisely in terms of its content. For instance, in the essay "Hölderlin and the Essence of Poetry" we read that the world is "the ever changing circuit of decision and work, of action and responsibility, but also of caprice and commotion, decadence and confusion." [17] In the essay "The Origin of the Artwork," the world is "the unity of those paths and relations in which birth and death, disaster and blessings, victory and disgrace, endurance and decadence, secure the shape and course of the human being in his mission." [18] Or, in opposition to a conception which represents it as a "framework for a sum of beings on hand," the world is identified as "the always unobjective, to which we are sub-jected as long as the paths of birth and death, blessings and curses, hold us entranced in Being." [19]

This concept of world defined in terms of content now moves into a closer relation to truth. We have already described [20] how Heidegger regarded the creative occurrence of the erection of an artwork as a matter of truth fixing itself in the work, in which truth is understood as a primeval strife of unconcealment and concealment. The "content" that comes out of this primeval strife is the strife of "world and earth." [21] The world of a temple, for instance, is that unity of paths and relations whose content was cited above. In this coming to be of an artwork, "earth" is regarded as a counterpole to world. It is that which "holds itself back in the work," e.g., "the massiveness and heaviness of the stone" of a temple. This massiveness of the earth in the artwork gains access to the opening of a world, but, because it essentially denies any penetration into itself, it permeates the world as the "undisclosable" and therefore "inaccessible." [22] This contentious

16. *SZ* 66 ff.
17. *HD* 35 (300).
18. *HW* 31 (669).
19. *HW* 33 (671).
20. See above, p. 151.
21. *HW* 37 (675).
22. *HW* 36 (674).

"unity" [23] of world and earth is the "content" of the occurrence of art as an occurrence of truth.

The prevailing of the world, determined in terms of content, is at this stage in the development of the concept of world identified with "history." In the *Introduction to Metaphysics* Heidegger characterizes the "world becoming" in the first beginning as the "authentic history." [24] And in the Hölderlin commentary it is said that "only where world prevails is there history." [25] But beyond what is said in *Being and Time,* Heidegger has made no attempt to explain this identity of world and history. To say that world in its determination of content shows itself to "historical Dasein" or to the "historical folk" [26] does not explain that world "prevails" as history and why the world worlds only there "where the essential decisions of our history are made, are undertaken and forsaken by us, are mistaken and once again questioned." [27]

In Heidegger's later view, world occurs out of an even closer relation to language. The artwork as an occurrence of truth and world takes place, according to the essay "The Origin of the Artwork," "always already and always only in the opening of the saying * and naming." [28] Art is essentially poetry and thus ultimately to be understood only out of the openness that language brings. Language is "the saying of the unconcealment of being," the "projecting of the clearing, in which announcement is made of how being comes into the open."

This essay on art also conceives of the relation of world to thing in a new way. The thingness of the thing must be thought originally out of the work character of the artwork, out of the occurrence of truth in whose strife countervailing world and earth contentiously come forth. The interpretation of the thing-character of things must pay heed to the thing's belonging to the earth, the earthy, the "sustaining self-closure not pressed toward any goal" which unveils itself by jutting into the world of the artwork.[29]

If the most recent publications are viewed as the true expres-

---

* *Sagen:* Often prefixed by "soundless," "saying" in its reference to the language of Being, *Sage,* cannot be taken in the usual sense, since its ways are silent. It is man who must give it voice, by listening and responding to its silent ways.

23. HW 38 (666).
24. EM 48 (63).
25. HD 35 (300).
26. HW 31 (669).
27. HW 33 (671).
28. HW 61 (695).
29. HW 57 (691).

sion of Heidegger's forethinking, then one must first note how this forethought concept of the world is in its turn sharply distinguished from the one we have just developed. World is no longer the "self-changing circuit of decisions" nor the "unity of the paths and relations of birth and death, blessings and curses." Now the "words of Being" secured from the "dialogue" with Hölderlin's poetic work become the "building tool" for the "other sense of the Being and essence" of the "world essence." The earth and the heavens, the divine and the mortal, become the "neighborhoods" [*Gegenden*], near in the sense of being "over against one another," which in this way constitute the prevailing and worlding of the world.[30] The earth [31] is now "that which builds and bears, nurtures and ripens, cultivating waters and minerals, vegetation and wild life." The heavens [32] are "the course of the sun and the moon, the twinkling of the stars, the seasons of the year, light and twilight of day, obscurity and purity of night, fair and foul weather, the procession of the clouds and the azure depth of the aether." The divine [33] are the "hinting messengers of the divinity" whose "reign is hidden." Heidegger often spoke of these "hinting divines" in the Hölderlin interpretations.[34] They constitute the sphere which there and in the *Letter on Humanism* is called the "holy." [35] It is only within the "holy" that the divinity can "present or withdraw itself." Till now, Heidegger has always spoken of the divinity only in negatively guarded terms, that it is not a being, and not the "highest" being of theology and onto-theo-logy.[36]

Heidegger's inclusion of the essence of man in the "world essence" reveals how he now thinks of the "relation of Being and man." Here it is not a matter of the man of today but of the future man, for the "rational animals" must first *become* mortals.[37] Man still understands himself nowadays from the horizon of life (*zōē*) or *animalitas* and *logos* or *ratio*. In *Being and Time* and the subsequent writings, the essence of man was already understood on the basis of his "Being toward death" and defined from the ways in which the Nothing that "essences" prevails in Dasein. One decisive mode of this essencing Nothing is the "need" that

30. *US* 211.
31. *VA* 176.
32. *VA* 176.
33. *Ibid.*
34. *HD* 42 ff. (310 ff.).
35. *HB* 102 (294); *HD* 18, 44 (273, 313), 56, 58; *HW* 250.
36. *WM* 18 ff. (217 ff.); cf. *HW* 171 (121); *HB* 101 ff. (293 ff.).
37. *VA* 177.

necessitates Dasein to "be" the existing and comporting understanding of Being. In *Being and Time* Heidegger already saw
death not as an end but as the "ontological" *signum* of mortality.
Today he sees it as the enveloping that like a "shrine" [38] shelters
the nihilating modes of Nothing, which by essencing enable Dasein's understanding of Being as the "relational hold" of "Being
to Being." If we want to understand this later characterization of
the "mortality" of man in the essay "The Thing," it is necessary
to recall Heidegger's earlier definitions.

Let us now investigate how this forethought concept of world
refers back to what is "to be thought" of the sense of Being in the
first beginning. Only on the basis of such an investigation can
the "kind" of selfsameness as the basic trait of the sense of Being
in the first beginning be determined more closely or can the question be answered of the extent to which the basic traits of the
other beginning are still grounded in the "experiences" of the
first beginning and thus have their legitimate basis in them.

It must first be recalled that the coprevalence in the first beginning of the overpowering powers of *physis* and the violent
man was called a "world formation." The world is formed in a
creative setting-apart, the *polemos*. The initial opening of Being
occurred as a world opening, in which creative Dasein violently
harnessed the emergent power of *physis* into works, through
which the hitherto un-thought, un-heard, un-said came forth.

The forethought world of the other beginning points back to
this rethought coprevalence in the first beginning of *physis* and
Dasein, insofar as it is also an active occurrence, a "prevailing,"
whereby the neighborhoods of the world emerge in their unity.
Because of its active character, this prevailing is called "worlding." [39] But this prevalence of worlding in the other beginning
does not occur as a consequence of the battling coprevalence of
physis and Dasein, even though the human being also in the
other beginning belongs in this worlding, which is shown in detail later. Heidegger understands this worlding of the four world
neighborhoods as a "gathering." [40] It can therefore be said that
this basic trait of the world essence has been forethought from
the basic trait of *logos* in the first beginning. But the "gathering
collection" of the first beginning produced a highly contentious
kind of ordering of the countervalent. By contrast, [41] the world-

38. *Ibid.*
39. *VA* 178.
40. *VA* 170 ff.
41. *VA* 171, 172, 178 ff.

ing gathers the fourfold, which is already a "onefold united by itself." The gathering that rules here is so minimally a co-ordering of the countervalent that Heidegger thinks of it in the categories of "play," "dance," "mirror," "square," and "ring" and describes the way in which the world neighborhoods are together as "pliant" and "supple."

Let us now explore whether the mirror play of the fourfold points back to what is to be thought in the early Greek *alētheia.* This question can be answered in the affirmative to the extent that the "mirroring" is expressly understood by Heidegger as a "clearing mode," [42] a mode of "lighting," and the idea of the mirror, just like that of reflection, is oriented to the metaphor of light. However, the early Greek *alētheia* rethought by Heidegger not only means clearing and openness but also a relation to concealment, i.e., to disguise and to mystery, since every clearing always remains pervaded by concealment, and in this sense every openness is an *un*concealment. It was in this conception of truth as a relationship in which "light and darkness" are "equal partners" that we saw Heidegger's contribution. It was thus that he radicalized Hegel's insight into truth as a relationship of "light and darkness" and sought not only to overcome "light metaphysics" but also to make room for the coming of the new and unprecedented.

It is true that Heidegger has recently [43] explained that, in prevailing against one another, the world neighborhoods are open in their "self-concealing," but he has not shown how such a self-concealing is consistent with the mirror play described in the essay "The Thing." But before we can make a final judgment as to whether the forethinking of the world essence abandons the rethought conception of the essence of truth and possibly returns to "light metaphysics," we must examine the forethought "relation of world and language," since for Heidegger the "truth of the world" is now based on the essence of language.

All of these basic traits of the forethought occurrence of the world thus point back to what is to be thought in the rethought occurrence of Being of the first beginning, even though the content of the world neighborhoods comes from the dialogue with Hölderlin. This specifies the "kind" of selfsameness of the Being of the first beginning more precisely. It sustains this basic trait not only insofar as it "grants," at the end of the "eschatological" development, the possibility of experiencing the essence of tech-

42. *VA* 178.
43. *US* 211.

nology as its "withdrawal configuration"; it also "grants" the light of the creative basic traits of the first beginning to which fore-thinking returns. But the "selfsameness" that prevails here by no means binds forethinking exclusively to the Being of the first beginning and to the experiences of the early Greeks that underlie it. Rather, as we saw, forethinking has made extensive use of its transmuting power, and what is forethought thus finds its legitimate basis in great measure in the experiences which Heidegger himself has had with Being.

We have not yet asked whether and how the *temporal* sense of the world essence was forethought out of the temporal sense of *eon*. It may be recalled that the prevailing of the temporal *eon* was defined as *the present* of an "abrupt while," and that it was in this sense that it was translated into the German *Anwesen* (presenting). In the ensuing "history of Being," the sense of "Being" was likewise situated in a "presenting," even though the character of this "present" was altered from an "abrupt occurrence" to a process which was "stable" in various ways. But as long as "Being" retained the meaning of presenting, the predominance of the present was assured. In the lectures *What Evokes Thinking?* Heidegger now declares: [44] "We commit an error if we believe that Being of being means only and for all time the presenting of what is present." This seems to express the intention to transmute the initially incipient temporal sense of Being by forethought. In *Being and Time* Heidegger sought to break the preponderance of the present by showing that it dominated the course of the understanding of Being only in a derivative way and that the "authentically" existing understanding of Being is made possible by a "future" which is to be thought in a definite way, a future which lets "momentousness" arise together with "what is as having been." But these determinations are attributable only to Dasein, and referred only to the understanding of Being, and hence could not consider a temporal sense conceived as coming from Being itself, a temporal sense which would overcome the predominance of the present, the sense of Being as presenting. In the essay "The Thing" Heidegger declares that the gathering "worlding" of the world essence has its own "while." [45] It must be inferred from the essay "The Essence of Language" [46] that here we are no longer dealing with a "while" of the first beginning. For the "while" of the world essence is not a presenting

44. *WD* 143 (235).
45. *VA* 172.
46. *US* 213.

in the sense of a predominance of the present but rather is a "contemporaneity" of "having been, presenting, for-ward" [*Gegenwart*] (i.e., future). Here it is explained in a very brief remark that time, which in the whole of its essence rests still and tranquil, temporalizes itself by arranging, together with equally still space, a "temporal playing field" [*Zeit-Spiel-Raum*] for the play of the world. This remark is at any rate unequivocal in showing the tendency of Heidegger's thought to overcome not only the temporal sense of metaphysically conceived Being but that of initially incipient Being as well. If the temporal sense of "worlding," of the "world play," "the while," were no longer that of a "presentness" but of a "contemporaneity," then *Being would no longer have the sense of presenting.* It would in fact be transmuted "from the ground up," as Heidegger endeavored to do in the *Introduction to Metaphysics.*[47] Yet this comment ultimately brings us to the difficult problem which to date has only been suggested by Heidegger somewhat cryptically in terms of the question just treated, the question of the relationship of "Being" and "world." It seems to us that it is now Heidegger's intention to think of Being in general simply as world. Supporting this interpretation is perhaps his proposal [48] to give up "the alienating and separating word" "Being" just as decisively as the term "man." Perhaps another indication in this direction is the fact that he has recently written the word Being as crossed out. In the essay *The Question of Being* [49] he explains that this crossing-out indicates, among other things, that Being is the place in which the four neighborhoods of the world play are gathered. This is the positive sense of the crossing-out. But if Being always "essences" only as the gathering of the four world neighborhoods—and Heidegger did not say that Being should be crossed out only on occasion—then it presumably always "is" as the "worlding" of the world. *Then the "other sense of Being and essence" which we seek in Heidegger would lie primarily in Being as the "world essence," the essence of the world.* But world "essences" in its relation to "thing." This relation of world and thing must now be discussed.

47. *EM* 155 (203).
48. *SF* 28 (77).
49. *SF* 31 (83).

2 / World and Thing

IN THE ESSAY "THE THING," the statement is made that hitherto the thingness of the thing has actually never yet been thought. It remained "hidden" and "forgotten," making no claim on thought. Especially within the dominion of the essence which now prevails, that of the "com-posite," which in reciprocally provocative positioning lets everything real come forth without "truth," simply as "disposable stock," the essence of the thing, its thingness, continues to be "denied." On the other hand, Heidegger is convinced that, within the dominion of this com-posite, the "turn" to the Being that pertains to the other beginning has already taken place. For the basic traits of a creative Being of the first and of the other beginning were "commissioned" to his thinking after it experienced the oblivion of Being. He also calls the experience of the withdrawal of the creative sense of Being the experience of "nearness." It is at a time in which all extensive distances are increasingly eliminated through technological advances, so that everything becomes "uniformly close," that it becomes possible to experience the withdrawal of that which really "pertains" to us and thus "approaches" us. Because the "approaching" can approach only out of nearness, a thinking which is concerned with the essence of what is withdrawn must "think over" the essence of nearness. This happens in the essay "The Thing," where the essence of the thing is exhibited as that "which is in nearness." Heidegger thus at the same time hopes to determine the essence of nearness as that which "approaches" thinking.

In *Being and Time* the essence of the thing and the essence of nearness were also examined together.[1] As the being within the

1. *SZ* 102 ff.

world, the thing has the mode of Being of handiness. There is in this "near at hand" of handiness the character of a nearness that cannot be ascertained by measuring distances but is instead defined on the basis of Dasein's circumspective and preoccupied handling. Dasein has the tendency to overcome distances. In this sense of overcoming everything far, it is "far-fetching" * [ent-fernend] and thus makes possible the nearness in which it can encounter beings.[2] But these conceptions of the essence of the thing and of nearness are governed only by the viewpoint of "serviceability for" Dasein. They are obtained from Dasein and not from the essence of the thing and of nearness. For the referential relations of handiness simply constitute the context of meaning of a usefulness that pertains to the daily "environment," and this particular meaningful whole bears reference only to the "for the sake of" Dasein.

Now, by contrast, the determination of the essence of things and of nearness is attempted strictly outside the viewpoint of serviceability and not at all from Dasein. Accordingly, Heidegger proceeds in such a way that he lets himself be "approached" by the essence of a particular thing in the nearness, by the essence of a jug, for example, and in this sense lets himself be "conditioned" or "thinged" [bedingen] [3] by the essence of a thing or the thing as such, instead of "representing"[4] it in the everyday and scientific ways or apprehending this thingness absolutely or "unconditionally," and thus "unthinged."[5] Our investigation will again test whether the essence of the thing and of nearness are determined from basic traits that were taken from the rethinking of the sense of Being in the first beginning, as well as the degree to which these basic traits were transmuted by forethinking.

Heidegger sees the essence of things, the hitherto unthought "thingness," in a verbally understood occurrence as "thinging."[6] The exclusive aim of this thinging is to draw the world nearer to us.[7] The prevalence of *physis* in the first beginning also led to the formation of the world, but only when its powers were violently harnessed into works by Dasein. The thinging of things is neither violent like the power of *physis* nor in need of the violent deeds

---

* In the sense of "making the far vanish . . . by bringing the distant near" (SZ 105).
2. SZ 106.
3. VA 179.
4. VA 170.
5. VA 179.
6. VA 172.
7. VA 176, 178 ff.

of a Dasein. If one wants to maintain that thinging in the other beginning still retains basic traits of the *physis* of the first beginning, then one must at the same time point to this difference. Here we have a decisive *transmutation*.

This thinging is a "gathering" in the whiling of the fourfold.[8] Insofar as it is thought as a gathering, it refers back to the rethought sense of the basic trait of Being in the first beginning, to the *logos* as laying "collection." In the essence of a thing of the "style of a jug," [9] a twofold gathering takes place. The "taking" and "holding" of the hollow of a jug gather themselves in the "gift of the gush" uniting these two modes.[10] This gift of outpouring brings about a renewed gathering that constitutes the thinging and therefore the essence of the thing, which cannot be experienced merely through representation.[11] Only "essential thinking" experiences [12] how, in the gift of the pour of water, the earth in its dark slumber in the stones of the spring is gathered with the heavens, the dispenser of rain and dew. Or it experiences in the gift of the pour of wine how the nurturing earth gathers itself with the heavens, which through its sunlight brought the vine to blossom. The pour of the gift of water and wine at the same time always includes in its gathering the one "for whom" such an outpouring is made. As a "libation," it is originally given as a sacrifice and offering "for the divine ones," i.e., for the sphere of the "holy" in which the divinity shows or hides itself. As a "draught," the gift of the pour is for the "mortals"; it livens "their leisure and cheers their conviviality."

Just like the worlding of the world thought in the other beginning, the gathering of thinging which is forethought here is not a matter of the deployment or the "holding in contention" of a "primeval strife of the countervailing," as it was in the basic trait of *logos* in the first beginning. Forethinking has thus completely *transmuted* this basic trait of *logos* in this context as well.

The gathering of the thinging thing is a "whiling of the world." [13] This whiling brings the while that pertains to the world essence into a "particular while" [*je Weiliges*].[14] With this, Heidegger seeks to express how the world essence "individualizes" itself, how it incorporates itself in a particular thing like that "of

8. VA 172.
9. VA 176.
10. VA 170.
11. VA 172.
12. VA 170 ff.
13. VA 172, 178.
14. VA 172, 179.

the style of a jug." But this brief allusion merely suggests that this individualizing process of the world occurrence is the "temporalizing" of a contemporaneity. Unfortunately, no further details are given as to how the while of the worlding world temporalizing itself as "contemporaneous" temporalizes itself "in" an individual. However, in the essay "Building, Dwelling, Thinking," the "spatial" sense of this individualizing process has received a more detailed specification as the "nearing" of a nearness.

This nearing has a "spatial" character which, however, cannot be represented as the *spatium* or *extensio* of quantitatively measurable distances, extensions, and intervals.[15] The proximity of handy gear as discussed in *Being and Time* also had a specific spatiality. The "place" of a tool is specified there on the basis of the totality of places related to one another as the "there of belonging to," in which this totality was in turn conditioned by a "whereunto" which ultimately came from the circumspectively preoccupied handling of "far-fetching" Dasein. By contrast, the peculiar kind of spatiality that rules in the nearing that gathers is based on the thinging of the thing, e.g., of the "style" of a bridge. A bridge [16] "things," in that it appoints a "spot" to be a "site" in which the four world neighborhoods can while. Inasmuch as the bridge things as a spot, it brings near and gathers, which here means that it arranges or "spaces in" a space in which the earth and the heavens, the divine ones and the mortals, are "let in." It gathers the earth as a landscape around the stream and the heavens to themselves, in that it keeps the streaming of the stream close to the heavens and ready for its weather. It gathers the mortals to itself by guiding them on their ways. And since the mortals basically aspire "to bring themselves before the hail of the divine," the bridge also gathers "as the overarching passage before the divine."

Given our concern in the history of the problem, let us now stress that this reflection on the relation of world and thing from the proximating thinging of the worlding essence of the world must be viewed as Heidegger's attempt to fulfill the "positive aim" which, according to *Being and Time,* lay behind all the "destructions" of the traditional determinations. The determinations that concern us here are substance and subject. The categories of "play," "mirroring," "square," "round dance" and "ring," "nearness" and "gathering whiling," which aim to define the essence

15. VA 156.
16. VA 152 ff.

of the thing anew, are *Heidegger's "positive" answers to the question of what will take place of substance and subject* after these traditional models are destroyed. Instead of an Aristotelian teleological *kosmos* of substances, instead of the "world" of an "infinite context of grounds and grounded" thought in Hegel's way "in the element of thinking," the world reigns here as a wholeness that surpasses the dimensions of beings within the world and their coordination, a world which does not ground and found, which is rather a "groundless" play and round dance.

But precisely because this world essence in its relation to the essence of the thing is different from the essence conceived as substance and subject, attention must be given to specifying the basic traits which constitute this "sense." While we are "applying" Heidegger's own "method" to the forethought world essence in its relation to the thing, we may also ask which basic traits underlie these "categories" of the other beginning. This can be done with the guideline of the basic traits which determined the inner-worldly Aristotelian *ousia* and Hegel's thought-laden "Being," the basic traits of necessity, selfsameness, intelligibility, and eternalness.

To be sure, the circling of the "round dance" of the world play does not proceed in the same way as the circular course of the "method" of categorial-dialectical reflection, which orders itself to itself. But this groundless play also has its order. The "ring" of the fourfold is a self-enclosed circle of wholly determinate and noninterchangeable world neighborhoods. The earth, the heavens, the divine ones, and the mortals are not only "united by themselves" and "entrusted to one another," they are also held in a "singular onefold." [17] There is in this order a definite "kind" of "necessity." As a result of it, the play [18] of one world neighborhood must always mirror the other three, in the course of which it must at the same time be restored to itself from the mirror image of the other three. Otherwise, the mirror play cannot play. And, because of this necessity, the "saying" of a world neighborhood is compelled to say the other three out of the onefold of the Four.[19] Manifestly, there is in this necessity a definite "compulsion."

And likewise, the play of the world essence in its relation to the thing bears the basic trait of a certain "kind" of selfsameness. In a brief remark in the lecture "Hölderlin's Earth and the Heav-

17. VA 178, 179.
18. *Ibid.*
19. VA 177.

ens" that explicitly refers to German idealism, Heidegger calls the onefold simplicity of the four world neighborhoods the "infinite relationship." [20] The infinite relationship is Hegel's good infinity, which is based on the basic trait of selfsameness. Heidegger presumably views this relationship in such a way that every world neighborhood is the same and yet, at the same time, when opposed to the other three, is another. It is extremely noteworthy that he finds his way back to Hegel's decisive conception of the structure of Being, even though for him Being or the world is not just in the "element of thinking." So far, he has not shown how the movement of good infinity is possible outside the element of thinking. Furthermore, the thinging that gathers the world neighborhoods "whiles" the world sense of the four neighborhoods as always "the same." As a bridge it gathers the four world neighborhoods in its way, and as a jug in still another way, and yet it is always a matter of these same four neighborhoods. We have here a very significant distinction from the traditional selfsameness. While the selfsameness of the Aristotelian *ousia* excluded the *genesis haplōs* and Hegel's conception of selfsameness yields no new realities, this "selfsameness" of the world relationship does not prevent the advent of "new" things. Thinging also permits the advent of these four neighborhoods in "other styles" of things. The drawbacks of this "advantage" of this selfsameness will be pointed out forthwith.

The thinging and worlding world essence bears in itself the basic trait of a certain "kind" of intelligibility. The world neighborhoods certainly do not have a noetic, an eidetic, or a logical Being and accordingly cannot be experienced by a noetic, eidetic, or logical determination of essence. And since they are not "concepts," they cannot, moreover, be grasped by an "absolute conceiving." Only the "world-open" attitude, which in "stepping back" has renounced everything "unconditioned" and lets itself be "conditioned," experiences the "truth" of the world essence in its mirror play. This concept of truth seems once again to approximate the "total intelligibility" of "light metaphysics," since the category of mirroring hardly leaves room for the concealment that always pervaded the "clearing" in the truth concept of the first beginning.

Finally, the world essence in its relation to the thing has a "kind" of "eternity." Here, to be sure, it is not a matter of Hegel's "eternity" nor of the "extratemporality" of the Aristotelian *telos*,

20. The long-play record of the lecture of January 18, 1960, part IV.

nor of the kind of presence that we recognized as the temporal sense of the Aristotelian *ousia* of a *synholon*. The while of the worlding world essence and the whiling of thinging in the "particular while" come about—according to Heidegger's brief suggestions—from a time that rests calm and still, and they are temporalized from a contemporaneity. Whatever way the sense of this "time" may be more precisely considered, it seems that in any case Heidegger does not regard the world essence as a "mission." One may thus ask whether *he now "brings history to a standstill and puts it out of play" in this "cosmological"* turn, whereby he does not arrive at an extratemporal "eternity" but at a contemporaneity which for him resides in a time that rests still in itself.

The sense of the "other Being and essence" of the world essence in its relation to the thing essence thus bears basic traits that recall the basic traits of the "tradition." This may be maintained, because this "sense" perhaps corresponds to the subject matter itself. For it is still the task of thinking to think the things as they are "in truth." Precisely because this is the task, one may further ask whether these "world and thing categories" are suitable for the determination of the essence of our things in every respect.

Aristotle thought of Being and essence only with regard to being and from being. He did not deal with being emerging from Being and only from Being. Heidegger, on the contrary, thinks the thingness of a thing so much "from Being," and this means "from the world," that the essence of a thing seems to lie only in its gathering the four world neighborhoods within itself. We must ask whether this radically anti-Aristotelian direction of Heidegger's inquiry has not led to an inappropriate neglect of those essential modes that also "enable" a being and determine it in its sense. This question may be elucidated more closely by a glance back to the form of the first *ousia*.

As the *hypokeimenon*, the Aristotelian essence was the underlying, the forelying, the self-supporting and standing-in-itself, which stands in a mobile relation to the possible and contingent coincident modes, to the accidents. Its epoch-making "performance power" rested above all in its being thus a relational "bearer of properties" and "core" of a being. This conception of the structure of beings, in particular the lifeless things of nature and things of use, has for two thousand years determined the Western history of thought, in which the "relational character" of the *ousia* grew more and more rigid. Heidegger takes the position that this Aristotelian model was not thought through but was merely a "represented" structure of the thing in accordance with the "framework of the simple sentence," i.e., the relation of subject and object.[21] But this view is unsatisfactory. Moreover, at the end of the Aristotelian tradition, Hegel expressly demonstrated that it is a necessity of "thinking" to define the thingness of a thing as a "bearer of properties." This does not preclude "thinking" from understanding with equal necessity these properties as "independent materials" as well, for the thing exists—as Hegel showed—"logically-categorially," i.e., "necessitated by thought," as this "contradiction." [22]

Since Heidegger does not recognize Hegel's conceiving as a "thinking," let us point out that this self-supporting character, the standing-in-itself in natural and artificial things, is also phenomenally evident. Heidegger's essay "The Origin of the Artwork" acknowledged this phenomenal character of things at least for the natural thing, characterizing it as a "resting in itself" and defining it as the "earthy." [23] Here, therefore, the thing was not yet thought exclusively "from Being" or "from the world" but was granted a certain measure of "standing on its own." By contrast, in view of the forethought conception operative in the later Heidegger, a thing can no longer be conceived as "properly standing on its own" and accordingly also no longer as "having properties." According to the Aristotelian model, the properties of a jug, e.g., its "Being large" or its "Being colored," could be defined according to the "schemata of categories." One asks oneself how, according to Heidegger's forethought model, this or other character traits of a specific thing, e.g., of a specific jug, are to be understood. Heidegger has responded to the difficult problem of the individuation of the world essence in its temporal aspect only by way of allusion.

The Aristotelian *physis ousia* was an "enabling unity," a "whole" that made it possible from the inside out, so that what "lies before" is, e.g., a specific house and not a pile of bricks in disarray. By contrast, it is difficult to see how the wholeness of the four world neighborhoods "enables" a specific jug in its specific content of meaning. The onefold character of the heavens and the earth, the mortals and the divine ones, which are gathered, e.g., in the "gift" of wine, displays a sense that could lead a potter to produce another "style" of "container" or even

---

21. HW 13 (654).
22. PG 90 ff. (162 ff.); *Logik II* 105 ff. (484 ff.).
23. HW 57 (691).

another "style" of thing, e.g., a bridge. Surely this sense is not the enabling element of an "individual" jug. But since only individual things actually "approach" us, the problem still seems to lie precisely in proving how the "wholeness," the world, is capable of determining or enabling the sense of individual things.[24]

Furthermore, the other ways in which Aristotle thought of *ousia* seemed to Heidegger to be inadequate to the subject matter. He thus explicitly rejected the *eidos-hylē* determination as an "assault on thingness." [25] This determination at best concerns useful things, whose "original determination" lies in their "serviceability," which in turn is said to be based on a "reliability" which is to be understood in a certain way.[26]

It was the "genetic" viewpoint which was of course predominant in Aristotle. The problem of how being "is" after its production was hardly discussed. The peculiar "direction" of the Aristotelian inquiry toward individual being did not really lead him to the problem of whether and how the *ousiai*, the "wholes," were determined by that encompassing "wholeness" in which they belong, by that totality which he himself called the cosmos. It is this question which Heidegger now seeks to pose. He thinks from another direction, from the "turn," beginning with this "wholeness," the neighborhoods of the world, and from here wants to determine the essence of "things." But it seems to us that this shift in emphasis in the inquiry has led to a "neglect" of important modes of the essence, without which no individual thing can be "near" to us.

In conclusion, the question may still be raised as to whether the categories of "world" and "thing" in the other beginning are really pertinent and applicable to the plurality of "things" among which men now live. The essay "The Thing" gives a "catalogue" of those things which the four world neighborhoods are capable of gathering by thinging.[27] Among those named are the path, the plow, the heron, the deer, the horse, the bull, the mirror, the buckle, the book, the picture, the crown, and the cross. The two "things" already mentioned in another context, the jug and the bridge, also belong here. It is thus a matter of both "natural things" and "things of use." Oddly enough, no "art objects" are listed, even though it can be said, perhaps above all of them, that they are capable of gathering the four world neighborhoods.

24. Cf. E. Fink, *Spiel als Weltsymbol*, pp. 59, 61, 114, 128, 210.
25. HW 19 (660).
26. HW 23 (662).
27. VA 181.

It is indisputable—nor is it disputed by Heidegger—that the "utensils" which technology in increasing measure places at our disposal simply do not gather the four world neighborhoods. Among these belong several of the utensils already listed as "things." Bridges, jugs (i.e., drinking utensils), houses, and plows, which now and presumably likewise in the future are factory-made, are no longer "things." And for that matter, a jug made by hand or the Heidelberg bridge in the midst of present-day traffic could hardly still gather the neighborhood of the divine ones. Just because "once upon a time" the gift of the jug was a libation of offering and sacrifice does not mean that the "dimension of the holy" opens itself to us now or in the future in this gift of an outpouring. And to say that the men who today cross the Heidelberg bridge "at bottom aspire to bring themselves before the hail of the divine" appears dubious since, even according to Heidegger's own view, men have not yet "become mortal" in the sense in which he understands this.

Our discussion of the sense of Being in the first beginning came to the conclusion that this sense does not even seem to hold true for the kind of "being" which the early Greeks encountered in their daily rounds but that it is only a matter of the sense of Being which lay at the basis of their "creative world" and the "works" of "creative men." We recognized here an important "limit" to the dominion of the sense of Being in the first beginning. Similarly, the sense of Being of the other beginning seems to hold only for things of art and for very few things of nature and of use. Moreover, Heidegger himself has explicitly declared that the "thinging things" are "few in number." [28] Hence our thinking along with Heidegger here also encounters a very decisive "limit" to the dominion of the sense of Being of the other beginning. One must proceed on the assumption that this fore-thought essence of world and thing *is meant* to be valid only for a definite "creative" realm, that it thus is a matter here of a limitation which Heidegger sets on the "other sense of Being and essence." Otherwise—at least from the present perspective—Heidegger's sense of Being of the other beginning must be judged as downright "utopian." But if the dominion of the sense of Being of the other beginning, of the world essence in its relation to the thing, is restricted to things which have come forth "creatively," then the question arises as to how to regard the essence of all the other "things" with which man now and in the future dwells

28. *Ibid.*

"under the heavens and upon the earth." Then we have the grave problem of relating these "creative" and "uncreative" *regions* to each other. As a result, it further follows that Heidegger has really only partly answered the question of what to put in the place of the "destroyed" categories of substance and of subject that he therefore has fulfilled the "positive aim" of his destruction only in part.

3 / The Essence of Language

IN OUR PRESENTATION of the forethought essence of language we also wish to pay attention to how far its essential traits still rest on the basic traits of the first beginning obtained in rethinking and how far these have been "transmuted" by forethinking. Rethinking proceeded from the assumption that the early Greeks "dwelt" in the experience of language as a nonhuman occurrence and that they "suspected" its "essential intertwining" with Being. It exhibited the essence of language from the *logos* as a "gathering that lays forth and lays open," from the *physis* as an overpowering power that pervades the essence of man, and from the *alētheia* as a concealing clearing. Language in the first beginning showed itself particularly as an "occurrence of truth," since it was the "primeval poetry," the opening "coming to word of Being," the "originary saying" which through "linguistic works" lets a "world" of meaningful relations come forth.

The basic traits of this presence still determine the forethought essence of language as well. But forethinking penetrates deeper into the "structure" of the linguistic essence."[1] Within this structure [*Aufriss*], it is above all in the "soundless saying" which precedes every enunciation that Heidegger sees the nonhuman occurrence. The sense of this saying is specified as a "pointing-out," as a "letting-appear, a clearing-concealing-releasing proffering of world."[2] Here is where "the essencing in saying" lies.[3]

The basic traits of Being in the first beginning, of the *physis*,

1. *US* 251.
2. *US* 214, 200.
3. *US* 200.

the *logos,* and especially the *alētheia,* can be recognized without difficulty in these determinations. The *alētheia* is forethought by transmuting it into "saying," which by "proffering" and "pointing out" brings the four world neighborhoods near, "lets them appear." [4] In that it addresses itself in a soundless way to the poet and thinker, it yields "the free of the clearing" [5] in which the four world neighborhoods can be present in their specific sense. The soundless saying "essences" as this opening "occurrence of truth," in that it "moves" [*be-wegt*] [6] poetizing and thinking, i.e., sends them on their way, so that they must "listen" to it and translate what it soundlessly says into the spoken word. All this will become clearer after the role of the human being is determined in more detail. Now it is only a matter of seeing that the soundless saying, the silent exhortation to the creative man, is the forethought *alētheia* and that as such it constitutes the "truth of world and thing." This means that the saying belongs to the "Being and essence" of the other beginning. Heidegger has recently formulated this belonging thus: "The essence of speech: the speech of essence." [7] Language belongs "in the essencing," because the essencing itself is "saying." [8]

This conception implies that the worlding of the world and the thinging of the thing are in their "truth" only through the saying. World and thing are called forth only when the soundless saying addresses itself to poetizing in its "summons" [*Geheiss*].[9] Things thing "creatively," gather the four world neighborhoods, only because they, in originating from the soundless saying, the summons, are heard by the creative human being, "brought to language," and laid down and preserved in linguistic works.

Just as the *alētheia* was conceived as a nonhuman occurrence, so also the soundless saying, the summons, as the "essencing" of language, is nothing "human," but it addresses itself to the creative man and must be heard by him and brought to enunciation. Inasmuch as world and thing come to their "truth" only in and through the saying, Heidegger's conception refers to a peculiar "relationship" between "Being" and the "essence" of man. When Heidegger declares that the essence of the other beginning is "saying," when world and thing originally require the summons or "con-vocation" [*Ge-heiss*], then the essence of

4. *US* 257–58.
5. *US* 258.
6. *US* 201.
7. *US* 200.
8. *US* 263.
9. *US* 21 ff., esp. 32.

man which is capable of "hearing" this saying and summons must "belong" to Being in a special way. Language points to the realm of an "essential for-each-other" of Being and man. Our thinking along with Heidegger must follow this indication and reconstruct the "relationship" whose determination is the central thrust of his repeated efforts at rethinking and forethinking. Here we must break off our presentation of the essence of language and pick it up again within this "relationship."

PART VI
The Essence of Man

1 / The "Relationship" of Being to the Essence of Man

In the presentation of the basic traits of Being and essence, the determination of the essence of man has been deferred up to now. This may have given the erroneous impression that for Heidegger there is first a "Being and essence in itself" and second an "essence of man" which stands opposite to Being in a dogmatic and precritical way, as if it were a matter of two entities separated from each other. Heidegger endeavors, however, to apprehend the belonging-together of Being and essence with the essence of man much more closely than did transcendental philosophy.

Our discussions of the history of the problem stressed that both Aristotle and Hegel defined the essence of man from Being. Aristotle thought of it from the basic trait of the "total intelligibility" of *ousia*. Man is essentially noetic because he is coordinated to noetic Being. And in the performance of his spiritual modes of Being, he remains a "servant" of the noetic ousiological order. Neither as a philosopher nor in praxis as an ethical, political, or artistic man does he cocreate in this order. The possibility of a cocreative role is also contradicted by the basic traits of the selfsameness and eternalness of *ousia*, which exclude any new creation of essence.

Hegel also defined the essence of man from Being, inasmuch as its "truth" lies in its capacity as "infinite spirit" to realize in absolute knowledge the "self-thinking idea," the "concept of philosophy." The role of man is not radically "creative" or "cocreative" because there is no "new" reality in the process of reality. Man in Hegel also is essentially a servant, but his service

212 / PART VI

was conceived differently than in Aristotle, since his thinking has the task of "idealizing" reality.

In order to clarify how Heidegger differs in his determination of the essence of man from Being, we need not repeat how the basic constitution of man was determined in the various analyses of *Being and Time*. Even though *Being and Time* set forth how Dasein is pervaded by nullity and is in many respects finite, it nonetheless gained access to dimensions which were to a large extent denied to the tradition.[1] For what does it mean to assert that Dasein is always already "Being-in-the-world," that it is always already "in the truth" and has all along understood the "sense of Being"? Dasein constitutes this "Being-in," it constitutes its disclosure and, to an extent, that of worldliness, the unveiledness of the sense of Being and the overtness of beings within the world.[2] In an original "transcending act," it brings the worldliness of the world before itself and in the antecedent overthrow throws the projected world over being. In this "transcendentally" antecedent way, Dasein therefore has something essential to do with a world being given, as well as with the worldly character of being. Thus Heidegger has expressly declared that the "world-entry of being" is dependent upon this occurrence of "transcendence," upon this constitution of Dasein,[3] and that "ontological truth," the unveiling of the sense of Being, is an occurrence of giving [*gibt es*] only [4] "so far and so long as Dasein is." Without the Being of Dasein, without "Being-understanding," without "disclosure," without this truth in the original sense, the sense of Being cannot show itself. It is true that Heidegger guards against interpreting this "relativizing" [5] of truth thus understood to the Being of Dasein as a mere "subjectivizing," since no "sub-

---

1. See above, p. 71, note 171. The producing of the *general* transcendental subject was carried out *categorially* and to that extent remained bound to the tradition. This applies to Fichte's "deed-act" as well; the doctrine of science can derive only the traditional categories (substantiality, causality, reciprocity, etc.) from it. And yet it can be said that Fichte's conception of the "primacy of practical reason," together with Hegel's determination in the *Phenomenology of Spirit*, began to view man as a *doer* in a way which goes beyond the traditional limitations to his power. The post-Hegelians (Feuerbach, Marx, Stirner) already stand outside the history of thought which is customarily called "the tradition." But it is questionable whether they consciously "freed" their thinking sufficiently from the traditional categories and whether they came to a philosophical foundation of categorially unbound modes of being human.
2. *SZ* 130 ff. and 219 ff.; *WG* 14 ff. (21 ff.).
3. *WG* 36 (89).
4. *SZ* 226; cf. also *SZ* 212.
5. *SZ* 227.

ject" has ever decided which constitution of Being it will have. But it must still be noted that the specific way in which Heidegger formulated the relationship of Being and man in *Being and Time* can be conceived not only as an ontological but also as an ontic relativizing of the "ontological" to the "ontical." [6] For, as expressed there, the Being of man "is" the "power." The Being of being is not only dependent on this power insofar as its sense could never show itself without the understanding of Being. It is in addition dependent on there being a Dasein actually and ontically on the earth.

Thus if one wishes to speak graphically of a distribution of "power" and "lack of power," [7] then it must be said that Heidegger evidently recognized the enormous danger that lies in this formulation. For it delegated too much power to man and did not do justice to the fact that the Being of man as well, his understanding of Being, his disclosure and "truth," must still reside in the Being that is more than the essence of man. That he has since then vacillated in his distribution of the "power and impotence of man" need not make us wonder, in view of the immense aim of these endeavors. For here it is a matter of nothing less than the attempt to apprehend the role of the essence of man in a new way, a way which deviates radically from the tradition. Even in the later writings, which stress the impotence of man much more strongly, man retains, compared to the tradition, a great "power."

If we now turn, within the limits of our specific concern, to a description of these determinations of the relationship of Being and the essence of man in Heidegger's later writings, it should be stressed at the outset that what is at issue here is certainly not the relationship of Being to "ontic" man. In *Being and Time* as well, what mattered most were the "existential" structures and not the "existentiel" modes of human behavior, just as in the tradition, e.g., in the *idea* or *eidos* of man or in Kant's "transcendental consciousness," it was not a question of something "human" but of the conditions that "enable" man and that are, in this sense, "nonhuman." The relationship or the reference of Being to the essence of man, which the later writings treat again and again, concerns this nonhuman dimension which first enables man.

This nonhuman enabling dimension is called "Dasein." While

6. *SZ* 212; cf. K. Löwith, *Heidegger*, pp. 26 ff.
7. Cf. here W. Szilasi, *Macht und Ohnmacht des Geistes*, pp. 261 ff.

in *Being and Time* this term designated the being, it is now a
title for Being. And in a further contrast to *Being and Time,* it is
now used only for the highest mode of consummation of the
human essence, in its capacity of creative interplay in the
occurrence of Being. The "everyday" modes of the Being of man,
which played such an important role in *Being and Time,* are as
such no longer studied. Nor is it asked how the creative modes of
man might determine the everyday modes or whether and how
these everyday modes are "derived" from the creative modes. The
problems of the "self" in its capacity to stand on its own remain
undiscussed.

The question of the relationship of "Being, essence, and the
essence of man" is thus now narrowed down to the question of
how the reference between the "creative occurrence of Being"
and the "creative essence of man" is to be conceived. A "relationship" is commonly thought to be a reference between two independent sides. Heidegger strives again and again to express the
idea of the "relationship" for this particular case in a much more
restricted way. In order to avoid the customary conception of
the meaning of a "relationship" and to apprehend it in its unique
mode, he circumscribes it by way of example as follows: [8]

> We always say *too little* of "Being itself" when, in saying
> "Being," we leave out the presenting *to* the human essence and
> thereby fail to acknowledge that this essence itself coconstitutes
> "Being." Also, we always say *too little* of man when, in saying
> "Being" (not being man), we posit man all by himself and only
> then bring what has thus been posited into a relation to "Being."
> But we also say *too much* when we mean Being as the all-encom-
> passing and thereby represent man only as a particular being
> among others (plants, animals) and put both into the relation.
> For the essence of man already implies the relation to that which,
> through the reference, the bearing in the sense of behooving, is
> determined as "Being," so that its presumed "in and for itself" is
> abolished.

The sense of "behooving" was already defined by us [9] in such
a way that it first brings the behooved into its essence and holds
it there, hands it out to its own essence, but holds it in the protecting hand. On the basis of this "behooving," the "reference" or

8. *SF* 27 (75).
9. See above, pp. 126 ff., and the translator's note.

"bearing" [*Bezug*] * of creative Being to the creative essence of man is understood as a "relationship" or "hold" [*Verhältnis*] *sui generis*.

If this is so, then the basic traits of the rethought initially incipient and forethought other incipient sense of Being must also indicate, by their structure, that and how Being "behooves" the essence of man. We shall now reconstructively investigate how the creative modes of the essence of man were described by Heidegger as "behooved" by the initially incipient and other incipient sense of Being. We shall also show how the "metaphysical" conceptions of the essence of man are for him historically determined in their "mission" by the "oblivion" of this relationship of Being and the essence of man.

* "Bearing" in the sense of "bringing forth," "giving by carrying and bringing," e.g., "Bear welcome in your eye" (*Macbeth* I.v.65), and "bearing gifts." According to Heidegger, the original meaning of *Bezug* involves "pulling in something and providing it from someplace" (*HW* 260). Note its connection with *Zug*, "pull," normally translated here as "trait," which presumably is the issue (*Austrag*) of such a bearing.

2 / The Basic Traits of the Essence of Man in the First Beginning

LET US FIRST ASK TO WHAT EXTENT the *eon*, the "unifying power of the distinction of Being and being," "behooves" the essential modes of man. Heidegger has concentrated particularly on the interpretation of Parmenides' Fragment B 6(1) since it is here that the "relationship" or "hold" of *eon* or *eon emmenai* to human *legein* and *noein* has "come to language."[1] For our purposes, the result of this interpretation is that the occurrence of the participial unity of the difference of Being and being could not come forth (*alētheuein*) as prevailing if there were no modes of the essence of man to "let it lie forth" and "take heed" of it. Such a "letting-lie-forth" constitutes for Heidegger the sense of the *legein*. The *legein* lays the occurrence of the difference of Being and being before the *noein* that structurally belongs to it, so that the *noein* can "take heed" of it. It is in this way that the *eon emmenai* "behooves" the essence of man.

By contrast, the essence of metaphysics is determined by its character of not laying forth this twofold of Being and being and taking heed of it.[2] This does not mean, according to Heidegger, that it did not "experience" the "summons" of this difference of Being and being. The essence of man during the dominion of metaphysics should thus have been determined by the "experience" of being "behooved" in this particular way. But the metaphysical thinker did not "think" this essential trait of man in his determinations. It was Heidegger who for the first time sought to think the difference as difference, as the prevailing distinction

1. Cf. *WD* 105 ff., esp. 125 ff., 136 ff. (167 ff., 208 ff., 225 ff.). Cf. also *EM* 85 ff., 105 ff., 129 ff. (111 ff., 137 ff., 168 ff.); *VA* 242 ff.
2. *WD* 127, 136, 145 (211, 224, 238); *VA* 264 ff.; *HW* 336.

of Being and being. He thus experiences himself being "be-hooved" by the difference in a special way.

Heidegger has not asked whether and how the temporal sense of *eon,* presence as "abrupt while," shows that the essential modes of man are "behooved." There is a suggestion concerning the relationship of the subsequent "epochal" stampings of this initially incipient "present" to the essence of man. The "epochal essence of Being" is said to stand in a "relationship" to "Dasein," insofar as the Dasein appropriated by it and belonging to it pre-serves this "epochal" character of Being in ek-sisting. There is in this "preserving" a "being behooved." [3]

Physis,[4] the overpowering prevailing, opening, coming forth, and appearing, "behooves" the "actively violent" modes of the essence of man,[5] the wielder of power, so that it can "come to stand" in what is present.[6] *Technē,* the creative and battling "cognitive activity," is needed [7] if Being, *physis,* is to be "fixed in the work," if the overpowering as "articulation of Being" is to be "harnessed" in works and a world is to be formed. *Physis* as initially incipient sense of Being "behooves" the "Da-sein of historical man." [8] Likewise, the creative occurrence of presence "behooves" the creators, poets, thinkers, and statesmen.[9] In a "reciprocity" [10] with them, the "un-heard," the "hitherto un-said and un-thought," [11] something "new," [12] originally comes forth for the first time.

The *technē* through artworks violently brings a specific being forth into Being and makes it "shine" as something beautiful. But it is not only the artwork that harnesses *physis* but also the act of power of the statesman which brings about the "here" of Being as "historical Being-here" within the *polis,* the "site of history." [13] And the thinker, who through his *legein* and *noein* also appre-hends Being as *physis,* as the appearing in its appearance, and takes heed of it, is "behooved" by Being for just this. But the one who is "behooved" above all is the poet, who violently harnesses the overpowering powers of *physis* into linguistic works and

3. Cf. *HW* 311.
4. *EM* 124 (162–63).
5. *EM* 115 ff. (151).
6. *EM* 47 (62).
7. *EM* 122, 123, 47 (161–62, 62).
8. *EM* 124 (162–63).
9. *EM* 47, 101 (62, 132).
10. *EM* 126 (165).
11. *EM* 47, 123 (62, 162).
12. *EM* 110 (144).
13. *EM* 117 (152).

thereby "names" them. The subsequent historical determinations
of the essence of man, in particular that of *zōion logon echon*,[14]
are all characterized by the "forgetting" of this "creative reciprocity" of *physis* and *technē*.

It is in the conflict of the first beginning, in the *polemos* of
physis and the violent essence of man, in this bringing-to-light of
the sense of Being as *physis*, that "truth" (*alētheia*) occurs. The
human essence is in this occurrence of truth "behooved" in a
special way, since it itself is "the site" of the opening of Being,
the site that is "necessitated by Being."[15] In *Being and Time*,
Dasein, which "is cleared in itself in its own here," was called
"the clearing." But, since then, this clearing has been conceived
"from Being," as a basic trait belonging to the presenting process
itself. The essay "Aletheia"[16] further determines the "relationship" of the essence of man to the initially incipient Being occurring as clearing. The "relationship," the "hold" to the clearing,
is said to be nothing other than the clearing itself. For it gathers
in gods and men into the clearing. Out of this clearing, man is
not only enlightened but is "lighted up toward it." Out of it he is
"cleared up" in his essence. Because of this, he in *his* way is able
to bring the clearing into the fullness of its essence and thereby
to guard the clearing.

This "holding relationship" of the initially incipient Being to
the essence of man, rethought as *alētheia*, is determined more
closely in the *Letter on Humanism* and in the essay "The Origin
of the Artwork," so that it can become "what is to be thought" for
forethinking, which will again transmute this thought. The
Letter on Humanism[17] shows to what extent the clearing as the
"truth" of Being itself is this "holding relationship." Being holds
existence in its ecstatic essence to itself and gathers it to itself as
the "place of the truth of Being in the midst of beings." The
"here" is the "clearing of Being" into which man stands out as
Being-here, as ek-sisting, thereby taking this "here" into custody.
Because of this "nearness" to Being, Heidegger here calls man the
"neighbor of Being."

These turns of phrase aim at showing that *alētheia* experienced as clearing in the first beginning belongs to the occurrence
of presence and at the same time coconstitutes the essence of

14. EM 134 (175). Cf. also WD 27 (61); HB 66 (277); SZ 49.
15. EM 156, 124, 130 (205, 162, 170).
16. VA 278.
17. HB 69, 71, 75, 77 (278, 279, 281, 282); cf. also HW 42 ff.
(678 ff.).

man in a decisive way. Man is "behooved" by it to such an extent that the occurrence of presence could not be accomplished as an occurrence of truth without the essence of man. By contrast, metaphysics conceived "seeing" and "knowing" as a "subsequent" reference to what is already unconcealed. The seeing of the ideas in Plato as well as the *noein* of the *noēton* and the *eidenai* of the *eidos* in Aristotle are directed to what has already appeared and is thus "on hand." And this also holds for the comprehension of understanding and of reason in the later development of metaphysics. There is no longer any "original" cocreative opening here. The "forgetting" of this original relationship to the occurrence of truth leads to the metaphysical determinations of the essence of man.[18]

Our deliberations on the history of the problem showed that the Aristotelian *ousia* as a *noēton* is structured toward the *noēsis* and that Hegel's "fulfilled Being," the self-knowing idea in absolute knowing, "realizes" the highest mode of the Being of man. But the Being of the first beginning is not a noetic, ousiological, teleologically predetermined order, nor is it a substantially determined occurrence of the thought of a subjectivity which orders itself to itself. Accordingly, the relationship of the essential modes of man to the initially incipient occurrence of presence cannot be an expression of a merely subservient role in the occurrence of *nous* or of the "good infinity." The talk of being "behooved" must not obscure the point that man in his essence is simply not a "servant" of the occurrence of Being, no matter how conditioned he may be. Since Being in the first beginning, according to Heidegger, is not determined by the basic trait of the traditional selfsameness but, as ousiologically unbound *poiesis*, permits the advent of the "new" in the sense already explained, the man who is "behooved" by this radically creative occurrence of presence is also radically "creative." This was just confirmed for us by the insight into the reciprocity between *physis* and *technē*. This is also the way in which the human essence as ek-sistence, in standing out into the clearing of Being, "takes Being into custody." The reference is "cocreative." [19] Such an ek-sisting standing-out into Being is an active "action." [20] The ek-sistent modes of the essence of man were also characterized as a "letting-be," and indeed in explicit contradistinction to the customarily passive meaning of this characterization. In *Being and*

18. *PW* 35 ff., 42 (262 ff., 265); *EM* 142 ff. (186).
19. *EM* 121 (158).
20. *HB* 53 ff. (270 ff.).

Time this letting-be with reference to the *alētheia* was called the *alētheuein*, and later it is called "unconcealing."

The great difference from the traditional conception of the essence of truth is that, as we have already seen, for Heidegger the *alētheia* as a basic trait of Being in the first beginning is not only the light, inasmuch as the clearing refers essentially to concealment, and the powers of error and sham pervade it and "mystery" permeates it. *Being and Time* already pointed out that Dasein is co-originally "in truth" and "in untruth" and that all of its "discovering" or *alētheuein* is a combat in which truth must be torn from untruth, *lēthē*. The essay *On the Essence of Truth* further explained how all unconcealing that "lets be" is always pervaded by the powers of concealment, by mystery and error. And likewise, the initially incipient *alētheia* as concealing clearing "behooves" the human modes of Being, which are essentially pervaded by mystery, error, and sham.[21]

At this point, we must emphasize the truly "uncanny" and "perilous" character of the role that Heidegger assigns to man. If man is not a servant of an order bound to substance but rather is a cocreator in an occurrence that creatively brings forth the new, then it is extremely significant that this cocreating remains essentially determined by the "unmitigated harshness of error."[22] The *noēsis* in Aristotle, as a result of the basic trait of the intelligibility of *ousia*, can never err. But unconcealing in Heidegger remains subject to the power of error. If one considers that for Heidegger man as thus erring is "behooved" by the occurrence of presence, that he thus opens the sense of Being by cocreating and as poet, thinker, and statesman helps to "fix" the truth of Being in the work, then one first recognizes the consequences of this conception, which lets man into dimensions from which the tradition had excluded him. To say that man "takes the clearing of Being into custody" means, in Heidegger's description of the first beginning, that the creative men through their works help to form the world, which constitutes the historical "unity of the paths and references" of a people. Threatened by error, the human essence thus cocreates these paths and references and therefore the measures for all "ethical" action.

In "the epochs of error," of "metaphysics," man forgets his role, in which he has to creatively take the occurrence into custody by cocreating. But even in his modes of Being which are growing more and more uncreative he has to deal with those

21. EM 78 ff. (103 ff.).
22. HW 43 (679).

significations of sense which are dominant. The "unconcealing" that occurs in the unconcealment of Being prevailing today is totally uncreative.

The work provoked by the unconcealment of the "com-posite" is limited to provoking Being and unconcealing it in the disposability of stock. These essential modes of man, which are determined by the power of error, are also "behooved," and even decisively, inasmuch as they for the first time let the belonging-together of Being and the essence of man come to the fore. As Heidegger sees it, the currently prevailing unconcealing is the "prelude" [23] to the other incipient relationship of Being and the essence of man in which man experiences himself being "behooved" in a "creative" way.

The basic trait of initially incipient Being rethought as *logos* indicates in a very special way how the essence of man is "behooved" in the occurrence of presence. According to Heidegger, during the time of the first beginning the nonhuman occurrence of presence conceived as *logos* was experienced in different ways in its relationship to the essence of man. Heraclitus' Fragment B 50 bears witness for him that the *logos* as a "selective laying," as a gathering that lays forth, out, and down, "behooved" the "letting-lie-forth," i.e., the human *legein*.[24] The role of the human *legein* as a *homologein* was limited to "listening" to the nonhuman occurrence of *logos* in a collected way. As regards that which fore-lies and gathered through the prevailing of the *logos*, the human *legein* must for its part "let it forelie" as the selfsame.[25] The *homologein* is certainly in no way the *logos* itself, but it "belongs" [*gehört*] to the *logos* in the twofold sense that it must listen [*hören*] to it and that it is "appropriated to it," "behooved" by it.[26] If that which is present is to "shine and appear" in the presenting through the "letting present" of the *logos*, the human *homologein* is "behooved" to "respond" to what is gathered and laid down. This relationship of the initially incipient *logos* to the *homologein* includes for Heidegger what is to be thought of the essence of language as well as of the essence of man. Heraclitus already "experienced" the essence of language in this relationship of the nonhuman power of *logos* to the *homologein*, but neither he nor the other Greeks had "thought" the essence of language out of the essence of Being in its relationship to the

23. ID 29 (36).
24. VA 207 ff.
25. VA 217 ff.
26. VA 226.

essence of man. It has already been shown how Heidegger conceives of the essence of language, and it has yet to be shown how he "forethinks" the role of man within the realm of language. For the time being, let us only stress that man according to this interpretation of Heraclitus' fragment plays a rather "passive" role within the occurrence of presence, at any rate in comparison to the role which he had as a result of Heidegger's translation of the *Antigone* chorus and on the basis of Heidegger's interpretation of the following fragments of Parmenides.

Fragment B 6(1), *chrē te legein te noein t'eon emmenai*, especially bears witness for Heidegger that man essentially had to violently take over the gathering of Being in the overpowering *physis*.[27] The essence of man is defined here as that of a violent "assembler" [28] who harnesses and conserves the overpowering *physis*. Through this violence, man reveals himself in his strange and tremendous uncanniness. To be sure, it is emphasized that this violent assembly is "necessitated" by Being and that it happens only as an "acceptance" and "administration for" Being.[29] But this role, which is expressly characterized here as cocreative, distinguishes itself from the one in which man through a *homologein* is merely an obedient listener to the *logos*. And it distinguishes itself even more radically from the determination of the essence of man by metaphysics, which has forgotten this originative and creative cocreating. Already with Aristotle, the *legein* became the statement and the categorial definition of what is already on hand.[30] The initially incipient determination of the "relationship" in any case awards man a "power" which is indeed enormous. This becomes particularly clear when notice is taken of how this initially incipient role of the essence of man, who opens Being in his wielding of power, is carried out in the realm of language.

The opening of Being happens [31] through language, through its originative "naming of the word," which opens up and preserves being in the articulation of its gathering. Through this poetic utterance of man, being is opened up and named *as* sea, *as* earth, *as* animal. It is harnessed into linguistic works and meaningfully formed in its entirety into a "world." Even though Heidegger declares that speech is not a human ability, here it is

27. *EM* 129 (168–69).
28. *EM* 132 (173).
29. *EM* 120 (156).
30. *EM* 131 (171).
31. See above, pp. 159, 205 ff.

not merely a matter of man's being able to listen to the *logos*, the primeval saying, to which he can only "respond." If man is mighty enough to harness the overpowering Being by founding through his naming the meaningfulness of particular beings as well as the totality of beings, then the prevailing "order of essence" would also be something "made" by man. This enormous power could again be denied to man only if language itself—in a way independent of man—were to consign to him that to which he must listen and respond. It is in this direction that fore-thinking explicates the essence of language and the essence of man.

3 / The Basic Traits
of the Essence of Man
in the Other Beginning

THE "TURN" FROM THE OBLIVION of Being takes place when the essencing of technology, the com-posite in its reciprocal positing of Being and the essence of man, can be experienced as the togetherness of Being and man. It places a "demand" on Heidegger's thinking to forethink this relationship in its reference to language and "responsively" develop the essential modes of Being human. Man in his essential modes can no longer be considered in Aristotelian fashion as a *zōion logon echon,* as the animal which "has language." Rather, his essence must be defined in terms of the "dialogue" [1] with the nonhuman "claim" and "appeal" of Being, the dialogue which man *is* in his essence.

It is within the "structure" of the whole of the essence of language that the "soundless saying" preceding every enunciation "shows" itself. The saying, the Being forethought as world essence, "behooves" listening just as the Heraclitean *logos* "behooves" the *homologein.* But the saying also "behooves" human speaking insofar as it replies, answers, and speaks through the "sounding of the word." [2] The soundless saying must therefore be brought "on the way to language" by coming to sound.

The essence of man must therefore be defined from the essential human ability to let that which soundlessly addresses itself to him come to sound. And it must further be understood that the saying approaches the essence of man as a claim, reaches out to him and moves him on his way. [3] That man can "listen" to Being and its claim shows that he "belongs" to Being

1. *HD* 36, 37, 40 (301, 302, 307).
2. *US* 260.
3. *US* 201, 261 ff.

[225]

and must find his determination from this attuned belonging. Parmenides' Fragment 5, *to gar auto noein estin te kai einai* (Heidegger's translation: For the selfsame is attentive learning [thinking] as well as Being), which expresses a coordination of Being and attentive learning as the unity of an order, is accordingly forethought as a "listening" way of *belonging* together.[4] Because man is capable of listening to the claim and appeal of Being, he has an essence which lies in Being's "turning toward him or turning away from him."[5]

The forethought "relationship" of behooving, i.e., of the *to chrē* of the first beginning, is called the *appropriating event* [*Ereignis*].* This "key word" of forethinking is called upon now to determine the distribution of "power and impotence" between Being and the essence of man. It is intended to indicate how, corresponding to the original sense of the word,[6] the "focused" [*eräugte*] essence of man as "glimpsed" can only "respond" to that which addresses itself to him in the realm of language, in an address that comes soundlessly as a claim and appeal of Being or of the world essence. But in this "constellation" of Being and the essence of man,[7] man himself retains much more "power" than the tradition had ever consigned to him. As the "prelude" of the event of appropriation, which essences as com-posite,[8] already indicates, the noncreative human labor is itself a cocreating within the occurrence of Being. For being could never come

---

* *Ereignis* ordinarily means "event," but here the stress falls on the *eigen* ("own, proper") and thus on an appropriating. To stress the relationship of mutual appropriation between Being and the essence of man which "takes place" here, in a domain where each comes into its own, *Ereignis* is translated as "event of appropriation." To stress the process according to which the event "gives" (*Es gibt; das Ereignis er-eignet*) the modulations of this belonging-together, it is translated as "appropriating event." At times it will also be helpful to stress the emergent unconcealing character of the "e-vent," which is no ordinary event but the source of all events. "Appropriation" here connotes both give and take, both the allotting for an exclusive and proper use and the taking and making one's own that which properly belongs to one. Heidegger traces *Ereignis* back to the medieval *er-äugen*, "to eye," which here is being taken in the sense of "to focus," i.e., "to single out," once again serving to stress the uniqueness of the *proprium*, that which is most one's own (*eigen*). For *Ereignis* still bears a manifest resonance with the *Eigentlichkeit* of the unique and single individual, who anticipates his own death according to the descriptions of *Being and Time*, who enters into the event as a "mortal" in this later stage of Heidegger's thought.

4. ID 20 ff. (29 ff.).
5. SF 27 (75); cf. also VA 129 ff.
6. ID 28 (36).
7. ID 28 (36); VA 41.
8. ID 29 (36).

forth within the currently prevailing unconcealment as the disposability of stock if man could not listen to the currently prevailing demand and produce what is present through his labor. The creative modes of human response already designated by Heidegger in forethinking, namely, poetizing, thinking, building, and dwelling, are all no longer violent, but they are nonetheless, each in its own way, the expression of an enormous power of man.

Heidegger's attacks on the Cartesian image of man, on the modern man of reason, on the representing, planning, and self-certifying style of thinking, his attempt to "counterthink" all of these anthropocentric tendencies and to forethink a change in the essence of man, prompts us to forget that this essentially changed man retains a privilege of enormous power. That Heidegger now thinks of man as essentially "obedient" to Being or in a "composed letting-be" [*Gelassenheit*] of Being or as submitting to the mission of Being in a "befitting" manner, that he thinks of the essence of man as "focused" by the appropriating event, all of these seemingly "passive" characterizations should not blind us to the fact that man is allotted the role of cocreating creatively in the occurrence of Being. Man is thought by Heidegger as a necessary and creative *coplayer* in the play of the world. Without his creative supporting play, the world play, the worlding of the world and the thinging of the thing, could not take place; without him there would be no meaningful senses and significations. To be sure, man as coplayer cannot by himself create the world as his "product." But to think of his relationship to the world as an "event of appropriation" indicates that his essential modes must "come into play" in a creative way in order that the truth of world and thing may "take place" in this appropriation.[9] The scope and limits of this power as Heidegger defines it can be precisely known only by now investigating in detail the essential modes of man.

The poetizing and thinking modes of man,[10] which saying bestirs and "brings on the way to language," are decisive for this forethought essential determination of man. They characterize the essence of man as appropriately evented, glimpsed, or focused.

9. When Heidegger writes, "The thing is appropriated in the event" (*VA* 180), or that the mirror play of the world is "appropriating" (*VA* 178), the reference to the human essence is presumably implied.

10. *HW* 50 (685). Heidegger has to date not forethought the mode in which a state is founded.

Heidegger has defined the relationship of thinking and poet-izing in different ways.[11] But common to them all is that both the thinker and the poet are "custodians" of the "house" of Being, i.e., caretakers of language.[12] They are within the "soundless say-ing"[13] like "neighbors" who "dwell on separate summits."[14]

Hölderlin has *poetized* the "essence of poetry," while Heideg-ger has *thought* it in the other beginning. It first comes to the fore through the "dialogue of thinking with poetizing." In supple-menting what has already been presented in the course of this treatise as well as Heidegger's own characterizations, for a de-termination of the structure of this dialogue and of "essential thinking" in general we must fall back on the essence of Heideg-ger's own thinking, since he obviously is the only one so far who has actually done it.

Heidegger has "forethought" the relationship of human thinking to the nonhuman occurrence of Being, just as he had "rethought" in the Heraclitus fragment the relationship of the human *homologein* to the nonhuman occurrence of *logos*. The *transmutation* of the rethought into the forethought here lies in understanding this relationship as the expression of the "e-vent of appropriation" within the realm of language, as the relation-ship of "responding" to the soundless saying. Thinking is essen-tially a listening and belonging in the e-vent, an answering ap-propriated by it and taking place through the sounding word. Such a listening and belonging can, however, be reached only by a "leap."[15] Thinking must leap away "from all that is familiar" and from the metaphysical representations of the stampings of Being and leap into the realm in which the saying addresses its "words of Being" to the listening that obediently "belongs" to them, and bestirs what is heard on its way to sound.

But the role of the essence of man in its relationship to Being according to this characterization of the essence of thinking seems to be merely that of an obedient and attentive servant. For in formulating the relationship of the "words of Being" to "thinking," Heidegger insists that it is the words which have all the power. The word not only "names" the "topic" [*Sache*] but "nominates" it, "gives" it, and lets it "be present."[16] Thinking

11. VA 138 ff.; WM 46 (386); HW 303 ff.; US 38.
12. HB 53 (271).
13. US 202.
14. WM 46 (385).
15. See above, p. 115; WD 4, 48, 140 ff. (7–8, 13, 236); ID 32 ff. (39); US 159 ff.
16. HW 60 (694); VA 190; US 232.

must accordingly think the topical realm in the way "the word speaks to it." It must think the topic "in the hold it has in the early word meaning and its change" and pay attention to the "context of meanings" in which it has been "explicated throughout the history of thinking and poetizing." [17] So, for example, Heidegger thought the topic of the thinging thing with reference to the Old High German meaning of the word *Thing* in the sense of "gathering" and thus forethought the topic, here the "thinging," from the word in its "approaching and nearing" gathering. [18]

If the word is that which "nominates the topic," then the word seems to be more important than the topic. Accordingly, Heidegger claims that thinking catches a glimpse of what is said by a "glance that leaps" to the word that nominates the topic. [19] The words are the "wellsprings" to which thinking must go again and again; [20] they are the "fountainheads" [21] in which even the "unspoken of the saying," the "mystery," [22] prevails. These words are "signs," i.e., "hints," [23] which hint at what is "to be thought over," the "essence of a topic," [24] to those who think.

Despite this priority now granted to the word, thinking is still obliged to glance from the words to the topic. For—writes Heidegger [25]—"the mere ascertaining of the old and often no longer living meaning of words, the apprehending of this meaning with the intention of employing it in a new usage, leads to nothing but arbitrariness." Nothing would have been more important than to determine, over and above this cautioning remark, just where the task of the thinking which attends to words in relationship to the topic now lies and to point the structure of thinking in this direction, in order to show the "binding character" of the thinking that he now carries on and of its results to date. Precisely because the word that "nominates" the topic plays such a significant role, and thinking must hold to the word hints that suggest it, it becomes all the more urgent to ask just how one can really decide whether the relevance of a topic has been thought in a strict way. We have no "criteria" by which to decide whether an "elaboration of the *topos*" [*Erörterung*] or "delibera-

17. *VA* 48.
18. *VA* 172.
19. *WD* 141 (233).
20. *WD* 89 (130).
21. *US* 131.
22. *US* 233.
23. *US* 114 ff.; *WD* 91, 107 (138, 174).
24. *VA* 190; cf. also *HW* 338.
25. *VA* 48.

tion of sense" [*Besinnung*] is in accord with the topic [*Sache*], whether such an "essential thinking" or "dialogue" is carried out by Heidegger himself or by some other thinker. Whether a thinker has listened, in response to the topic, to a saying that soundlessly addresses itself to him, and whether he has responded to it in a correctly "sub-missive" and "obedient" way and has found the "correct" sounding word, can in no way be tested.

But perhaps even the wish for such a test seems to miss the point. Perhaps this correspondence of address and response is really a matter of an occurrence which can only be compared to "poetic inspiration." Now we readily concede to a poet that his works are "inspired," and we do not demand a demonstration of the "structure" of his poetizing. But here there is not even a problem of "binding force." There can be no doubt that this question disturbs Heidegger himself. Granted all of their common interests, he has nevertheless distinguished thinking from poetizing. The *Letter on Humanism* declares that the thinking of Being is not "arbitrary," since it is bound to a "law of thought" whose "strictness" lies in remaining "in the element of Being." [26] And the "element of Being" has since then been identified as the essence of language, the soundless saying. But this means that the plurivocity of the saying, its play of meanings, is bound and retained "in a hidden rule," in a "highest law." [27]

But Heidegger has so far not shown how thinking is capable of hearing, within the multiplicity of meanings, the meaning which is "in accord with the topic" and of responding to it with the appropriate word. The problem of binding force is not concerned with the question of the lawfulness of the interplay within the saying but the question of whether there is a "game rule" according to which thinking must be "properly" done, i.e., in accordance with the topic.

But it may be that, for the question of whether Being "shows" itself, and how it shows itself, and whether it has been appropriately brought to language, there *can* be no "game rules." For here it is no longer a matter of the problem of the "verification" of a projecting and discovering interpretation of possibilities "forthcoming in their having been" in the how of the discovery. After the relationship of historical Dasein and historical possibility was reversed for Heidegger, the question of whether the empowering possibility (the "topic") shows itself to his thinking or disguises and even hides itself is perhaps purely and simply

26. *HW* 56 (690), 118.
27. *SF* 42 (105).

"unverifiable." If this is so, then it would be better not to speak of "laws" and of the "strictness" of the "rules of the game," which in their very meaning always refer to a positive verifiability. This is not to cast doubt on the fact that Heidegger in his thinking has experiences which assume a measure of "constraint." But his contemporaries must perhaps resign themselves to the fact that they can never verify this constraint of "necessity" and that the question of the binding character of his thinking cannot be asked.

If we accept Heidegger's last determination from the essence of language as an answer to our question of the limits and scope of the power of man in his relationship to Being, then it holds true that man is only a very passive "coplayer." His creative and cocreating activity is limited to a correct hearing and a correct response. But it seems very strange that for the opening of Being in the first beginning, Being itself had "necessitated" a highly active and violent human essence, while for the opening of another incipient sense of Being it seems to "behoove" only a passive and submissive human essence. And the style and manner in which Heidegger himself thoughtfully prepares for this other oncoming sense of Being completely contradicts, after all, his own determination of this thinking. The rethinking which translated the basic traits of Being from the experience of the first beginning proceeded in a deliberately violent way. Only in this way, according to Heidegger, could the hitherto unthought as the having-been become present to thinking in such a way that, as the "having once been of the forthcoming," it was transmuted into what is to be thought. Forethinking is understood as an active transmuting and a "building," which accordingly is not the expression of a passive service. It is in fact a "supreme action" [28] which, in order to help to prepare the advent of another mission of Being, "coplays" in the play of the world. Heidegger's own thinking, the only example we have of "essential thinking" and "dialogue," indicates that—contrary to his recent emphasis—the forethought essence of man also possesses a very great power.

The violently active kind of essential thinking is particularly evident in the "dialogue" with Hölderlin's poetry,[29] which involved the transmutation of the "words of the holy" in poetry into "words of Being," which provide the necessary "tools" for the forethinking of the world essence.

28. *HB* 53 (271).
29. Cf. B. Allemann, *Hölderlin und Heidegger,* pp. 94 ff. and 172 ff., and Else Buddeberg, *Heidegger und die Dichtung,* pp. 21 ff.

4 / The Essence of Poetizing and "Poetic Dwelling"

THIS ESSENCE OF POETIZING, which the new type of thinking had *thought* and Hölderlin had *poetized*, determines for Heidegger the role of the essence of man and thus also the limits and scope of its power. It is true that Heidegger has declared that thinking is "the original mode of poetizing," [1] "the original *dictare*" that precedes all poesy.[2] But this priority of thinking over poetizing was in the first instance valid only for the first beginning, since it was here, after all, that language initially and at one time had to come "to language, i.e., to its essence." [3] But the preparation of the other beginning likewise seems to include the requirement that poetizing become in its way a thinking way [4] and that "there must first be thinkers, so that the poet's word can become audible." [5] On the other hand, Heidegger looks to poesy or, more generally, to the "fine arts"—and thus not in the first place to thinking—to cultivate the advent of the saving world essence in its growth, to reawaken and to institute the granting.[6]

The 1936 lecture entitled "Hölderlin and the Essence of Poetry" [7] conferred an extraordinarily great power and a decisive role upon poetizing. The exposition of Hölderlin's line "But that which remains is instituted by the poets" showed that it is the poets who, through the "essential word," initially "open" being in

1. HW 303.
2. *Ibid.*
3. *Ibid.*
4. Cf. *Trivium*, IX, no. 1 (1951), p. 8.
5. HD 29 (288).
6. VA 43.
7. HD 31 ff. (293 ff.). Cf. K. Löwith, *Heidegger*, pp. 34 ff.

its Being. Through this naming, being is "initially nominated to what it is." What we later talk over and dispose of in everyday language is "freely created, posited, and granted" through poetry. The poet's instituting of Being through words is an institution of what remains, which here is explicitly called "the persistent." For only the persistent can remain within "torrential time" as the "one and the same," as the measure which has been "wrested from confusion" as the "simple" and "brought to stand against the torrent" as the remaining.

But the poets not only have the power to institute the measures which pervade and sustain "being as a whole" or, to put it another way, to form a historical world. This instituting of the essence of things at the same time brings the historical Dasein "in" man into a firm relation and is in this sense a "solid grounding."

This conception of the role and power of man is compatible with the characterization of the essence of man during the first beginning as a violent cocreating. There, also, it was through language, the "primeval poetry," that the opening of Being took place. There, the power of man was held in check by the conception that he was only a "trustee" of language, a trust which he had simply "taken on" in its overpowering power. In the conception of the other beginning, "language, that most dangerous of possessions" is said to belong to man, and he is therefore essentially a "dialogue." To be sure, the poet, for all his freedom, is still bound to an "utmost necessity." In him, the saying is brought to language by the "gods themselves," who address him through "signs" which he receives and transmits. His poetizing is thereby bound to the "voice of the people."

Let it be noted that here too Heidegger has not examined how one can decide whether any particular instituting word is an "essential word" or a "mirage." Precisely because—as Heidegger himself stresses here—language is "the most dangerous of possessions," which creates the "manifest site of the menace to Being and its error and so the possibility of the forfeiture of Being," the question of when an act of poetizing is a genuine saying is of the utmost urgency. If it is the poets who are consigned to this tremendous task of instituting that which endures, the measures, the historical world of a people, then it would be well to know what determines whether the poet actually heard the "signs" of the gods and was capable of interpreting the "voice of the people" correctly.

At a later stage, in the elucidation of the poem "As when on the feast day . . ." (1939),[8] the power of the poet is appreciably diminished. Here, the poetic naming says only what "that which has been evoked out of its essence requires the poet to say."[9] The poets are now called the "respondents." What they essentially respond to is the dimension of the "holy,"[10] which was thought out of the initially incipient basic word *physis,* as its "other." Holy is the original "hale," the "omnipresent and enrapturing Nature."[11] The hale or holy is not a "property borrowed from a fixed God"[12] but "the element of divinity" and, in this sense, "the aether of the gods or of God."[13] As this aether, the holy is therefore only the "trace" which the "departed gods" have left behind and which may lead again "to the divinity."

Hölderlin experienced the holy as the trace of the missing God, as the "lack of God,"[14] and poetized from this experience. In the world night that now prevails, in the "time of need," even the traces to the traces of the absent God are almost obliterated. The world has become un-holy, and only "a few mortals" actually still recognize "the unholy as unholy," as "the peril,"[15] and are capable of seeing "the saving element" in it. They are the ones who—like Heidegger—above all keep in mind how, through thinking, "historical ek-sistence may be led into the realm of the emergence of the hale"[16] and who think the "essence" of poetizing, so that man may again open himself to the hale and the holy. But this cannot be "forced." Poetizing likewise is possible[17] only when the holy "gives the word" and thereby "itself comes in the word." Only then is the word—as Heidegger already asserted here—an "e-vent" of the holy. Only then does the "work in words" let the "belonging-together" of gods and men appear, in the sense that they can respond to the demands made on them.

In relation to the poetizing human being, it is the holy that now seems to have all the power. It has "poetized beyond all poetizing."[18] The poet can only "hail" the holy, and even this only "because he himself is the hailed."[19] As the one who hails the

8. *HD* 47 ff.
9. *HD* 56.
10. *HD* 56, 58.
11. *HD* 58 ff.
12. *HD* 58.
13. *HW* 250.
14. *HD* 27 (286).
15. *HW* 272.
16. *HB* 112 (298).
17. *HD* 63, 67 ff., 74.
18. *HD* 139.
19. *HD* 94.

"messenger of the holy, the angel,"[20] he is "behooved"[21] and "compelled" to be a "trail blazer" [*Zeigender*].[22] He performs this "pointing-out," into which he is "com-missioned," in an appropriately "sub-missive" way when he thinks "what has been as the oncoming holy,"[23] when he in this sense rethinks. The feast commissioned by the holy, the holiday, takes the poet out of the context of everything ordinary and urges him to think what "has been" so that it is forthcoming to him, and he must unfold it as the oncoming holy.[24] Thus he displays the holy in order that, through his poetizing, the gods "bring themselves to appearance in the dwelling place of man on this earth."[25] The "instituting of that which remains" is now situated in the thinking of the holy, which remains fast and festive through such thinking. It is in this way that the "coming" of "another beginning of another history"[26] is made possible. If, in the elucidation in "Hölderlin and the Essence of Poetry," that which remains was the measure which persists at present in "torrential time," so now it becomes a coming of the holy which calls man to the "essential decisions" of his history. In the later elucidation entitled "Remembrance," the instituting of that which remains is understood simply as the way in which the poet finds his way to his own essence and dwelling. In order for poetizing as rethinking to take place, the primordial dwelling, the poetic in the realm of the holy, must be made fast again and again, fixed, and in this sense instituted as remaining. This happens only when the poet again and again takes the awesome path to the "source," to the "proximity of the origin," to the "ground," to the hale and holy which opens itself to him as he "holds his ground and points,"[27] and hails him with its "word." Though the poet himself no longer institutes the persistent measures, Heidegger nevertheless still characterizes poetizing as a matter of "taking measures." In the commentary first delivered in 1951, ". . . Poetically Dwells Man . . . ,"[28] poetizing is characterized as the "measure-taking." This peculiar measuring measures—beyond any spatial metric—the dwelling of

20. HD 16 (268).
21. HD 109.
22. HD 92.
23. HD 94.
24. HD 101 ff.
25. HD 116.
26. HD 73.
27. HD 136 ff. Heidegger did not distinguish rethinking here from authentic forethinking.
28. VA 187 ff., esp. 196.

man "between" the heavens and the earth and thereby bestows the measure for the breadth of the human essence in general. But poetizing as such a "measure-taking" is possible only because the divinity grants the poet the measure by which man can measure himself. In a time in which God conceals himself as the "unknown," the heavens provide the awesome spectacles from which the poet takes his measures.

The poetizing appropriated by the holy is, in this most recent interpretation of Heidegger, no more violent than thinking is at this stage. One is thereby easily led to overlook the significant change which it still undergoes in comparison to the tradition, even in this diminished role. In order to see what is new or "other" in the role of poetizing in Heidegger, we must above all keep in mind that poetizing is the producing of a *work*. The great significance which is attributed to the artwork in Heidegger's over-all view has already been indicated. Through the artwork "truth" is founded in a new and unprecedented way, a "world" is formed, sense and meaning emerge. As a consequence of Heidegger's conception of the essence of language, the poetic work has a very special position in this occurrence of *poiēsis*. It is evident that more than just a passively understood "listening" and "responding" must take place if "works" are to come out of poetizing. What Heidegger has said about the creating of works in "The Origin of the Artwork" must therefore also hold generally. Without cocreative actions on the part of man, artworks as created cannot be "forced" into their meaningful "configuration." [29] In the linguistic work as well, the poet must actively and creatively put to work the "evocative distinction" of world and thing. The sounding of the word cannot be an imitating of the saying but must be understood as the way in which world and thing come to language in a "new" way. It is thus that the poet creatively takes part in the emergence of significant meanings. The Aristotelian artist "merely imitates." The artist in Hegel simply realized the infinitely absolute spirit. And since there can be neither a "new" *ousia* in Aristotle nor a "new reality" in Hegel, the poets in this tradition could never take part in the emergence of a new meaningfulness. Their "works" therefore do not have the uncanny role which the poetic work acquires in Heidegger's view. If the poet can also—according to the later formulations— bring the measures of divinity to language in his works, these are nevertheless works cocreated by mortals, works which provide

29. *HW* 51 (686).

the measures for the sojourn of the earthly. The power of the poet and his work is in fact so great that even in Heidegger's present view it is *poiēsis* which first grounds the genuine "dwelling" of man, his true sojourn, and in this sense his "existence."

According to Hölderlin's dictum,[30] "poetically dwells man," there can be a genuine dwelling only if poets have first measured the dimension, the "between" of heaven and earth, according to the heavenly measure, the measure of the hidden God. Only when the poets have already poetized the fourfold does it become possible for a mortal to inhabit it, in the sense that he has learned "to heed it in its essence." Otherwise the sense and meaning of the earth and the heavens, the divine ones and the mortals, would remain closed to him.

Do the mortals dwell poetically today? Do they heed the essence of the fourfold? Heidegger has replied negatively to this very question,[31] even though Hölderlin had already measured off the dimension and thereby "let the dwelling be," and even though Heidegger's thinking had expressly thought this dimension as the fourfold, the world. We need only compare the more precise description of such a poetic dwelling with the present and presumably future state of affairs in order to see that man dwells utterly "unpoetically." And this holds for the dwelling of the few really creative men as well as that of the many uncreative men.

For to dwell on the "earth," i.e., to heed it in its essence, means to guard it as "the serving and sustaining element," as "that which blooms and bears fruit, dispersed in minerals and waters, emerging for vegetation and animal life." [32] But today the earth is simply not heeded in this, its own essence. Instead, it is belabored and exploited. Under the dominion of the essence of technology, it is positioned for its energy and raw material. It is provoked into delivering the energy of nature for industry.[33] Under the dominion of metaphysics, the earth is "devastated," it is forced to yield "the impossible." [34] But to dwell poetically on the earth means "to receive the benediction of the earth, to become acclimated in the law of this reception, in order to guard the 'mystery' of Being and to watch over the inviolability of the possible." [35]

30. *VA* 187 ff.; also *VA* 145 ff.
31. *VA* 187.
32. *VA* 149.
33. *VA* 23 ff.
34. *VA* 98.
35. *Ibid.*

To dwell "on the earth" always means to dwell "under the heavens" as well. The heavens as poetized by the poet, under which poetic dwelling should take place, is "the arching course of the sun, the path of the changing shape of the moon, the wandering brilliance of the constellations, the seasons of the year and their turning points, light and twilight of day, dark and bright of night, fair and foul weather, the procession of the clouds and the azure depth of the aether." [36] The man employed in the business world under the dominion of the "com-posite," who is housed like a stock item in the metropolitan buildings of Gothams, certainly does not dwell poetically under the heavens. And it is even more certain that he does not dwell in the "presence of the divine," of the "hinting messengers of the divinity." He therefore cannot "await the hints of their advent and not mistake the signs of their absence," because—as Heidegger explained—in the world night that now prevails the very trace leading to the divinity has been lost.

Men no longer live as "rational animals" but as "mortals" if they—while living—have learned "to die," i.e., when they relate themselves to "death *as* death." [37] But of whom will it be said during the reign of technology that he actually experiences this Being-unto-death as "the relationship" in which Being—in this ultimate way of concealing itself—unconceals itself to him?

Man dwells poetically when he dwells among his "things." In Heidegger's view, [38] things "are" insofar as they, by thinging, permit the presence of the fourfold, the unifying unity of the world neighborhoods. Man dwells authentically among things and with them when he "lets" them be "as" things in this, their essence. This occurs when he nurtures and tends "growing things," preserves the fourfold in them, and thus lets them be in this, their own "truth," i.e., in the way they are unconcealed. And this also occurs when he receives "directions" from the unifying unity of the fourfold for the erection of sites in which the fourfold can while, in which it acquires an abode, as in the cited examples of the jug, bridge, and house.

But we have already seen that there are very few "things" to which the capacity of "permitting the whiling of the fourfold (the world) by thinging" can be attributed. But what seems to be even more of a rarity today is the man who is capable of dwelling poetically with things, so that he permits himself to be

36. *VA* 150.
37. *VA* 150; see above, p. 187; *VA* 69; *HD* 62.
38. *VA* 151 ff., 155 ff.

"thinged" (conditioned) by them and experiences their proximating as their mirror play. Who today can honestly say of himself
that he, in being mindful of his death, crosses the Heidelberg
bridge in such a way that he comes "before the hale of the divine"? Or who today experiences the presentation of the divine
in the gift of the jug?

Heidegger would not dispute the point that there is no poetic
dwelling on the earth today. This in fact is the "peril" which essences as com-posite. The menace to the essence of man and the
neglect of his things are its immediate essential consequences.
But Heidegger is convinced that the "turn" from the oblivion of
Being, from the withdrawal of creative Being, to the world essence has already "e-vented" itself, that his thinking is appropriated by Being into the thinking of its truth, that the "saving element" has begun to grow. Heidegger has declared more than
once that he already sees "the signs" of a turning point.[39] These
signs should bear on the Being of man in his present sojourn
with things. It may be asked whether or not all signs indicate instead the intensification of the currently prevailing tendencies,
so that man is becoming more and more alienated from the earth
as earth, from the heavens as heavens, so that the "aether of divinity" is closing itself off more and more and so that man has
less opportunity to "learn to die," i.e., to live "as a mortal." Even
Heidegger of late seems to resign himself to a future of fewer
and fewer "thinging" things. For, as the correct attitude toward
the things of the technological world, he recommends a posture
which he calls "composure toward the things," which lets them
"be" as they are. And this posture must be integrated with an
openness for the mystery of Being, the very "sense" which technology conceals. This "composure toward the things" and "openness for the mystery" already grant a glimpse of a "new autochthony" of man.[40] But these two attitudes which are possible for
him today hardly constitute a "poetic dwelling" within the fourfold of the world. Heidegger's over-all view appears questionable
if it cannot be shown how the old autochthony now disappearing
can be developed into a new autochthony, in which the world essence holds sway in the way in which he has described it.

These deliberations, which have attempted to think along
with Heidegger, have tried to clarify the disturbing character of
the "result" of what he has forethought. If the turn in Heidegger's sense has really evented itself, would not this have entailed

39. Cf. VA 69; HD 62.
40. Gelassenheit, p. 25 (54).

the beginning of the dominion of the other sense of Being and essence in one form or another? Would not the fourfold of the world "address" itself not only to his thinking but also to the thinking and poetizing of his contemporaries? Would not the actual building have begun to "correspond" to the fourfold of the world, and would not the dwelling of man on the earth have become at least somewhat more poetical? Although everything "actually" points to exactly the opposite development, Heidegger holds fast to the conviction that the turn has already occurred. To be sure, Heidegger rightly asserts that the "actual" is not the "exclusively real." But with respect to our questions of the legitimation and the binding character of his thinking, it may be asked whether Heidegger can with such certainty claim to know our impending future in terms of what it holds as the "exclusively real."

Conclusion

THE AIM OF THIS WORK consisted in the first place in finding an answer to the question of where the *other* sense of Being and essence and of the essence of man—"other" as compared to the tradition—is to be found in Heidegger.

This *otherness* of the sense of Being and essence and of the essence of man in Heidegger was elaborated and viewed from the vantage point of the distance existing between them and the basic traits of Being and essence in Aristotle and in Hegel. It manifested itself in a triple direction: as the other sense of Being and of the essence of man in the *first beginning*, as the—against the traditional conception—*other essence of metaphysics* (in its history of Being and its determinations of man), and as the other sense of Being of the *other beginning*—the world essence and the essence of man as open to the world.

These efforts were occasioned and guided by the specific question of whether Heidegger's work represents a contribution to the "present need of philosophy." We saw this need above all in holding the question of the *essence* of essence in motion. It must be acknowledged without qualification that it was Heidegger who first actually got this question moving. On the other hand, presumably because of the special style of his inquiry, the movement initiated by him has been taken up and carried on in a fruitful way in contemporary philosophy only in isolated instances. Accordingly, we have attempted to place the problematic under question once again and in various respects, in order thereby to pave the way for a *further thinking*, a thinking that carries on.

Let us repeat that we consider the enormously difficult task

[243]

of our generation to lie in thinking the essence of essence in such a way that the advent of the *new* is found to be possible. And the advent of the new will have to be thought in a way which gives man a role in the occurrence of this change without thereby "humanizing," historicizing, or relativizing the essence again. The other sense of Being and essence which is to be thought must properly comprehend the decisive modes of the Being of man and redefine the essence of "things" from the "wholeness" which encompasses them, in order to curb their increasing "reification." Has Heidegger responded to these problems?

He regarded the sense of Being in the first beginning as a highly creative presence. This is borne out by the inner mobility of the twofold character of *eon* and its temporal sense, the "abrupt while." This is further demonstrated by the sense of *physis* as a self-emerging prevalence, as a "poietic" coming-forth and appearing, as well as by the sense of *alētheia* as a clearing permeated by countervailing concealment. And it is borne out by the way in which Being as *logos*, as a contentious gathering, lays forth and lays down. Presence is considered as "changeable" in itself, so that here change itself seems to be posited "absolutely." In particular, change in this creative occurrence is "absolute" in the sense that it is not a "product" of man. And yet a role has been ascribed to man within this self-changing presence. His creative modes of essence are "behooved" by presence. Accordingly, his essence resides in his being a "violent" cocreator. This creative presence in its interplay with the creative man brings forth "works," it forms a creative "world," a "wholeness" which encompasses and suffuses every being.

Heidegger then proceeded to think of a "change of essence" in the "eschatological" development of metaphysics, in the history of Being. Here, to be sure, it is not a matter of the advent of the creatively new, certainly not during the dominion of the essence of technology. But this conception of a history of Being takes into account the existence of our "historical consciousness" without thereby historistically relativizing or humanizing this change of essence, for the man of a given epoch has no influence over the particular unconcealment of the "stamping of Being" that governs it. And yet, without knowing it, man does play a role in the presence which is hidden in the prevalent stamping of Being. For example, he responds to the presence which is operative today, inasmuch as by laboring he reveals all that is present as uncreatively disposed. At the end of this history of Being, there is no "world" from which the "things" could be determined in their sense and in their truth; they are instead "neglected," and thus without truth.

Heidegger next considered the sense of Being of the other beginning, the "world essence," in a way which enables the advent of the new. The thinging of the thing in the mirror play that appropriates leaves open the possibility for the world neighborhoods to gather themselves into new "variations," into new "modes" of things. This change is not "made by man," although the creative man, the poet and thinker, plays a role in this world insofar as he listens to the "soundless saying," in which the world play addresses itself to him, and thus brings the saying into "sounding language." It is out of this "openness of the world" that the essence of man is determined. In all of these respects, therefore, Heidegger seems to have responded to the "present need of philosophy." But before a final judgment can be made, we must once more recall the various objections which have emerged in the course of these investigations.

It was shown that there is a "limit" to the dominion of the sense of Being in both the first and the other beginning. The poetic and creative sense of presenting in the first beginning did not adequately cover the many everyday things which must also have been given to the early Greeks. And the thinging of the other beginning which gathers the world neighborhoods can account for only a very small number of "genuine things," and not for the ever increasing quantity of the "things" of universally dominating technology. Heidegger must have intentionally limited the ruling scope of Being in the first and other beginnings, for otherwise one would be compelled to reject his over-all project as absolutely "utopian." But if the creative sense of Being holds only for the creative realms, then Heidegger has not responded to the present need of philosophy in every instance, insofar as he has up to now not exhibited the sense of Being which might adequately take the noncreative realms into account. Nor has he addressed himself to the difficult regional problems which necessarily arise through this delimitation. He has therefore only partially answered the question of what specifically is to take the place of the "destroyed" categories of substance and of subject. The delimitation of the project of Being in both beginnings is also to be found in the restriction of the discussion to the role of creative men and their essential ways. By contrast, *Being and Time* began with the everyday modes of man's Being, in order to demonstrate their derivative character in relation to the authentic modes of Dasein. In the late writings no attempt is made to set forth the ways in which the creative modes of man could specifically influence the everyday modes of behavior.

Another objection is that the exclusive way in which the project of the sense of things is determined in the other beginning, from "wholeness," from the meanings of the world neighborhoods, leads to a neglect of their capacity to stand on their own and of other important modes of the Being of things. This even pertains to those few "genuine" things which Heidegger cites.

In order to be able to make a final judgment as to whether Heidegger's later thinking can be viewed as a contribution to the tasks listed above, we must also recall once again that all of these modes of a creative sense of Being were explicated by a special kind of "thinking." This thinking experiences itself as enabled by "empowering" Being, "granted" by the sense of Being of the first beginning. But Heidegger has not shown how the "power of the possible" in *Being and Time* became the "empowering" Being (in *Letter on Humanism*) from which rethinking and even forethinking are legitimated. For all that, our investigation came to the conclusion that the forethought basic traits still refer back only in slight measure to the "granting" of the sense of Being in the first beginning, to the experiences of the early Greeks, and that instead they must be based largely on the experiences which Heidegger himself has had with Being.

But Heidegger has not provided any "rules of the game" for rethinking and forethinking, according to which one might be able to decide whether that which addresses itself in "soundless saying" is properly heard and properly brought to language. It is thus that the problem of the binding character of this thinking arose, which to a lesser degree also persisted for the "retrieving" interpretations in the early works. This problem persists—notwithstanding the many extraordinarily illuminating determinations in Heidegger's works—because the relationship of essential thinking to the self-showing and self-concealing topic has been treated only sparingly.

The objections which lie in these references to the problems of the legitimation and the binding force of rethinking and forethinking become particularly disquieting when one realizes that the decision as to whether the turn to the other beginning has taken place (whether, in other words, the forethought sense of Being of the other beginning, the world essence, has already "arrived") depends on whether this "kind" of thinking and the experiences that proceed from it are binding or not. Add to this the difficulty, which Heidegger has not clarified, of why the essencing of technology, this withdrawal configuration of the creative basic traits of the first beginning, did not in fact draw his thinking back to that first beginning but instead required the exhibition of the quite distinct traits of another beginning.

It is of course possible to set aside these objections and to view Heidegger's over-all interpretation as the extremely significant statement of a great individual and simply accept it in the way we acknowledge the works of a great artist, without investigating it in terms of its legitimation and without challenging the artistic creation with inquiries into its binding or arbitrary character. Whoever is ready to accept Heidegger's work for its own sake, without troubling himself too much with the problems of its origin, will—indeed within the limited realm indicated by us —adjudge it to be an important contribution to the present need of philosophy.

Aside from these questions, it appears to be necessary to emphasize once again the special danger present in Heidegger's conception of the role of man and to point out the extremely disquieting consequences of Heidegger's conception of the essence of truth.

Heidegger was able to radically think through to the end the development for which Hegel had paved the way. If Hegel had already viewed the occurrence of Being as an occurrence of truth, as a coming-to-light of Being, and had also thought of the reference of light to darkness as a "relationship," he still primarily gave predominance to the "light," to reason and spirit, following the traditional presuppositions and approaches. It was Heidegger who first actually overcame the traditional "light metaphysics," inasmuch as he considered the "powers of darkness" in their own right and thought of them as equal partners in a countervailing strife with the "powers of light" and thus conceived the essence of truth as the relationship of a concealing clearing.

Heidegger's insight into the "mystery character" of the essence of Being is very important. The idea that everything which comes to light, which appears, continues to be pervaded by the mystery would profoundly affect and alter not only the scientific relationship of man to Being but all the modes of his behavior and his own self-understanding. The dangerous element which lies in this, as in every reference to "the dark," the essentially unknowable, and the mysterious, should not be underestimated. But even greater than this danger is the aggressive self-security of present-day Western man who, convinced of the total intelligibility of Being by a long tradition, has lost all his sense of awe before the unknown and, with ever increasing claims to superiority, has given himself over to the way of a universal and total science. The danger is all the greater as the predominant standards that came from religions are officially discredited in large parts of the West and in other parts are largely secularized.

No further comment is needed in order to show that in this situation Heidegger's coordination of the powers of error and sham with those of the luminous presents an extreme danger. The chief reason for this is that Heidegger—to put it in a traditional way—could give no rules for either the realm of theory or the realm of practice with regard to how to distinguish between a truth in which error and sham dominate and a truth which these "equal partners" have not disguised. Furthermore, in place of the moral commandments which—according to Heidegger— have evidently been overcome and dismissed, forethinking has arrived at no standards which can decide whether a specific interpretation or action is "good" or not.

The most extreme consequence of this conception for the theoretical domain would be to throw doubt on Hölderlin's poetizing or Heidegger's thinking as well, since it cannot be decided to what extent the poet and thinker were subjected to the "affliction of error." For according to Heidegger,[1] he who "thinks great" must also "err great." In *Being and Time* authentic Dasein was capable of becoming master over his immersive ways to a considerable degree. By contrast, the later Heidegger has never asked how creative men, who take custody of the truth of Being, might guard themselves from the error and sham which are always involved in this essence of truth. Instead, he has himself repeatedly stressed the danger of poetizing and thinking, if only because they guard "that most dangerous of possessions," language.

At this time, we might recall once again that Heidegger has released the creative essence of man into dimensions from which the tradition largely sought to exclude it. Whether it is the violence of the first beginning or the appropriately submissive listening of the other beginning, the poet and thinker are involved in the origination of the meaningful significations which hold sway at any particular time. For it is through their works that a

1. *Aus der Erfahrung des Denkens*, p. 17.

"world" is formed and through their correct listening to the soundless saying that "the world comes to language." Now consider the possibility that the poet and thinker bring to language a truth of Being in which error and sham are involved. This possibility is present because the error would not be an error, nor the sham a sham, if it expressly manifested itself as such. An error thus cannot really be averted or discovered later; and since there are no rules anyway, the poet and thinker cannot even be made responsible for such an error, nor need they feel guilty themselves. They have submissively responded to the commission of a truth of Being, in which error and sham are essentially involved.

It is difficult to decide whether "only" a secularized traditional morality, especially in the area of practice, is scandalized by these consequences of Heidegger's concept of truth. It is in this area of practice that "the ethical" traditionally belongs. We might therefore still mention the remarks in the *Letter on Humanism* [2] in which the attempt is made to think the "ethical" as an occurrence of truth as well. Both the "hale" and the "evil" appear in the clearing of Being. They appear together because Being is "contentious." The emergence of the hale in this clearing or truth of Being along with the emergence of the evil in it is thus conceived precisely as the relationship of the undistorted to distorting error and to sham. Within the countervailing and contentious truth of Being, the good and the evil are coordinated equal partners. But man ek-sists (stands out into) this truth of Being which is equally pervaded by good and evil. And from it he obtains the allocations of those directions which "must become law and rule for him." Heidegger does not speak of whether and how man can distinguish between the good and the evil within the truth of Being, or whether he should seek, for example, to do good and avoid evil. He foregoes the "setting-up of rules," since it is more essential "for man to find his sojourn in the truth of Being."

If it is therefore only a matter of listening to the directions of Being, whatever they may be, and of responding to them, then this evidently does away with the entire realm of problems which the tradition since Socrates and, more intensively, since Augustine had grappled with again and again and had cultivated under the headings of "ethics" and "morals." Aristotelian ethics, which

2. *HB* 112 ff. (298 ff.).

250 / HEIDEGGER AND THE TRADITION

up to the present day has left a deep impression on the Christian image of man in the Thomistic synthesis with the biblical faith in revelation, would also lose its influence. It would no longer be a matter for man to learn by long practice to overcome his "natural" hedonistic tendencies and to bring himself into a state of character, a *hexis,* by which he, as a "good man," an *agathos,* is capable of striking the mean between excesses and thus acting virtuously, *kat' aretēn.* The problems of responsibility for one's own actions (*archē*), the freedom from external compulsion (*hekousion*), the deliberation of the right means (*bouleusis*), and the right choice (*prohairesis*) no longer play any role. Likewise, this would do away with those problems of the soul which Christendom, influenced by the Judaic moral teachings but also by the Stoics, had cultivated in such a profound manner: the problems of sin, freedom of the will, divine grace, the efforts to conform with divine providence, as well as the problems of the responsible struggle with temptation and with the moral decision, which still determine Western man today in secularized form.

Heidegger's later writings do not deal with everyday men but with creative men. Accordingly, Heidegger's remarks on "ethics" are presumably only for them. But the biographies of creative men very often bear out that the gift of listening to good directions and responding to them, and of avoiding evil directions, more often than not seems to be granted to a man of simple heart rather than to the creative man. More familiar is the case of the creative man who easily falls into error and sham and becomes one-sided in his venture into alien regions. According to the inherited morality, creative talent would in no case "justify" evil or deviant behavior, although it would "pardon" it. In Heidegger's vision there is no room for this question of justification or pardon. The consequence of Heidegger's conception that scandalizes us lies precisely in the fact that the poet and thinker can fall into evil, error, and sham "with impunity," just when they are occupied with the execution of the highly responsible mission of aiding in the emergence of sense and meanings and measures which are to become "law and rule" for their fellow man.

Traditionally, the "political" belongs in the realm of practice. Heidegger conceived the institution of the *polis* in the first beginning, on the basis of *alētheia,* as an occurrence of truth in which man is violently involved. Likewise, in the "basic event of the realization of the National Socialist State" he saw an "incipient" foundation of a state, a "state-founding act," which he expressly characterized in the essay on the artwork (1935)[3] as one of the ways in which "truth essences." That the "National Socialist revolution" as the "total upheaval of our German Dasein"[4] could only take place violently, and that it was pervaded by evil as well as by error and sham, for Heidegger might thus have simply resulted from an "occurrence of truth." And it might have been for him only a consequence of the coordination of evil and good in the clearing of Being, so that the founders of the state followed the directions of evil without his being able to hold them guilty on the basis of "moral considerations." These references touch on the difficult, disturbing, and painful problem of the relationship of this thinker to National Socialism and the effect of his related speeches, writings, and actions[5] only insofar as they cast doubt on the often heard view that he "erred" with regard to the violence and evil of the National Socialist revolution. On the contrary, he must have a priori assessed it correctly, since he viewed it as an "occurrence of truth."

These deliberations are especially appropriate in bringing to light the extremely perilous character of Heidegger's concept of truth and at once to evoke most forcefully the question of whether Heidegger has actually considered the matter correctly when he recognized not only "the mystery" but also error, sham, and evil as equal partners within the occurrence of truth. Do the *fact* of the sciences and their results not show that error and sham can be overcome and are therefore of lesser rank than undisguised luminosity, and this without detriment to the true insight that these results themselves continue to be pervaded by the mystery, which denies itself to these sciences? And for all our skepticism, do we not encounter a sufficient number of modes of behavior in extreme human situations which demonstrate that the good has priority over evil, just as in the bodily realm health unquestionably has priority over sickness? Perhaps a significant task for a thinking that carries on that pursues Heidegger's insight into the mystery character of truth lies in demonstrating, from the topic itself, that the undisguised has an essential priority over the disguised in the relationship of light and darkness.

There are many other tasks in the endeavor to think further.

3. *HW* 50 (685).
4. "Bekenntnisse der Professoren an den deutschen Universitäten und Hochschulen zu Adolf Hitler und dem Nationalsozialistischen Staat," in G. Schneeberger, *Ergänzungen zu einer Heidegger-Bibliographie*, p. 15.
5. See above, p. 13.

Such a thinking, whose concern would simply be to supplement and improve Heidegger's over-all view, might try to add to what is unfinished and even on occasion to what is inconsistent and unclarified, to which numerous references were made in the course of this investigation. It might therefore assume the following tasks:

In order to overcome substance and subject convincingly and finally, it should be shown that *all* of the decisive conceptions of substance and subject in the tradition are inadequate for the proper thinking of the essence of man and the essence of the things with which man lives in ordinary commerce.

The problem of the verification of "retrieving" interpretations should be taken up in a thorough way, precisely because they are necessarily violent.[6] But, above all, it should be shown just how the historically extant possibilities for Dasein can become the historical "empowering" possibility which appropriates Dasein and is the "granting element" for his thinking.

With regard to the basic traits of initially incipient Being, the temporal sense of *eon* and the subsequent modes of "presenting" must be clarified further. Special attention should be given to those basic traits that constitute the sense of the Being of everyday uncreative being. And the regional problem between the creative and uncreative sense of Being should be studied.

The specific developments in the history of Being of the initially incipient basic traits as well as the specific conceptions of the various stampings of Being should be reconsidered, and inquiry should be made into whether there is a "kind" of necessity in the sequence of the stages of the historical epochs of the "eschatology." Also, the "influence" of the "Meta-physical" on the social institutions of the various epochs should be demonstrated more concretely.

With regard to the other incipient sense of Being, the relationship of Being and world must be studied. The basis for the various changes of the world concept, especially the one for the world as the "mirror play of the fourfold," should be shown. Here, too, a thinking that carries on, which takes over the sense of Being which is regional because of its creative character, should try to think another sense of Being suitable for the region of ev-

6. This task has now been carried out in great detail by H. G. Gadamer's work, *Wahrheit und Methode;* this independent investigation also goes into the problem of Heidegger's method of interpretation. Cf. Gadamer, pp. 245 ff. and 250 ff.

eryday being and to solve the problem of how these regions belong together. Further thinking would, moreover, have to pay attention to the hitherto neglected modes of "genuine" things. It should in addition seek to show the structure of the transmuting power of rethinking and forethinking and to cite the rules for this thinking. And in case this should prove to be impossible, then perhaps the relationship of the word to the topic and of thinking to the state of affairs could be given further clarification.

With regard to the essence of man, a thinking that carries on should concern itself with determining the distribution of the power and impotence between Being and the essence of man more definitively. For example, it should pursue the question of whether there is an inconsistency in the assertion that initially incipient Being "behooves" a violent man, while the other incipient Being seems to "behoove" a submissive and obedient servant, even though their "dialogues" have necessarily remained violent.

Such a thinking, which has to do only with a completion and clarification of Heidegger's writings, should perhaps also continue the efforts which have been begun here, insofar as we have explicated the basic traits of Being in the two beginnings. Finally, Heidegger's suggestions with regard to the temporal sense of Being in the other beginning should above all be clarified, since this is where the decisive tendency to overcome the temporal sense of initially incipient Being, the "presenting," manifests itself. Our other references to this tendency should also be pursued further. Finally, beyond Heidegger's own indications, a thinking that carries on should also deal with the problem of the individuation of the world essence in temporal and other respects.

But the endeavor to think further could proceed, on the basis of the following consideration, in an entirely different way: In an age in which the Greek cosmic model of a mobile order can no longer determine thinking, in which religious order is secularized and Hegel's belief in the self-organizing power of thought is profoundly shaken, Heidegger has sought to find, in the works transmitted to us and the initially incipient experiences underlying them, categories which could grant Western man a new commitment. In a heroic effort, he sought to find a last "absolute" in mundane "history," after the efficacy of the absolute beyond the world and the absolute of pure thought seemed to have become increasingly meaningless. But our investigation has shown that Heidegger held the foundation of his historically oriented thinking, the movement of rethinking and forethinking, in the element of the mysterious, and that thinking made widespread use of the transmuting power relegated to it in its explication of the Being of the other beginning and especially its basic traits.

But this means that the "absolute" and the new categories which it seeks are not legitimated exclusively on the basis of the experiences and works of our historical beginning but rest largely on Heidegger's own experiences with Being. If this is so, then the particular historical "method" and structure of Heidegger's thinking and what he has thought has perhaps lost its justification, and a thinking that carries on might resolve to abandon it. This perhaps all the more so, as our investigation has shown that the forethought basic traits of the other beginning of Being again recall the traditional basic traits of Being. And Heidegger himself no longer seems to understand the world essence as a "mission," so that we asked whether he wishes "to lay history itself still" in a "cosmological" turn.

Then, to be sure, a number of decisive moments within the over-all project would be abandoned. But just as the abandonment of Hegel's system of thought did not impair his significant insights into many phenomena, so also many of the important and very productive and penetrating thoughts of Heidegger would remain, even if they should be taken from their particular "historical" binding. Also, without referring to rethinking and forethinking and their specific range of tasks, a thinking that carries on could receive inspiration especially from Heidegger's significant insights into the essence of truth, language, and art. We have already given several indications as to how the essence of truth should perhaps be thought further. Heidegger's insights into the "structure of the essence of language," his statements concerning the soundless saying, listening, and responding, must, if possible, be more adequately demonstrated out of the topic, in order to allay the suspicion that it is only a matter here of an individual man extraordinarily gifted in listening and speaking. A thinking that carries on will have to dedicate its special efforts toward an explication of the truly significant insights of Heidegger into the essence of art. We are convinced with Heidegger that the increasing contraction of the creative meanings could perhaps be checked by art and that thinking by a reflection on the essence of art should help in this task.

But a thinking that carries on should above all follow Heidegger in thinking the "other sense of Being and essence" as the essence of world and in defining the essence of man as well as the thingness of things from the bearing of the world on them. It should therefore retain the "category" of "mirror play." For it expresses in a felicitous way that, and in what way, the world is an occurrence and how it brings the basic traits to a "kind" of necessity, intelligibility, eternity, and especially to a "kind" of self-sameness which permits the advent of new things. But it would provide an even better response to the present need of philosophy if the meanings of the world neighborhoods could be changed and broadened so as to clarify the universal dominion of the world in its uncreative as well as in its creative modes. The world neighborhood of the mortals would have to be changed and broadened so that it refers to man not only in his many social relations—in everyday as well as authentic ways—but as an active living being. Generally speaking, a thinking that carries on would have to try to go beyond the basic relationship of world and man and to explicate the modes of human behavior concretely. The thinking that comes "from the world" will have to reach far back so that it can do justice to the fact that man not only "stands out into Being" and is "open to the world" but that he is in many respects a "self," an individual, that he—thus understood—is a "subject." Heidegger's significant determinations in *Being and Time,* in which he dealt with the problems of Dasein as a self, its individualization and individuation, should all be taken into consideration from the vantage point of the world. This non-Cartesian and nonidealistic "kind" of "subjectivity" should be determined in detail.

A thinking that carries on would likewise have to pay attention to the problem of the individuation of things, their capacity to stand on their own and their property character. For the things not only gather the world neighborhoods but also show many "substantial" structures. This "kind" of substantiality should be developed. In these tasks, such thinking should not close itself off from the deep insights of the tradition into the structure of the thingness of things, the self, and the "Being" thought from the self. Without giving up the "turned" direction of thinking and without linking itself to a wholly ousiological and Cartesian viewpoint, it should bear in mind that the categories of substance and of subject can impart a self-grounded order to the understanding of being and Being. Accordingly, with every new determination this thinking will carefully test whether it is really pertinent and therefore necessary to fully overcome the tradition in the sense that Heidegger demands in order to determine the essence of Being and world, man and thing. Against the "existentiel" either-or, what may in the end prove to be the truth of Being is that Being in its immeasurable richness grants the world as creative *and* uncreative, the thing as worldly *and* substantial, man as open to the world *and* subjective, and holds them together in their manifold relations. The true concern of a thinking that carries on would then be the concrete demonstration of these relations.

Appendix

THE RECENTLY PUBLISHED "interpretations" of Nietzsche's fundamental ideas (M. Heidegger, *Nietzsche,* Volumes I
and II [Pfullingen, 1961]) appear to follow the "method" which
Heidegger had developed in *Being and Time*.[1] Although the "predisposition" and the "preconception" of the interpretations are
not expressly determined, the "preview"[2] of the whole of the
"project,"[3] which comes "from us,"[4] is explicitly treated. Corresponding to the method of the initial writings, the task is to
bring to light the "unsaid" in Nietzsche's work[5] as a still "operative power."[6] This is possible only if the interpreter lets his own
ideas "grow in the face of" Nietzsche's ideas,[7] if he "listens" to
Nietzsche in order to think "with him, through him, and thus *at
the same time against him.*"[8]

In full accord with the conception of *Being and Time,* these
"interpretations" involve a discovering "occurrence of truth"
which is necessarily "violent."[9] The movement of interpretive
thinking seems to remain oriented to the "retrieving and countermanding rejoinder"[10] which is described there; thinking must go
forward in order to experience the backwards,[11] for the thinker

1. See above, pp. 107 ff.
2. *I* 430.
3. *I* 341.
4. *I* 341 and 653, but cf. *II* 264.
5. *I* 158; cf. also *I* 426.
6. *I* 13.
7. *I* 403.
8. *I* 33—emphasized in the text.
9. See above, p. 108.
10. See above, p. 107.
11. *I* 398.

[257]

"himself is the moment which proceeds into the future and thereby does not let the past fall behind." [12]

And yet the interpretive method of *Being and Time* can no longer simply be the dominant one here. For, in the meantime, Heidegger's thinking had made the "turn"; [13] when it interprets texts, it proceeds according to the "history of Being," [14] the "mission." Now it is simply a matter of determining the "sense of Being," [15] of inquiring into the specific manner in which Being has withdrawn itself in the particular conception of the metaphysical thinker and as it thus comes forth as a mere "stamping of Being." [16] And furthermore, this is done only in order to bring the truth of Being to language [17] as it prevailed "creatively" in the first beginning and as it is to prevail in the other beginning that is to be forethought. [18] More precisely stated, these "interpretations" of Nietzsche's basic ideas wish, first, to describe the consummation of the entire development of the withdrawal of creative Being, a process which began with Plato and Aristotle. From the vantage point of this level of consummation, the preceding stampings of Being could then be viewed as prior levels developing "eschatologically" toward this consummation. [19] Second, from this stage of consummation, the aim is to reach the "free" [20] character of the "truth of Being," [21] in order to obtain the creative basic traits of Being in the first beginning by rethinking and the creative basic traits of Being in the other beginning by forethinking. [22] It is thus obvious that what is attempted here is not just another of the customary interpretations of Nietzsche.

This treatise was exclusively guided by Aristotle and Hegel. Accordingly, a discussion of Heidegger's understanding of Nietzsche would have been outside its range of tasks. This new publication of Heidegger has, however, a second aim that does concern the interests of this work. According to the foreword, [23] to the publication of his various Nietzsche lectures and the discus-

12. *I* 311; cf. also *I* 431, 446, and *II* 9.
13. See above, p. 173.
14. See above, pp. 163 ff.; *II* 389 ff., 481 ff.; cf. *I* 37, 234, 340, and *II* 97, 180, 264.
15. *I* 26, 80, 633; cf. also *II* 13 and 17.
16. See above, p. 119.
17. *I* 19.
18. See above, pp. 125 ff., 183 ff.
19. Cf. *II* 390, 458 ff.
20. *II* 397.
21. *Ibid.*
22. *II* 490.
23. *I* 10.

sions and outlines of the history of Being Heidegger also adds the intention "of providing a glimpse into the way of thought" which he followed from 1930 to 1947. Though the following references can for the greatest part be only a matter of compilations in catalogue fashion, they may nevertheless be apropos for the further clarifications of the development of Heidegger's thinking. At the same time, some of the texts cited might further elucidate and supplement the determinations examined in this treatise. This applies especially to Heidegger's determinations of the "history of Being" and the "essence of metaphysics" (A). Since the Nietzsche interpretations review, from the vantage of the consummation of metaphysics, all of the preceding stages and the whole of metaphysics, many determinations receive a greater precision than in previous publications. The development of Heidegger's thought shall first be exemplified by several examples (B) that show how he sought to rethink metaphysical determinations in the direction of the question of Being. Second, a series of references (C) will prove that during this phase he had already developed determinations for the other beginning, without of course having attacked the authentic task of forethinking.[24] Especially important in this developmental history are the determinations of the "creative" which this "dialogue" with Nietzsche provoked, published here for the first time (D).

A. References to the History of Being

I. The "Essence" of "Metaphysics"

1. General determination of the essence of metaphysics (*I*, 478; *II* 33, 378 ff.)—cf. here the concept of the "metaphysical basic position" (*I* 271 ff., 448 ff.)—also the delimitation of the "guiding question" (*I* 15, 455) from the "basic question" (*I* 25, 26, 80). On metaphysics as the "truth of being as a whole" see, e.g., *II* 33 ff.; on the problem of the determination of factual relationships through "metaphysics," cf. *II* 343.
2. The determination of the sense of Being that underlies the metaphysical stamping of "Being."
   a) "Presenting as stability": *II* 8, 13, 19, 229 ff., 335 ff., 403; to note why, and in what sense for Heidegger himself, becoming in Nietzsche has the character of permanence see *I* 648 ff., *II* 19; on the history of the origin of the priority

24. See above, pp. 117 ff.; cf. also *II* 481.

of "whatness" over "thatness" and on the changes of "reality," cf. esp. *II* 410 ff.

b) "Being" as objectivity: *II* 462 ff.

c) "Being" as will: *I* 44 ff., 70 ff., 76, 467 ff., 648 ff.; *II* 235 ff.

d) "Being" as value: *I* 34 ff.; *II* 44 ff., 71 ff., 100, 113, 120, 229 ff., 341 ff.

3. The characterization of the essence of metaphysics from the "essence of representation."

a) The structure of representation in Descartes: cf. esp. *II* 148 ff., 166 ff.

b) The growing determination of representing by "willing": *I* 68 ff., 161; *II* 17, 166, 169 ff., 340, 460, 467, 472. To what extent for Heidegger this development already begins in German Idealism: *I* 45, 450; *II* 7, 299, 342, 471.

c) The subject-object relation and subjectivity: cf. *II* 297 ff., 382 ff., 450 ff.

d) The change of the "truth of being" into a certainty for knowing: *I* 551 ff.; *II* 171, 230, 465. Truth as correctness (*I* 511) and as adequation (*I* 512).

II. The "Consummation" of Metaphysics

1. General determination: *II* 471 ff. Exclusion of the question of the essence of Nothing: *II* 54.

2. The loss of confidence in logic and the categories of reason: *I* 530 ff., 533 ff., 591; *II* 76 ff., 180 ff., 185.

3. Thinking in horizons and perspectives: *I* 573; *II* 104 ff.

III. The Essence of Metaphysics as "Nihilism"

1. General determination of nihilism: *I* 35 ff., 436; *II* 340 ff., 88, 113.

2. There "is" "nothing doing with Being": *II* 338 ff., 342, 353. The will wills nothing: *II* 65.

3. The "justification" of might and power: *II* 95. The "justification" of brutality: *II* 200.

4. The "justification" of evil in German Idealism: *I* 73, 159. The "justification" of evil in Nietzsche: *I* 315; *II* 200.

5. The identification of "truth" and "error" in Nietzsche: *I* 39, 166 ff., 247 ff., 251, 498, 499, 508, 620; *II* 197.

IV. The Essence of Man in Self-Consummating Metaphysics

1. Man as a center of relations (*II* 24)—he "posits the essence of things" (*II* 122); he has an unconditioned right of domi-

nation (*II* 130) and conducts the battle for the domination of the earth with consciousness (*II* 261).
2. The consummation of subjectivity: *II* 26 ff., 82, 186, 382, 450 ff., 465 ff.
3. The "humanization" of all being: *I* 356 ff., 653. On the concept of "machinations": *II* 23, 26, 117, 487.

B. Examples of the Attempt to Rethink "Metaphysical" Determinations in the Direction of the Question of Being

1. In *Being and Time* the temporality of Dasein's inauthentic understanding of Being was used as a basis for the determination of the temporal sense of "eternity" (see above, p. 99). By contrast, here the attempt is made to pose the temporal sense of the "eternity" thought by Nietzsche as the question of the temporality of "Being" (*I* 28). Heidegger, however, does not enter into this "most difficult idea of philosophy" (*ibid.*) in a way that goes beyond the determinations which he had developed in *Being and Time* for the understanding of Being on the part of authentic Dasein (*I* 357, 399). On the more precise connection of "eternity" and "moment" cf. *I* 296, 314, 348, 357; on the determination of eternity as the "now that rushes back into itself" rather than as the *nunc stans* cf. *I* 28.
2. Heidegger finds that "truth" and "error" are identified in Nietzsche (*I* 39, 166 ff., 247 ff., 251, 498, 499, 508, 620 ff., and *II* 197) and that "evil, suffering, and destruction" belong to the "truth of being" (*I* 73, 159, 315). His "interpretation" radicalizes this turn away from the traditional conception, in which truth excludes error and sham (see above, pp. 38 ff.) and the "powers of light" have predominance over the "powers of darkness" (see above, p. 57). Here he forethinks the structure of the "truth of being" in the direction of the conception which then becomes determining for the "truth of *Being*" in both the first and the other beginning (see above, p. 145).

C. References to the Basic Determinations of Being in the Other Beginning

1. Determinations which were examined more closely in Heidegger's later writings and in the present treatise:
a) Withdrawal (*II* 355, 383, 390); forgottenness of Being (*II* 390 ff.); Being "holds to itself" (*II* 383); the concealment and the denial of Being (*II* 354).

   b) Being as mission (*II* 339).
   c) Being as that which "empowers the possible" (*II* 377).
   d) Nothing as the "veil of Being" (*II* 42, 353).
   e) The "ontological difference" and the "issue" [*Austrag*] (*II* 203 ff., 209).
   f) The "truth of Being" over against the "truth of being" (*II* 352 ff.).
   g) The "essence of Being" (*II* 403; cf. also 344 ff., 388).
   h) Being as "event" (*II* 402, 485).
   i) Being "loses its names" (*II* 336, 340).
   k) Being as "world essence" (*I* 377) and as "world play" (*II* 381 ff.).
   l) The coordination of Being and thinking (*II* 342 ff., 356).
   m) The essence of man as the "behooved" (*II* 391) who is relegated a "share" (*II* 342).
   n) Man and language (*I* 363–64; *II* 337); hints (*II* 383); "the other strictness of saying" (*II* 336).
2. Determinations of the other beginning which are no longer mentioned in the later writings:
   a) The determination of the essence of man from the "distinction of what and that"; on this and on the question of the origin of this distinction see *II* 14 ff., 344 ff., 400 ff., 458 ff.
   b) The determination of the essence of man as "stay," "locality," and "intervent of the advent" of the "mystery" of the "promise of Being" (*II* 368, 370 ff., 390 ff.).

D. The "Creative" in Nietzsche

The present treatise was guided by the fundamental conception that for Heidegger the sense of Being and of the essence of man is "creative." [25] This conception is confirmed by the following determinations, published for the first time, which arose from the "dialogue" with Nietzsche's ideas.

Heidegger defines the essence of *creating*. Creating "allots and imparts a *new* Being to the hitherto existing being." [26] Such an allotting and imparting is carried out as an original *transmuting*, to which the "having to destroy" also belongs. [27] Creating is undertaken by the creative men, i.e., the artists [28] and the new

25. See above, pp. 106 ff., 139 ff., 155 f., 218 f., 227 f., 237.
26. *I* 389, and also 466; see above, pp. 151, 156, 198.
27. *I* 45, 73, 263, 337; see above, pp. 116 ff.
28. *I* 82.

philosophers.[29] Artists are "productive";[30] they are capable "of positing what is not into Being."[31] The thinking of philosophers is "constructive,"[32] eliminative, and annihilative,[33] it is a "grounding that makes way and erects in a decisive manner."[34] The creative men are the "precursors of the future,"[35] the "cofashioners of future Dasein."[36] Inasmuch as they think beyond themselves,[37] they think "possibilities."[38] They posit the "essence of things."[39] Heidegger conceives the role of the creative men together with that of things; insofar as the creative men *are*, being in its entirety is already transmuted as well.[40]

These determinations of the "creative,"[41] of creating and creative men, suggest the characterizations in which Heidegger had developed the essence of the creative and of creative men in the first beginning.[42] But the decisive distinction is that, in the creating that was thought in the first beginning, it was a matter of a "cocreating" with the "creative occurrence of Being." Such a cocreating is impossible during the dominion of metaphysics, since "creative Being" is withdrawn in it. This withdrawal comes to fullness during the consummation of metaphysics, in Nietzsche's thinking. The "Being" that comes forth has the sense of a presence of ultimate stability:[43] as "will to power," it is a "becoming" which is realized as the "eternal recurrence of the same."[44]

And yet, in this total withdrawal of the creative sense of Being, thinking according to the "history of Being" can experience and determine not only the essence of creating and creative men but also the essence of Being itself as "creative." The insight into the creative essence of Being is evoked or activated for Heidegger out of his "dialogue" with Nietzsche's conception of the essence of art. Of course, for Nietzsche art is only an ultimate

29. *I* 37.
30. *I* 84.
31. *I* 82.
32. *I* 640.
33. *I* 642.
34. *Ibid.*
35. *I* 153.
36. *I* 155.
37. *I* 466.
38. *I* 392, 406, 410, and *II* 317.
39. *II* 122.
40. *I* 394.
41. *I* 154, 155.
42. See above, pp. 217 ff.
43. *I* 542, and *II* 8, 13, 19.
44. *I* 41 ff., 44 ff., 70 ff., 255 ff., 414 ff., 425, 448, 464 ff., and *II* 19.

"value" and is subservient to "Being thought metaphysically," to the "will to power." [45] But to the thinking according to the history of Being, which apprehends art "from the essence of Being," [46] it manifests itself as the basic occurrence [47] and the "basic character" [48] of being. If Heidegger here thinks of art as "a mode of the Being of being," as a "configuration of Being in general," [49] this implies that for him Being is "artistic" in the sense of "poietic," and therefore creative.

It may be questioned whether Heidegger gained these insights into the essence of the creative directly from the dialogue with the ideas of self-consummating metaphysics. In the later writings he declared that "what endures incipiently out of the dawn is the granting." [50] And in a series of academic years before the first lecture course on Nietzsche, Heidegger had in fact rethought the initially incipient experiences that the early Greeks had deposited in their basic words.[51] Apparently then he came to the essence of the creative in Nietzsche in the light of his insights into the creative sense of Being and of the essence of man in the first beginning and, therefore, from "that which endures out of the dawn." As Heidegger determined the essence of the creative in Nietzsche's work in the horizon of the first beginning, it seems to have become evident to him that this creative element has completely withdrawn itself in Nietzsche's metaphysical conception of "Being." This experience of total withdrawal is for him the experience of the "need" to forethink the sense of Being creatively. The consummation of metaphysics therefore represents an end which for Heidegger "*is* the need of another beginning." [52]

45. *I* 82 ff., 243 ff.
46. *I* 253.
47. *I* 253, 86.
48. *I* 125.
49. *I* 94.
50. VA 39; see above, p. 165.
51. For example, in the lecture course of the summer semester of 1932, "Die Anfänge der abendländischen Philosophie" and later in the lecture course of the summer of 1935, which was published under the title *Einführung in die Metaphysik.*
52. *I* 657; cf. also *I* 470.

Bibliography
of Works Cited

I. WORKS BY HEIDEGGER, WITH CORRESPONDING ENGLISH
TRANSLATIONS

(Listed in approximate chronological order of first public
presentation.)

A. *Major Works*

Sein und Zeit (1927). 6th ed. Tübingen: M. Niemeyer,
1949. Translation by John Macquarrie and Edward
Robinson, *Being and Time.* London: SCM Press, 1962.
With marginal pagination of the German edition.
Kant und das Problem der Metaphysik (1927). 2d ed.
Frankfurt: Klostermann, 1951. Translation by James
S. Churchill, *Kant and the Problem of Metaphysics.*
Bloomington: Indiana University Press, 1962.
Vom Wesen des Grundes (1928). 3d ed. Frankfurt:
Klostermann, 1949. Translation by Terrence Malick,
The Essence of Reasons. Bilingual edition. Evanston,
Ill.: Northwestern University Press, 1969.
Was ist Metaphysik? (1929). 5th ed. Frankfurt: Kloster-
mann, 1949. (Postscript added to 4th ed., 1943; Intro-
duction added to 5th ed., 1949.) Lecture and post-
script translated by R. F. C. Hull and Alan Crick,
"What Is Metaphysics?" In Werner Brock, *Existence
and Being,* pp. 355–92. London: Vision Press, 1949.
Introduction translated by Walter Kaufmann, "The

Way Back into the Ground of Metaphysics." In Walter Kaufmann, *Existentialism from Dostoyevsky to Sartre*, pp. 206–21. New York: Meridian Books, 1957.

Vom Wesen der Wahrheit (1930–43). 1st ed. Frankfurt: Klostermann, 1943. Translation by R. F. C. Hull and Alan Crick, "On the Essence of Truth." In Werner Brock, *Existence and Being*, pp. 317–51.

Einführung in die Metaphysik (1935). 1st ed. Tübingen: M. Niemeyer, 1953. Translation by Ralph Manheim, *An Introduction to Metaphysics*. New Haven: Yale University Press, 1959.

Erläuterungen zu Hölderlins Dichtung (1936–44). 2d ed. Frankfurt: Klostermann, 1951. Translation of the first two essays (pp. 7–30, 31–45 in the German) by Douglas Scott, "Remembrance of the Poet" and "Hölderlin and the Essence of Poetry." In Werner Brock, *Existence and Being*, pp. 251–90, 291–315.

Holzwege (1936–46). 1st ed. Frankfurt: Klostermann, 1950. Translation of its first essay (pp. 7–68 in the German) by Albert Hofstadter, "The Origin of the Work of Art." In *Philosophies of Art and Beauty*, ed. A. Hofstadter and Richard Kuhns, pp. 649–701. New York: Random House, 1964. Translation of its third essay (pp. 105–92 in the German) is now available as Martin Heidegger, *Hegel's Concept of Experience*, with a section from Hegel's *Phenomenology of Spirit* in the Kenley Royce Dove translation. New York: Harper & Row, 1970.

Nietzsche. 2 vols. (Vol. I, 1936–39; Vol. II, 1939–46). 1st ed. Pfullingen: Neske, 1961.

Platons Lehre von der Wahrheit (1942): *Mit einem Brief über den "Humanismus"* (1946). 2d ed. Bern: Francke, 1947. Translations of both essays are in William Barrett and H. D. Aiken, eds., *Philosophy in the Twentieth Century.* 4 vols. The essays in question here are in Vol. III, pp. 251–302. New York: Random House, 1962.

Vorträge und Aufsätze (1936–53). 1st ed. Pfullingen: Neske, 1954. Translation by Bernd Magnus of one of its essays (pp. 101–26 in the German), "Who is Nietzsche's Zarathustra?" *Review of Metaphysics*, XX (1967), 411–31.

Was heisst Denken? (1951–52). 1st ed. Tübingen: M.

Niemeyer, 1954. Translation by Fred D. Wieck and J. Glenn Gray, *What Is Called Thinking?* New York: Harper & Row, 1968.

Gelassenheit (1944–55). 1st ed. Pfullingen: Neske, 1959. Translation by John M. Anderson and E. Hans Freund, *Discourse on Thinking.* New York: Harper & Row, 1966.

Zur Seinsfrage (1955). 1st ed. Frankfurt: Klostermann, 1956. Translation by William Kluback and Jean T. Wilde, *The Question of Being.* Bilingual edition. New York: Twayne, 1958.

Was ist das—die Philosophie? (1955). 1st ed. Pfullingen: Neske, 1956. Translation by William Kluback and Jean T. Wilde. *What Is Philosophy?* Bilingual edition. New York: Twayne, 1958.

Der Satz vom Grund (1955–56). 1st ed. Pfullingen: Neske, 1957.

Identität und Differenz (1957). 1st ed. Pfullingen: Neske, 1957. Translation by Joan Stambaugh, *Identity and Difference.* New York: Harper & Row, 1969.

Unterwegs zur Sprache (1950–59). 1st ed. Pfullingen: Neske, 1959.

B. *Other Works*

Die Selbstbehauptung der deutschen Universität. Breslau: Korn, 1933.

"Verlautbarungen des Rektors," *Freiburger Studentenzeitung* (1933–34). Reprinted in Guido Schneeberger, *Nachlese zu Heidegger: Dokumente zu seinem Leben und Denken.* Bern: Privately printed by G. Schneeberger, 1962.

"Bekenntnisse der Professoren der deutschen Hochschulen zu Adolf Hitler und dem Nationalsozialistischen Staat." In Guido Schneeberger, *Ergänzungen zu einer Heidegger Bibliographie.* Bern, 1960.

"Zu einem Vers von Mörike," *Trivium,* IX, 1. Zurich: Atlantis, 1951.

Der Feldweg. 1st ed. Frankfurt: Klostermann, 1953. Translation by Thomas F. O'Meara, "The Pathway," in *Listening,* II (1967), 88–91 (Dubuque, Iowa).

Aus der Erfahrung des Denkens. 1st ed. Pfullingen: Neske, 1954.

"Vom Wesen und Begriff der *Physis," Il Pensiero,* III, no.

2–3, 1958. Recently published in Martin Heidegger, *Wegmarken*, pp. 309–71. Frankfurt: Klostermann, 1967.

"Hegel und die Griechen," in *Festschrift für Hans-Georg Gadamer*. Tübingen: Mohr, 1960. Recently published in Martin Heidegger, *Wegmarken*, pp. 255–72.

"Hölderlin's Erde und Himmel," *Hölderlin-Jahrbuch, 1958–1960* (Tübingen, 1960), pp. 17–39. Also available on long-playing record. Pfullingen: Neske, 1960. Originally delivered as a lecture on January 18, 1960.

II. WORKS BY HEGEL, WITH CORRESPONDING ENGLISH TRANSLATIONS

Phänomenologie des Geistes. 6th ed. Hamburg: Meiner, 1952. Translation by J. B. Baillie, *The Phenomenology of Mind*. 2d ed. London: Allen & Unwin, 1931.

Wissenschaft der Logik. 2 vols. 2d ed. Leipzig: Meiner, 1948. Translation by A. V. Miller, *Hegel's Science of Logic*. New York: Humanities Press, 1969.

Enzyklopädie der philosophischen Wissenschaften. Leiden: Bolland, 1906. (3d rev. ed., 1830, with add.) Translation of the first part (§§ 1–244) by William Wallace, *The Logic of Hegel*. 2d ed. London: Oxford University Press, 1892. Translation of the second part (§§ 244–377) by A. V. Miller, *Hegel's Philosophy of Nature*. Oxford: Oxford University Press, 1970. Translation of the third part (§§ 377–577) by William Wallace, *Hegel's Philosophy of Mind*. Oxford: Clarendon Press, 1894.

Geschichte der Philosophie. 3d ed. Stuttgart: Glockner, 1959. Translation by E. S. Haldane, *Lectures on the History of Philosophy*. 3 vols. London: Routledge & Kegan Paul, 1955.

Die Vernunft in der Geschichte. 5th ed. Hamburg: Meiner, 1955. (First published, 1837, as introduction to *Vorlesungen über die Philosophie der Geschichte*.) Translation of the third edition (ed. Karl Hegel, 1843) by J. Sibree (1858), *The Philosophy of History*. New York: Dover, 1956.

Hegels theologische Jugendschriften. Tübingen: Nohl, 1907. Translation by T. M. Knox, *Early Theological Writings*. Chicago: University of Chicago Press, 1948.

III. WORKS BY ARISTOTLE

Categoriae (cf. *Organon*, below).
De Interpretatione (cf. *Organon*, below).
Analytica Posteriora (cf. *Organon*, below).
Prior and Posterior Analytics. Translation by W. D. Ross. Oxford, 1947.
Organon. Translation by E. Rolfes. Leipzig, 1948.
Physics. Translation by W. D. Ross. Oxford, 1947.
The Physics. Translation by Ph. H. Wicksteed and F. M. Cornford. Cambridge, Mass., 1957.
On Coming-to-Be and Passing-Away (*De Generatione et Corruptione*). Translation by D. J. Furley. Cambridge, Mass., 1955.
The Nicomachean Ethics. Translation by H. Rackham. Cambridge, Mass., 1926.
De Anima. Translation by W. D. Ross. London, 1956.
Metaphysics. Translation by W. D. Ross. London, 1948.

IV. OTHER WORKS CITED

Allemann, Beda. *Hölderlin und Heidegger*. Freiburg: Alber, 1954.
Böder, Heribert. "Der frühgriechische Wortgebrauch von Logos und Aletheia," *Archiv für Begriffsgeschichte*, Vol. IV, Bonn.
Brand, Gerd. *Welt, Ich und Zeit*. The Hague: Nijhoff, 1958.
Buddeberg, Else. *Heidegger und die Dichtung*. Stuttgart, 1958.
Fink, Eugen. *Zur Ontologischen Frühgeschichte von Raum-Zeit-Bewegung*. The Hague: Nijhoff, 1957.
———. *Spiel als Weltsymbol*. Stuttgart: Kohlhammer, 1960.
Friedländer, Paul. *Platon*, Vol. I. Berlin: de Gruyter, 1954. Translation by Hans Meyerhoff, *Plato: An Introduction*. New York: Harper & Row, 1964.
Fürstenau, Peter. *Heidegger: Das Gefüge seines Denkens*. Frankfurt: Klostermann, 1958.
Gadamer, Hans-Georg. Introduction to *Martin Heidegger:*

20

Der Ursprung des Kunstwerks, pp. 102–25. Stuttgart: Reclam, 1960.

———. *Wahrheit und Methode*. Tübingen: Mohr, 1960.

Henrich, Dieter. "Uber die Einheit der Subjektivität," *Philosophische Rundschau*, III (1955).

Kojève, Alexandre. *Hegel, Kommentar zur Phänomenologie des Geistes*. Translated and edited by Iring Fetscher. Stuttgart: Kohlhammer, 1958.

Kullmann, Eugen. *Beiträge zum aristotelischen Begriff der "Prohairesis."* Basel, 1943.

Löwith, Karl. "Les Implications politiques de la philosophie de l'existence," *Les Temps Modernu :*, November, 1946; August, 1948.

———. *Heidegger: Denker in dürftiger Zeit*. Frankfurt: Fischer, 1953.

———. *Nietzsches Philosophie der ewigen Wiederkehr*. Stuttgart, 1958.

———. *Gesammelte Abhandlungen*. Stuttgart, 1960.

Marcuse, Herbert. *Hegels Ontologie und die Grundlegung einer Theorie der Geschichtlichkeit*. Frankfurt, 1932.

Marx, Karl. *Economic and Philosophical Manuscripts of 1844*. Edited by Dirk J. Struik. Translation by Martin Milligan. New York: International Publishers, n.d.

Marx, Werner. *The Meaning of Aristotle's "Ontology."* The Hague: Nijhoff, 1954.

———. "Heidegger's New Conception of Philosophy," *Social Research*, XXII (1955), 451 ff.

Müller, Max. *Existenzphilosophie im geistigen Leben der Gegenwart*. Heidelberg: Kerle, 1949.

Owens, Joseph. *The Doctrine of Being in the Aristotelian Metaphysics*. Toronto, 1951.

Schulz, Walter. "Über den philosophiegeschichtlichen Ort Martin Heideggers," *Philosophische Rundschau*, I (1953–54).

Szilasi, Wilhelm. *Macht und Ohnmacht des Geistes*. Bern: Francke, 1946.

Ulmer, Karl. *Wahrheit, Kunst und Natur bei Aristoteles*. Tübingen, 1953.

Tugendhat, Ernst. TI KATA TINOS. Freiburg: Alber, 1958.

van der Meulen, Jan. *Heidegger und Hegel, oder Widerstreit und Widerspruch*. Meisenheim: Hain, 1953.

———. *Hegel, die gebrochene Mitte*. Hamburg, 1958.

Index

Absolute, the (absolute idea, absolute knowledge), 44 ff., 49, 54, 79, 93, 104, 137, 253 f.
Actuality (*Wirklichkeit*), 61 ff.
Aition, 19, 23
Alētheia, xviii, xxiii, xxviii, 39 f., 41, 92, 142, 144 f., 203, 219. See also Truth
Allemann, B., 231 n
Appearance (*Erscheinung*), 54, 141 ff.
Art (artist, artwork), 37, 76, 151, 156, 185, 237, 254 f., 263
Augustine, 13, 58

Backtracking (*Rückschritt*), xxi, xxxi, 115
Becoming (*Werden*), 24, 46, 51, 132, 134
Beginning (*Anfang*, also translated as "inception" or "incipience," 116 n), xxi, xxiii, 116, 146
Behooving (*Brauch, brauchen*, 126–27 n), xxix–xxx, 127, 214 ff., 253
Being (*Sein;* also *Seinsgeschehen*, "occurrence of Being," and *Sein des Seienden*, "Being of being"), 3 ff., 17 f., 43 f., 59 f., 92, 95, 96, 107 f., 120 f., 125 ff., 139 f., 149, 158, 213
Being (at home) with itself in otherness (*Beisichselbstsein im*

Anderssein), 35, 58 ff., 93, 106, 111, 129, 137
Being-for-itself (*Fürsichsein*), 48, 67
Being-for-other (*Sein für Anderes*), 65
Being-in-itself (*Ansichsein*), 44, 65
Being-on-hand (*Vorhandensein*, 86 n), 86 ff., 132
Being-with (*Mitsein, Mitdasein*), 90 ff.
Binding character (*Verbindlichkeit*), 110, 118, 179, 229 ff., 246
Böder, H., 145 n, 154 n
Brand, G., 183 n
Buddeberg, E., 231 n

Category (categorial), 4, 19, 23, 35, 45, 57, 61 f., 95 f., 100, 126, 128
Causa. See Ground
Certainty, 53, 113, 135
Change, 34 ff., 61 ff., 163, 165
Chreōn, xxix–xxx, 126, 226
Circle, 22, 50, 106, 108, 111, 117, 140, 166, 197
Clearing (*Lichtung, Lichten*, occasionally translated as "lighting"), 88, 141, 146 ff., 151, 189, 219
Com-posite (*Ge-stell*, 176 n), xxvii, 176 ff., 193, 222, 226, 239
Concealment (*Verbergung, Verborgenheit*), 102, 142, 148, 166 f., 189

[271]

Turn (*Kehre*), 105, 117, 173, 176 f., 193, 240, 246, 258

Ulmer, K., 32 n, 33 n, 75 n
Understanding of Being (*Seinsverständnis*), 88, 92 ff., 96, 190, 212
Untruth (*Unwahrheit*), xxvii, 51 f., 55, 148 ff.

Verification (*Bewährung*), 110 f., 230
von Yorck, Count, xix

While (*Weile*), 27, 134, 190, 195, 199

Whole, wholeness (*Ganzes, Ganzheit*), 20, 23, 95, 101, 200, 244, 246
Will, xxvi, 170
Withdrawal (*Entzug*), xxxi, 119, 127, 164, 168 f., 174 ff.
Work, 116, 237
World, xxvii, 23, 78, 88 ff., 92, 183 ff., 193 ff., 255
World essence (*Weltwesen*), 187, 191, 195
World formation (*Weltbildung*), 141, 150, 167, 185 f., 218 f., 221
World play (*Weltspiel*), 197 ff.